Mysteries of the Mundane

Mysteries of the Mundane

The Films of Girish Kasaravalli

by

John W. Hood

Orient BlackSwan

MYSTERIES OF THE MUNDANE: THE FILMS OF GIRISH KASARAVALLI

ORIENT BLACKSWAN PRIVATE LIMITED

Registered Office
3-6-752 Himayatnagar, Hyderabad 500 029, Telangana, India
e-mail: centraloffice@orientblackswan.com

Other Offices
Bengaluru, Bhopal, Chennai, Guwahati,
Hyderabad, Jaipur, Kolkata, Lucknow, Mumbai,
New Delhi, Noida, Patna, Visakhapatnam

First published by Orient Blackswan Private Limited 2019

ISBN 978-93-5287-843-7

030361

Typeset in
Brioso Pro 11/13.5
by Le Studio Graphique, Gurgaon 122 007

Printed in India at
Akash Press, Delhi

Published by
Orient Blackswan Private Limited
3-6-752, Himayatnagar, Hyderabad 500 029, Telangana, India
e-mail: info@orientblackswan.com

To

Babli and Shiuli

Contents

Contents

Introducing Girish

More films are made in India each year than in any other country. Indian cinema is not only highly productive, but also immensely profitable. It is a very diverse cinema, and while most films are made in Hindi, films are also made in almost every major language of the country. Moreover, cinema has given rise to subsidiary industries such as the publication, in various languages, of 20 or so film magazines, and has engendered the production of vast numbers of CDs of songs from commercial movies. There is also a growing trade in DVDs of the films themselves.

It has long been accepted that Indian cinema is not one, but many. There has been a broad distinction between what is popularly known as *Bollywood* and the so-called *art* cinema, though some people consider *art cinema* a somewhat pretentious term and prefer to call it *Parallel* or *New Wave* or *Independent cinema*. *Bollywood* is a contraction of 'Bombay' and 'Hollywood,' suggesting that Bombay—now Mumbai—is the capital of a national film industry, thus positing another term for that industry: *Hindi cinema* or *Hindi commercial cinema*. Yet almost every state of the country makes popular, commercial films in the language of that state, and while Bollywood is predominant, it is, nevertheless, one of a plurality. We might note that art cinema has no centre corresponding to Mumbai, but serious films are made independently in almost every state of the country too.

It has often been said that the only meaningful distinction in cinema is between good films and bad films. This is an over-simplification, of course, ignoring the many shades of grey between the two polarities, but it does sensibly indicate a development that has been going on in Indian cinema for some years now, in that some very fine films have come out of Bollywood without the obligatory songs and choreographed fight sequences, and a number of independent films have been made with an apparent—and worthy—appeal to the front stalls. *Cinema* is becoming the predominant term while *commercial* or *art*, and all the rest, bear a diminishing significance.

Another distinction that would seem to carry more weight than it is worth is the application of the term *regional* to films not made in Mumbai. These films are indeed made in languages other than the national language, Hindi, and so are regional in a lingual sense, but better films will always aim at an appeal that is more global than local. There is a danger of being beguiled by externals; in addition to language, such things as dress, landscape or style of music might suggest a particular region, but good cinema offers much more below the apparent surface.

This more independent wing of Indian cinema should not be thought of as representing a 'school' or 'movement,' although a number of common features may be discerned. Most prominent is the reliance on literature for narrative inspiration, and in this regard, Girish Kasaravalli is far more typical than exceptional, as nearly all his films are based on novels or short stories by notable writers. The debt to literature notwithstanding, it must be stressed that the filmmaker is not a slave to the older muse, reproducing the original in some sort of celluloid incarnation, but an independent artist free to employ his or her powers of creativity to tell much the same story, but *as cinema*. A literary aficionado might be offended that a film bears differences and departures from the work on which it is based, but to take such offence is to miss the simple point that literature is literature and film is film, that neither is the handmaiden of the other. We might also observe that independent cinema engages, with varying degrees of candour or implication, in social criticism. A critical representation of the world of the filmmaker and his audience gives to cinema a dimension of controversy that has the audience involved beyond screen time. Here we might note that, in India, controversy can engender passions that might get out of hand, and extremists have, on many occasions, done damage to cinema halls and threatened much worse for the screening of films that do not cohere with their particular sensibilities about certain social issues, or the depiction of a popular historical figure, for example.

The same pleasure in name-play that gives us 'Bollywood' or 'Tollywood'[1] calls the cinema of Karnataka 'Sandalwood.'[2] Centred in Bengaluru, it is a very vibrant industry, with a steady production of popular films as well as more serious works by accomplished directors such as G. V. Iyer, who is renowned as the only filmmaker in India to make films in Sanskrit, M. S. Sathyu, B. V. Karanth, and the late Girish Karnad, who has made films in Hindi and English as well as in Kannada, and of course, Girish Kasaravalli.

Girish Kasaravalli may be said to be a regional filmmaker of the Indian art cinema, exploring in his films various themes that inform and interpret his world, quite without the trappings of contrived entertainment. However, there would be no need for any deconstruction of terms if he were more simply described as a prominent filmmaker whose films have a universal significance. It will be argued later in this book that while all of his films are set in his home state of Karnataka, are in the Kannada language, and carry many visuals that give them a Karnatic identity, they are also imbued with a profoundly global appeal. Moreover, while much of the subject matter is locally rooted, it too bears much universal appeal. The narratives very largely consist in the mundanities of life in a particular place, yet are bathed in mysteries that find expression in differently articulated mundanities elsewhere—yet, the mysteries are essentially the same. Much like the Bengali filmmaker Mrinal Sen, Kasaravalli seeks to explore the commonplace, looking for deeper meaning than what is evident on the surface.

There are two documentary films that provide some information on Kasaravalli's pre-cinema life: one by himself,[3] and

[1] Bengali commercial cinema; the major studios are in Tollygunge in Kolkata.

[2] The vernacular 'Chandanavana' is now preferred.

[3] *Ananthamurthy: Not a Biography but a Hypothesis,* 2012. See Chapter 14.

one by Om Prakash Srivastava.[4] He talks about his childhood as being rather lonely, in that rural life meant often being far from one's friends after school, and that, in a time long before television, literature was the most attractive complement to solitude. He was apparently a voracious reader in Kannada, developing a profoundly literary mind as preparation—although he hardly could know it then—for the flowering of his cinematic creativity. Perhaps that is also a partial explanation of the fact that all but one[5] of his films are based on literary sources.

Girish Kasaravalli was born in the village of Kesalur in Shimoga district in the mid-west of the state of Karnataka, in December 1950. His father, a former freedom fighter, was a book-loving landowner who encouraged reading among his large family of six boys and four girls. He was also an enthusiast of *Yakshagana*, Kannada folk-theatre involving music, dance and acting.[6]

While literature was the cultural staple of the young Girish in a village that was not electrified, he gained at least an awareness of cinema from the 'touring talkies' that would occasionally visit Kesalur. Another exposure to cinema came from his uncle, K. V. Subanna, a prominent cultural activist and founder of an acclaimed theatre company. After taking part in a film studies course, his uncle persuaded Girish that the prevailing snobbish disdain for cinema as an inferior art form was quite unwarranted, and so cinema started to find a place in Girish's mind. However, his life took a somewhat aberrant digression when his education reached the undergraduate stage, for the literarily saturated future master of cinema enrolled in the pharmacy course at Manipal University. After graduating, he went to Hyderabad for training, and here he was able to see so many films of quality that were quite new to him, discovering the Indian masters of cinema as well as some of the prominent

[4] *Life in Metaphors. A Portrait of Girish Kasaravalli*, 2016.

[5] *Bannada Vesha.*

[6] *Yakshagana* is the subject matter of *Bannada Vesha.* See Chapter 4.

international filmmakers. This experience was a turning point in his life. Cinema had become more than a cultural interest; it was now a rival to his professional life. Deciding that both could not be fully satisfied, he abandoned pharmacy and enrolled in the Film and Television Institute of India (FTII). He recalls the vibrant life at the Institute in Pune, particularly the huge tutorial benefits of the often impassioned discussions among the students, as their awareness and understanding of the art grew. Girish graduated in 1975 with the Institute's Gold Medal and, for his Diploma film *Avshesh,* the President's Silver Lotus Award for the Best Experimental Short Film of that year.

A remarkably prescient indication of what would come, *Avshesh* ('The Ruins') is a truly accomplished work, especially for a student. The film is as poetic in style as any of Girish's mature works would be and asserts a notion of 'pure' cinema—a preference for the visually directed narrative over that which is guided by dense dialogue. More than any other tool of the filmmaker's craft, the camera is vital to this film, and Girish's direction of it reveals an artistic genius well beyond the experience of the graduating film student. The camerawork is consistently superb and is enhanced by the musical backing; together they present a sensual unity, engendered by an extraordinary harmony between the visual and the aural.

The poetic delineation of some apparently simple yet quite profound notions makes conventional narrative generally inappropriate. Rather, a range of visual images offers to the viewer a depiction of some abstract ideas which, in a Hindu cultural context, allow the viewer to muse on the notion of the role and value of ritual, and some of the ways in which life may be contained and directed by it.

Avshesh is set almost entirely in an old, traditional *haveli* or large mansion, during the period of ritual mourning for the recently deceased *pater familias.* The house, and more particularly its ornate architecture, is portrayed almost as a character—'almost,' of course, for it *is* rather than *does,* but what it gives to the film is its underlying significance. The house represents tradition, the cultural superstructure of ritual, and the richness of that tradition is readily suggested by the beautiful shots of the house in its extensive splendour and in its ornate detail, especially the internal timberwork.

There is a sequence depicting the performance of the *pind* offering, a ritual for the salvation of the departed soul. The solemnity and devout concern for ritual detail bear stark contrast to the trivial engagement of the young women in their game of dice, too absorbed in their play to respond to a request to help the aged widow find a place in the sun. Their assertive selfishness offers another contrast, this time to the spontaneous care and concern of the little boy, Hari, who helps the old lady to a little comfort without having to be asked. And yet Hari's mother has quite firmly denied him the pleasure of playing with his young friend; evidently it is easier to impose standards of propriety on him than on the young women.

There is a heart-warming little scene in which Hari is showing off to his friend some of his grandmother's keepsakes, suggesting his fondness for her and also establishing another link with the past, a past whose emblems live on in the present. He recalls to his friend how he wanted to marry his grandmother, informing his father of this with a kind of tit-for-tat logic: 'You married my mother, so I'll marry yours.'

There are shots of the grandmother offering *prasad*, a symbol of her blessing, after the morning prayer. Hari reverentially accepts his, dressed only in traditional dhoti and wearing his sacred thread, the symbol of his Brahmanical status. Again, Hari shows a respect for the order sanctioned by ritual while his sister, absorbed in her game, asks that she be permitted to take her *prasad* by proxy; the old woman 'is blind and wouldn't know anyhow.' What is evident here is that forms or rituals might be truly meaningful to some, yet are mere motions to be gone through for others.

Amid all this action and observance of profound and sacred symbolism, the tackiness of family politics threatens to cheapen genuine spirituality, even more than the girls playing dice. Hari's father, the new head of the family, is in discussion with his younger brother about their mother's condition. The brother feels that he is better equipped to look after the old lady, implying a slight to his brother and sister-in-law, with the latter objecting that while he has never seen fit earlier to voice such a concern, so why now, when his mother's days are obviously numbered, should he be so solicitous? However, she is chided by her husband, who reminds her of the unseemliness of interfering in 'men's affairs.' What is unseemly, of course, is the worthless personal pride at the heart of such a discussion.

Worldliness has been shown in simple things, such as the girls' game of dice, Hari's friend wanting to play with him, the grandmother's keepsakes, and the family politics. A more natural expression of freedom is a shot of Hari running beside a river, a flag on a long stick he is holding stretched out full in the breeze. There is no impediment to his movement, which seems to be done for the mere joy of it, as suggested by the happiness evident on the little boy's face. However, the run does, in fact, have a destination—a temple, another obvious sign of tradition. Hari has come to meet his friend Munna, who is not there, so Hari wanders about for a while, evidently absorbed in the temple's mysteries, both spacious and solid.

The ritual mourning comes to a close with the *shraddha* ceremony, a ritual of reverential thanksgiving for the life of the departed. Details of the ceremony are picked out by the camera to highlight the notion of ritual and the tradition that upholds it, and then the post-funerary life begins. The film is given a suggested destination by the final shots depicting the little boy as a vehicle for the continuance of the Brahmanical tradition.

While Girish embraces some rather momentous elements in this short film, the work is unpretentious and unassuming. He chooses, most creatively, to allow the innocence of the little boy to be central to his arrangement of the other elements in the film. What is particularly remarkable about *Avshesh* is that it anticipates Girish's celebrated first feature film, *Ghatashraddha,* in both style and substance, though of course there are suggestions of notions and techniques that are found in most of his subsequent feature films.

After *Ghatashraddha,* Kasaravalli would go on to make 11 more feature films and two feature-length documentaries, which provide the substance of this book. However, it should be pointed out here that Kasaravalli made three more feature films. Two of them are unsubtitled (and this writer, alas, does not know Kannada) and the third, inconceivably, is lost.

In *Life in Metaphors*, U. R. Ananthamurthy insists that Kasaravalli is a philosopher, not an ideologist, meaning that his camera and script are observers that seek to facilitate understanding, rather than to propagate views and opinions. An audience is given the opportunity to critically engage with the film, and in all of his works, there is room for controversy. Moreover, he gives a voice to his protagonists, who would otherwise not be heard due to their inability, for various reasons, to articulate or even understand their problems. Also, those who are kept inarticulate and those who suffer alienation warrant his compassion and concern.

There is nothing remarkably inventive or exceptionally original in the substance of Kasaravalli's work. What is remarkable or exceptional in his cinema is his keen insight into the ordinary and everyday. His source is current—or relatively recent—India. Indeed, the images and the narrative details are drawn from Karnataka, and to a Western viewer, many of these might bear the appeal of the exotic to some extent. However, a basic universal import will indeed be appreciated.

Right from the time of the making of *Avshesh*, Girish Kasaravalli had a rare understanding of the relationship between camera, object, and the created image. He had also developed, largely through literature, a rich awareness of what makes a good story, and how it should be told. He is a man of genuine humanity, with a profound compassion for the unremarkable many—the deprived, the exploited, the bullied, the alienated, and the rejected. He is a man of his nation, critically and intelligently concerned with its history and tradition, and the society that has emanated out of that. He is not so lacking in realism as to overlook the ordinary, or to be content with simplicity in representing it. In all, he is eminently qualified to nurture at the core of his cinema the mystery of the mundane.

1

Why Are You Always Looking Sad?

Like many of the world's eminent filmmakers, Girish Kasaravalli announced with his first film a formidable artistic talent, a profound intellect and an incisive vision of his social and cultural inheritance. The strengths of this film would stand as the hallmarks of all his subsequent work, varied and diverse as it is, and some of its themes would reappear in the different social contexts and settings of other films.

Ghatashraddha (1977) is sometimes subtitled 'The Ritual,' sometimes 'The Excommunication.' While the latter might qualify the former, it also points more specifically to the film's substance. As in so much of Kasaravalli's work, the focal character is a woman and the developing theme is that of rejection; somewhat typically, the context is cultural tradition. It is the one Kasaravalli feature film discussed in this book that is in black and white, and is starkly memorable for that reason.

The setting of the film is a traditional Vedic school for the sons of Brahmans who are destined for a priestly vocation. This setting is also the central image of the film in that the school—its structure, its people, its associated behaviour and values—may be seen as a metaphor for Brahmanism itself. Visually, this central image is dominant as architecture, in its centrality to the village or small town, and in its contrast to the neighbouring jungle, while socially, it is dominant in the working out of the narrative and in the depiction of its characters, their behaviour and their engagement with one another.

The opening image (which tidily relates to the closing image as well) is not manmade but organic, and may on reflection be seen to endorse the metaphor of the school. It is the quintessentially Indian image of a banyan tree, much loved in literature for such favours as giving shelter to wayfarers, or offering shade to gurus and their disciples in quest of enlightenment. At the outset we see, only in close-up, the gnarled surface of the tree serving as backdrop for the opening titles. With the closing presentation of this image, the traditional notion of the banyan's loving and caring embrace will be seen as grim irony.

The visual impact of the image of the school does not strike us until a little way into the film. In the post-titles sequence, we are taken into its temple during an offertory ritual performed by one of the boys, while a discourse is being given to a congregation of men and women, seated according to gender. While in Hinduism, as in Judaism and Islam, such segregation is wholly unremarkable, this otherwise inconsequential portrayal of it is, nevertheless, a subtle indication of the institutionalised sexism that the film seeks to expose. This brief sequence also offers the first of an ongoing series of comments on the nature of the boys, who are the coming generation of the superior priests of Hinduism. The boy performing the ritual comes to stand beside one of his fellows, absorbed in a task of his own, and holds the offertory tray close to the other boy's arm, so that the tip of the flame of the lamp touches his bare flesh. This might be seen as a mere prank—they are boys, after all—but any generous feeling for its player sours when, a little later, he is seen pilfering some coins from the offering.

The visual impact of this opening sequence is impressive in the nature of the ritual itself, the costumes, the boys' formalised hair styles, and the elderly gentleman—who we will come to learn is Udupa, the principal of the school—occupied with what seem to be ancient manuscripts. There is nothing to suggest that what we see is necessarily set in the twentieth century. Indeed, semblances of antiquity are important here, for rationally or not, it is in antiquity that the authority of tradition is so often entrenched. Melded with this is the underlying imperfection of human nature, seen in the mischief of the officiating boy, and indicated in the only significant piece of dialogue in the opening sequence, in which one of the women in the congregation asks, somewhat pointedly perhaps, why

Yamuna does not come to the temple any more, coupled with the concern that she may be unwell. By simple eye contact, Udupa is drawn into engagement with the woman, and this also provides the continuity into the next sequence, after the pilfering, when we see him mixing some sort of a potion for a tired-looking young woman. So much has been introduced with such bare economy of action and dialogue.

The young woman is Yamuna, the widowed daughter of Udupa, and she sits in silence throughout the sequence, wan and melancholy. Two things come from Udupa: that Yamuna probably has a liver disorder, which will be cured by his potion in just a few days, and that one Sham Bhatta wants to enrol his son in the school. It will transpire that Yamuna's disorder does not pertain to her liver, and that Sham Bhatta's little boy will have a special relationship with Yamuna. Thus, two central pillars of the narrative are put in place. Udupa leaves the room, directing two boys to see that Yamuna has water. One of the boys is the mischief-maker and thief whom we have already met, and he obeys Udupa with what he describes as 'fun,' providing Yamuna with water that is boiling. Her obvious distress amuses him, and it is now evident that nastiness will be an element in the underlying emotional atmosphere of the film.

In the nature of things in such an institution as a Vedic school, Udupa had identified an auspicious day on which Sham Bhatta should bring his little boy, Nani, to be enrolled. Now we see the exterior of the school through the eyes of the new boy, as it were. The imposing entrance is the subject of a brief shot, focussing on the upper of two stories, and zooming out to reveal both stories and balcony, with carved pillars, ornate balustrades, and the wrought timber work of the ceilings. There is also a passing glimpse of Yamuna sitting inside a room alone.

Udupa receives Nani and his father, and without dialogue or much ado at all, Nani is accepted into the school. There is a shot of the little boy standing in isolation, dressed in his travelling clothes, then the same shot is offered again, but this time the boy is wearing the garb of the school—a short white dhoti and a white cloth across his otherwise bare upper body. This is followed by a shot that sees him engaged in some ritual activity with Udupa and some other boys (it is evident that he is much younger than the others).

There is then a cut to the river, which might suggest some interesting associations based on the image of water. Only a little earlier we noted the brief sequence involving boiling water. Now there is a shot of the river, with some boys washing their clothes. Soon after there is a shot of Sham Bhatta washing his and his son's feet before entering the school. Then, after establishing Nani's acceptance into the school, there is a shot of the river and boys swimming. So we have the simple image of water associated with cruelty, with cleansing and purifying, and with recreation. Further into this last sequence Nani is bullied in the river, and the life-giving substance is then associated with alienation. One may read symbolism and metaphorical intent into this if one likes, but it is important not to miss the narrative purpose that will see Nani being drawn increasingly to Yamuna in a relationship of mutual support, and a burgeoning callousness and pitilessness that will form the stumbling block which that relationship must confront and try to transcend.

The relationship is seemingly a substitutional one in that Nani stands in as the child Yamuna never had and she fills the place of his absent mother. When she finds Nani in tears after the departure of his father and his rough treatment in the river, her approach to him is maternal, as she cajoles him to stop crying and go to his lessons, tying his *dhoti* for him before he goes, and offering him sweets later on as a reward. Two things are revealed in the shot of her looking after him as he leaves: the obviously maternal affection in her eyes, followed quickly by her wince in apparent back pain.

Obviously, Nani has more to gain from this friendship than Yamuna has, but what develops is much more than a relationship of convenience for the boy, who will in turn prove himself to be resolutely loyal to Yamuna and protective of her. There is a sequence where he leaves the temple in hunger and runs to her. She feeds him with appreciable affection, but then is suddenly prevailed upon to deal with the neighbour Goda—the woman who was solicitous about Yamuna in the opening sequence—who has called to try to satisfy her concern (or curiosity) once again. All Nani has to do is say that Yamuna is not there and that he does not know where she is, and yet he cannot escape the guilty smile of one who is being duplicitous. However, he saves Yamuna from Goda's prying, and in so doing, his role in the relationship with Yamuna takes on a conspiratorial aspect. He does not realise the full extent of the significance of this, for he does not even know that there is something amiss with Yamuna's health, let alone what, in fact, her problem is. Quite some days later, when he goes to Goda's house to pick *bilva* leaves for use in the temple, he survives another grilling from her, quite truthfully pleading 'I don't know' to questions about Yamuna's health, saying little and giving nothing away, other than 'she was giddy' once. It is after these questions that he himself becomes concerned for Yamuna and asks, somewhat anxiously, if she is unwell. We soon find out what is wrong with her when she goes out clandestinely one night to meet a young man, the village schoolmaster, who offers her some sort of nostrum to effect an abortion.

The focus starts to fall more persistently on to Yamuna now. As she becomes manifestly more central to the narrative, she remains no longer the silent, melancholy woman in the background, or somewhere to the side. She will now be obliged to respond or react, or to do nothing, but she will never be an *agent,* never be able to take control over her own life and point it in the direction she wants it to take. She must submit to an inexorable course of victimisation, directed by self-righteous men and brutally mischievous boys. Inevitably, Nani will be gathered into this maelstrom.

However, before he lets the narrative show Yamuna in the emergent condition of victimhood, Kasaravalli examines more closely the social and potentially emotional isolation of the little boy, and this necessitates a more substantial treatment of the nature and devilment of the other boys, especially Shastri and Ganesha. The kindly Udupa, before setting out on a school business trip, expresses to Yamuna his concern for Nani's emotional security, as he is away from home at such a young age. She admits her worry that 'those two boys [Shastri and Ganesha] tease him so much.' She lets him sleep beside her, as would his mother, but soon he goes back to his own bed, beside Shastri. The boys tease him even while he is asleep, on one occasion putting religious marks in chalk on his forehead. Later, there is a shot of Shastri's hand doing some quasi-amorous wandering over Nani's body (the medium close shot shows clearly his filthy finger nails); Nani wakes up and flees in fright to Yamuna, who lies him down and covers him up on her bed. She is agitated, evidently, and is impatient with his questions of concern for her—'Why were you sitting outside?' and 'Why are you always looking sad?'

In fact, she is waiting for the schoolmaster to arrive and when he does, her quiet yet clearly panic-driven urging of him to come back some other time is observed with consternation by Nani, while it is spied on salaciously by the other two boys. Two things are suggested here. One is the helpless anxiety of Nani, aware—but, given his age, not intelligently so—that Yamuna, who is so kind and motherly to him, is profoundly unhappy. The other is one of the mechanisms by which gossip starts to evolve into scandal.

The camera shows Nani, when not with Yamuna, as an isolate or a reject. There are shots of him alone, lost, as it were, in the embrace of nature. We see him skipping about the jungle with the butterflies or observing from the cover of the trees the schoolmaster riding his bicycle down a rural road, all the while in his own world, keeping his own company. The pathos of his solitariness is pointed in one scene, where he chances upon the village school and watches through the window the schoolmaster miraculously managing what would normally be three or four classes in one. Clearly, Nani would rather be at this school with boys his own age, learning things that are useful and relevant to his life beyond an arcane religious system. There is empathy in his observation as he instinctively offers audible vocal help to a younger boy having difficulty in pronouncing a certain sound. Instantly, he realises that he is out of place and he hastens away, back to his solitude.

Nani's situation becomes more vulnerable when Udupa is away, for then an assistant, Upadhyay, takes charge, a man who appears cynical and uncommitted to his work, incurring the mild contempt even of Goda. He is hardly sympathetic or supportive of Nani, and even less kind. In front of the other boys, he belittles Nani with words steeped in sarcasm. When Yamuna comes in with a tumbler of water for him, Upadhyay expresses to her his scorn for the boy's lack of learning. Yamuna vigorously supports Nani and so brings a smile of gratitude to the little boy's face. Nevertheless, without the watchful and caring Udupa, Shastri and Ganesha have greater licence to tease and trouble him.

There is nothing in Shastri and Ganesha—or in any of the boys, for that matter—to suggest much that is redeeming in their natures. However, while they may be callous and negative, so too are many boys of their age. Kasaravalli would seem to find fault in the institution rather than its students. He has Shastri bemoan his boredom to Nani, citing the tedium of the syllabus, the activities, the people and the food, and it would be difficult to gainsay his complaints. While some boys might well be cut out for such an institution, most are not. The scene showing a group of them in a locked room, smoking and gambling with cards, might grate, given the moral high ground Brahmans are supposed to occupy, but like other boys, Brahman boys get bored too, even with things that are meant to engender virtue and moral upliftment. It is tedium rather than premeditated malice that brings Shastri, disguised as some kind of jungle savage, to genuinely terrify Nani on his way to collect *bilva* leaves. However, in the instance of touching the snake-stones, it may be thought that Shastri is doing Nani a favour in helping him overcome a mere superstition and the irrational fear that stems from it, but he then goes and spoils it by inventing some superstitious nonsense of his own in order to impose—albeit flippantly—his own power over Nani.

As Nani is troubled by Shastri, Yamuna continues to be troubled by Goda. Goda, too, is a widow, as may be supposed by the lack of a *bindi* on her forehead. While she is persistent in her curiosity about Yamuna's condition, there is no candid suggestion of any malice on her part. She might, indeed, be genuine in her concern. However, given Yamuna's pregnancy and the things that would serve to make it categorically repugnant—she is a widow and the daughter of a Brahman, one closely connected to the daily lives of sons of Brahmans in their education in righteousness—she is too emotionally distressed to be able to be anything but pessimistic about Goda's friendship. Goda reveals her suspicion that Yamuna is pregnant and claims to offer help, but in an emotional panic Yamuna loses her control and lets out a burst of abuse at Goda, and it becomes clear that Goda is, indeed, motivated by nastiness. In hellish fury, the woman scorned now reveals her indignation to all and sundry, and so the world starts closing in on Yamuna and, by association, on Nani.

(It is a very effective sequence of shots through which the camera suggests to us the extent of Goda's expression of rage. It is done mostly by means of high shots looking down on the village, with Goda's voiceover, as though she is actually walking through it, proclaiming her message publicly. The words come to an end, but an angry drumbeat is maintained, and the camera then sets its sights beyond the village to the surrounding countryside, the drumbeat still sounding, giving the suggestion that Yamuna's awful sin and its dreadful ramifications cannot be contained or suppressed.)

It becomes evident that Goda's rant has not been inconsequential. Upadhyay questions Shastri on Goda's allegations. He gives nothing away, nor does he clear the air in any way, and so Upadhyay decides to leave, entrusting the education of Nani to Shastri and Ganesha, which is, in effect, licence for further bullying. But word has travelled far, and Ganesha's father turns up unexpectedly to take his son away. The man pointedly ignores Yamuna's attempts at polite conversation, treads crudely over her offer of hospitality and turns aside from the water given to him by Nani. The reason for coming for his son appears clear. There is a shot of the pain on Yamuna's silent face, followed by a shot of the tumbler of water and the palpable insult that it represents. Strong in its symbolism is the shot of Nani raising the tumbler high and throwing the water on the floor.

Shastri too sees in all of this his own opportunity to break free and invites Nani to join him. Given the teasing and bullying that the little boy has borne from the older one, it might seem strange that he would even entertain the idea, but it is quite clear, in the light of circumstances such as Goda's rant, the sudden arrival of Ganesha's father and his contempt toward Yamuna, as well as Yamuna's own enhanced distress, that his situation would now seem to be uncertain. He seeks Yamuna's approval to leave, and she tries to constrain him with her hands and, ultimately, a hug, but Nani, confused and unable to interpret all that is happening, impulsively delivers a brutal kick to her stomach, causing her to cry out in pain as she lets him go. He does not run to join Shastri; rather, he backs very, very slowly away from Yamuna, unable to take his eyes off her in her suffering, which he has caused and which he cannot explain. He accidentally walks into a large copper vessel used to store water in traditional Brahman homes, and it crashes over. We know in that split second that he will not go, and the cut is to him sitting on the floor with her in the kitchen, playing with some utensils, trying to make things seem as though nothing untoward has happened. Eventually, a trace of a smile comes to Yamuna's face, and it is reflected on Nani's. He then takes the next step in the restoration of normalcy, telling her that he is hungry and so allowing her to show her affection for him in giving him food. They have come through a distressing episode together.

The focus of the narrative returns to Yamuna, where it will stay for the remainder of the film. And as we watch this hapless woman's plight, cruelly directed and enhanced by others, we see a remarkable moral growth in Nani, corresponding to Yamuna's complete loss of self-dominion.

There is a softening respite where the camera, focussing on Nani, might suggest that all is now well. We see the boy absorbed in his studies in the environs of some of the ornate features of the old building, seeming to blend with the structure and the shadows cast variously by it. Then some of the boys, with the intention of exposing Yamuna's 'affair,' come and ask Nani if he would go for a walk with them. He goes to seek Yamuna's permission, but she is not to be found and, sensing that something may be amiss, they all hurry off into the jungle to look for her.

The sequence that ensues is as dense as the jungle in which it is set. The boys find Yamuna, frightened and alone, outside the old temple. They take up positions for spying. The schoolmaster arrives and offers comfort, affection and a suggested course of action. We are not enlightened on the course of action, but it is enough for one of the boys to have all his suspicions confirmed. A cobra then slithers towards the couple, sending panic into Nani. We remember Nani's recently expressed fear of snakes and so it is a matter of surprise that he should rush out of hiding to warn of it, take up a stick and attack it. He takes Yamuna's arm and smiles reassuringly at her. Meanwhile, the loving and supportive schoolmaster has fled.

Of some interest is a brief interchange between two of the boys. One seeks to explain the presence of the snake as a result of 'the bitch' having defiled the temple. The other sees in this the reason for the anger of some god. The following sequence sees a deputation of men coming to Yamuna to make up for what the snake was unable to do. It is in this context that the schoolmaster's disappearance is significant. Evidently, in the case of an inappropriate pregnancy, which virtually by definition is an abomination, the woman is entirely culpable, while the man who, in the throes of physical delight, brought the abomination about would seem to be of no consequence at all.

This particular sequence is very dramatic and holds an element of tension in the fact that only a barred door keeps the parties apart. All the dialogue comes from outside the door, with Yamuna on the inside sitting in fearful silence and Nani, also silent, anxious and apprehensive. The men, wanting to confront Yamuna, demand that the door be opened. Her carnal sin has to be exposed and punished, but also Nani has to be rescued from his dangerous relationship with her. (It is, of course, unimaginable how unhappy he would have been had it not been for her.) The tension is further enhanced by the noise of their knocking and banging, somewhat surreally muffled to blend in with an ominous sound of drumming. Eventually the verdict of the elders of the temple is delivered: Udupa is to be informed that Yamuna is to be rendered outcaste.

The ludicrous lack of logic in this twisted morality is complemented by another cruel absurdity established in Hindu tradition. Nani has found Yamuna unconscious on the floor, beside a pool of vomit, and has carefully and with great maturity for his years attended to her. Later that night he falls asleep, allowing her to sneak out, apparently to invite death by putting her hand down a snake's hole. While she mulls over her disappointment at the failure of this plan, Kasaravalli introduces an Untouchable called Katira into the narrative. He comes to Yamuna for his nightly meal and is persuaded by Nani to help him look for her. Walking through the jungle at night, Nani gets frightened and pleads with Katira to hold his hand, but just as a caste Hindu would fear the pollution of an outcaste's touch, the Untouchable is also frightened of causing pollution to a Brahman boy. He resolutely refuses to hold Nani's hand, throwing down his flaming torch and inviting Nani to carry it instead, even though the torch, it may be said, carries the touch of the Untouchable. They find Yamuna and again, Katira is obliged to refuse to help Nani lift her up.

The course of action recommended by the schoolmaster is now put into effect. As the nostrums he had given Yamuna have failed to induce a miscarriage—or she has simply failed to take them—the only option remaining seems to be an abortion. And so the action shifts to Parbhu's squalid toddy-shop, where a hideous scene is played out as the means to resolve Yamuna's plight. An ironic visual element here is a baby in a cradle, an indication of a life beginning just where another is to be aborted.

There are three points of focus. One is the room in which Yamuna lies, submitting herself to the crone who will perform the hazardous operation. For a time, the schoolmaster is present here and, more briefly, so is Nani. Attached is a 'waiting room' where the schoolmaster and Nani, and later Nani alone, are confined. The third is outside the building and a short distance from it, where Katira and several other Untouchables consume without restraint Parbhu's toddy around a campfire. Kasaravalli asserts a degree of fluidity between these three areas by the nervous come and go of the schoolmaster, the proprietary role played by Parbhu, and especially by the anxiety-driven endeavours of Nani to be with Yamuna and his forceful removal by Parbhu. A connection is made between the shop and the campfire, as one of the drinkers approaches to obtain more toddy. There is also the mutual experience of pain. Yamuna is going through physical pain in order to rid herself of emotional and psychological pain, while in the next room the schoolmaster is suffering from anxiety, wanting this to be cleared up efficiently so that he can be on the early morning bus back to his village, far from the problem that he has created. Nani too is anxious, but his emotion is not self-centred and consists of genuine worry for the safety of Yamuna; he struggles physically to be with her and struggles violently when he is physically removed by Parbhu, asserting himself with anger and contempt by knocking away the mug of milk offered by the toddy seller. In the third arena, pain is present by implication, in that the group of Untouchables are trying to drink away the pain of their age-old inhuman condition.

The atmospherics of this section of the film are noteworthy. When Yamuna arrives at Parbhu's place with Nani, the anxious schoolmaster berates her for being late and for bringing Nani with her. (Nani, in fact, has brought *her*, taking the responsibility that ought to have been the schoolmaster's.) Then there is silence, with no sound other than a door shutting and the uttering of one or two words. Once Yamuna is laid out on a makeshift operating table, a percussive effect starts up, gradually increasing in volume toward the end to complement her expression of anguish and blending into the drum beat of the dance of the drunken Untouchables. The whole process is punctuated by snippets of dialogue, mainly concerned with the schoolmaster's interests, and with keeping Nani out of the way.

The episode is steeped in violence. It depicts an act against the natural way of things, performed illegally by an unqualified amateur. Nani struggles violently to be beside Yamuna, and struggles even more violently to free himself from Parbhu. The Untouchables outside are emblems of the victimisation by institutionalised social violence. And yet, the whole process is preceded with wonderful irony by a shot of the abortionist tenderly rocking the baby in its cradle, and a loving smile on the face of the toddy seller.

Smell is also offered among the atmospherics. Parbhu's place is, after all, a toddy shop, and the drink has a distinct smell, appealing to aficionados and not so appealing to others. It is understandable that a boy of Nani's age, totally unused to the presence of liquor, would find its smell repugnant, and so would cover his nose when it is brought close to him. One may also believe that the consumption of a strong drink would be anathema to the schoolmaster, yet when he covers his nose in disgust, we might sense an element of hypocrisy; he can hardly claim enough of the moral high ground to be contemptuous of the foibles of others.

There is some excellent visual presentation of Yamuna's torment and physical distress, accompanied and intercut with the dance to the beat of a drum of the group of Untouchables, who suppress the pain of their depressed social and economic condition by drinking and dancing. The intensity of all this is contrasted by the simplicity of the abortionist's efficient removal, between two banana leaves, of what might have been a life, and her consignment of it, presumably, to the comforting fire of the Untouchables.

As far as narrative is concerned, this section might be quite climactic. Emotions have reached a peak and the tangle of action has been unravelled. However, there must be more, for this is not simply the story of a woman and her mistake. In a realm where the individual is free, the story might now be over, but Yamuna does not live in such a realm. Her world is one of personal stratification, where tradition is over-reaching and in which laws are deferred to, not for the protection they offer to the vulnerable, but because they maintain traditionally determined right values, which are the bulwarks of a traditionally determined righteous society. To go against this tradition is to pollute it as surely as would the defiling touch of Katira, so forfeiting one's right to remain part of it. Yamuna may have gone through untold anguish, but a retributive tradition must still exact a final blow.

A striking feature of the last part of the film is the expressionless face of Udupa. Sitting on the floor, he seems not sad so much as utterly detached. The same air of detachment characterises him as he performs the rituals that effectually 'kill' his daughter. It might seem odd to some that the kindly old man, so concerned for his daughter's health and caring for the welfare of Nani earlier in the film, should transcend natural human emotions and familial sentiment and appear as a dutiful functionary of religious tradition. Yamuna, fully tonsured and cast out of home and society, cuts a tragic figure, one that Nani can hardly bear to look at as he sets out with his father on his journey home. But Udupa, too, is a tragic figure, brought to suffer through no fault of his own. He has lost his daughter, cast out by a ritual performed by himself, and he has lost his school. That the Brahman Ram Bhatta, met briefly at the beginning of the film, would like to marry his daughter to him suggests that his reputation is not seriously sullied; however, what it might say about the happiness of a 16-year-old girl is another matter.

The cruelty in the treatment of Yamuna is underlined by its injustice. Yamuna's 'sin' was created by the action of two people, a man and a woman. When we see the pitiable state of the tonsured, outcaste Yamuna at the end of the film, we may think of her co-offender, now a long way away in his home village, enjoying the society of family and friends, and probably formulating designs on at least one young woman there. There is no justice, not a shred of reason, in such a contrast.

The brief portrayal of Ram Bhatta's daughter is a simple and subtle way of suggesting a more general concern about women than the particular one highlighted by the tragedy of Yamuna. In much of Indian society, it is almost inconceivable that a girl growing into adulthood should have control over the direction she would like her life to take. Her father is obliged to ensure that she is married by the time she reaches a certain age, and as Ram Bhatta's daughter is 16, he sees the matter of her marriage as urgent. After marriage, she will be subordinate to her husband and, should she become a widow, to her sons. At no stage will she hold dominion over herself. Should Ram Bhatta marry his daughter to Udupa, he would be fulfilling his tradition-decreed social obligation, arranging his daughter's marriage with a truly virtuous man, yet condemning her to the imposed severity of a long widowhood, given the likelihood of Udupa dying well before she does. The fact that Yamuna is a widow and still very young suggests that she too might have been married to a much older man. Happiness in a marriage, while it lasts, is not a consideration.

The visual quality of *Ghatashraddha* is exceptional. There is a measured balance between the long shots that lend an awareness of context and the closer shots that imbue the film with much of its intensity. The natural disorder of the surrounding jungle and the design of the constructed interiors, often with ornate elements, offer a visual contrast, yet one which allows an easy transition from one space to another. The black and white photography allows for some very fine work with shadows and silhouettes, such as when Nani is sitting on a balcony absorbed in study, or in the shots of him and Katira running through the jungle at night. Black and white also allows much of the atmosphere to be imbued with an appropriate starkness. The precise camerawork and tight editing, which set up the triangular connection in the toddy-shop, create an atmosphere that is sinister and at times alarming. Again, in the final shots of the film, the precision of the camera facilitates, without dialogue, the irrevocable separation between the once seemingly inseparable Nani and Yamuna.

The central characters in Kasaravalli's films are not all women, though women feature prominently in every one of them. The treatment of women might be said to be a measure of a society's advancement, and a perceptive social observer must take a critical look at the position of women in society if social criticism is to be of any real value. In a society where values and protocols have been developed and established by high-caste men, in whom social authority is also vested, it would be unrewarding to seek an inclusive, democratic way of life universally enjoyed by all, even in the world's largest democracy.

Nearly 40 years after its release, *Ghatashraddha* remains one of the most memorable films of Indian art cinema. Its artistic excellence has not in any way been compromised by time, while in the matter of the tension between tradition and modernity, its substance continues to be strikingly relevant. Cultural conservatism is very strong in India, and it is of great importance that films such as those of Girish Kasaravalli should make it answerable to incisively critical examination.

On this abstract and essentially intellectual level, *Ghatashraddha* is a beacon film. On a more concrete and personal level, it is also laudable for its genuine humanity and its representation of human sensitivities, particularly those of the powerless. The quintessential sadness of Yamuna, preserved in her inability to give vent to its causes, and the emotionally agitated Nani, muffled by his innocence and inexperience, may be seen to represent a myriad of little people who are repressed by powers unwilling to listen, understand, or care.

2

I Have Never Been Able to Give You Anything

It has been estimated that at any given time of day, something equivalent to the population of Australia is travelling by train in India. Despite many glaring inefficiencies, the service seems to be nothing short of a miracle, rather like the Indian government. India has been the world's largest democracy by far since it attained independence in 1947 (except for the 21 months of the Emergency imposed by Indira Gandhi in 1975), and its continued flourishing might be considered miraculous too. Immensely more populous, much more extensive, but indeed more nightmarish than miraculous is the bureaucracy needed to make this democracy work. It is a vast chaos of manual typewriters, fountain pens and carbon paper, forms, reports, rules and regulations, and manila folders, whose antiquity and irrelevance may be gauged by the thickness of the layers of dust that they bear, and the profusion of cobwebs that embrace them. Set in this rebarbative world, *Tabarana Kathe* ('The Story of Tabara,' 1986) deals with the slow and relentless strangulation of a good man with an infinite supply of red tape.

In the main, the film is standard neo-realism, developing a narrative that implies a credible critique of Indian bureaucracy, but as that bureaucracy is very often a playground for all manner of human foibles, so too is Kasaravalli's film appropriately tinted with suggestions of the surreal, hints of the grotesque and a liberal measure of nightmare. The film's genius lies in the successful blending of these fanciful elements into a generally natural context.

Confusion, bafflement, unreason and the like are prominent throughout, so there is significance in the film's beginning at the end with a joke about not knowing the difference between an end and a beginning. Two men coming home from hunting see Tabara staring at the horizon. They refer to his 'madness' (how many innocent misfits have been explained away as mad?), an unkind description which, however, would seem to be somewhat corroborated by his telling them that he does not know whether the sun is rising or setting. To the two hunters—representative, let us say, of the 'general public'—such a difficulty in perception is not only amusing, but indicative of insanity. Eventually, we will come to perceive in the hunters—or whoever they represent—a blindness to the rampant moral derangement in a society that would readily conflate the sun's rising with its setting, if that were to serve its venal urges. Significant here is, on the one hand, the readiness of the hunters to jump to clichéd conclusions and, on the other, Tabara's standing apart from them in impressive dignity and mystery. And yet, a contradiction basic to him is central to Tabara's seeming separation from the rest of the world. While he maintains an admiration for the former rule of the British in India, the political system adopted after Independence, which gradually came to stifle and crush him, was essentially left by those whose rule he continues to admire. Singularly devoted to his own duty, he remains ignorant of politics. Thus, his confusion between sunrise and sunset is a suggestion of the failure of the Indian system of government and administration.

The narrative is based on conflict and impelled by emanations of randomness. In fact, it is an unforeseen play of circumstances that sets this story of Tabara in motion to start with. Krishnappa, Tabara's friend and colleague in the local or sub-district civil service, had wanted to be transferred from the apparently stressful coffee department and was somewhat dismayed, not just at having his request granted but also at its being executed as a simple swap with Tabara, who was then working in the more comfortable department of the toll gate. This is where the film actually opens, with Krishnappa bringing conscience-appeasing gifts to Tabara. Tabara, however, is in no way perturbed. He is a dedicated clerk and has been for decades, praised by the erstwhile British rulers for his integrity and efficiency. He trusts his belief that simply doing the job with integrity and efficiency will help him over whatever obstacles might come in his way.

What follows is quite unforeseen, especially by Tabara. The district's coffee planters are wealthy men and, with their concomitant power, are a formidable force when they declare their flat refusal to pay their due tax. Such disputations had been the cause of Krishnappa's discomfort and now will be the bane of Tabara's life. It is in Tabara's nature to carry out his work with care and good humour, so when a few of the planters come to harass him, he attends meticulously to the paperwork, engaging minimally, though with courtesy and affability, with their leader, Kalliah. However, wealthy bullies can turn nasty when their own interests are threatened, and so Tabara is intimidated, his paperwork is torn up and thrown in his face, and a bottle of red ink is used to exacerbate the spoilage. This is more than an act of bullying, for in the destruction of Tabara's paperwork, including a receipt for 360 rupees, the seeds of Tabara's own destruction are sown. The ageing clerk has always prided himself on his honesty but now, to his dismay, a strong suspicion of corruption is voiced by some of his superiors. Without the paperwork, who is to deny that Kalliah actually paid the 360 rupees and that it was filched by Tabara? He now has to depend on the decency of the planters, or the sympathetic understanding of his superiors, or find the spoiled and discarded paperwork—three options, all of which prove fruitless.

The coffee planters are seen generally as an anonymous presence, there to support Kalliah in Tabara's office, or revelling in drink, gambling and petty squabbling at their club. Two are presented in particular: the president of the planters' association, Gowda, and his would-be political rival, the bully Kalliah. When Tabara approaches Kalliah at the club, the liquor bill being run up would be far in excess of the 360 rupees—a month's salary for Tabara—at the root of the problem, but Tabara's sincere plea elicits only rudeness and humiliation. Towards the end of the film, Tabara approaches Kalliah for a loan to help pay for medical treatment for his wife, and is offered more rudeness, followed by a patronising offer of a donation.

Tabara's pride makes him reject the offer—he wanted a loan which he intended to repay—a rejection that Kalliah interprets as arrogance. Kalliah is good at misconstruing. Earlier, when he and his henchmen appear in Tabara's office, Tabara tells them, 'The British orders were to collect taxes without fear or favour.' Unimpressed, Kalliah asserts that the planters are being Gandhian in their employment of non-cooperation, implying that Tabara stands with the imperialists and against nationalist loyalists. The truth is that Tabara is very much a Gandhian, given his dedication to the truth, while there is little in Kalliah that is in any way morally redemptive or admirable. Gowda displays a veneer of class and decency, but it does not go very deep, and he is shown as not much more than a slightly polished version of Kalliah. Early in the piece, he sends for Tabara, who is obliged to stand waiting outside his house until he comes home. When Gowda does arrive at last, he walks straight past Tabara to make a phone call inside, after which he strides out and lays hands on Tabara, furiously accusing him of meddling, of being put up to it, and even of being in league with Kalliah!

Such misunderstanding of Tabara is seen a number of times. In fact, it is more a deliberate misrepresentation to protect a Gowda or a Kalliah or certain members of the bureaucracy by simple blame-shifting. This is one of the factors that serve to create an air of unreality in the film, a kind of pervasive madness which would seek to see the simple, humble and good Tabara for what he is not. All the talk of Tabara being mad really emanates out of his inability to cope with this more general societal madness.

After all, Tabara's personal qualities mark him off as something of an oddball in comparison with many. He is hardworking and not at all self-seeking. He lives happily, in very straitened circumstances, with his wife Appi, to whom he is a loving and devoted husband, and his adopted son Babu, to whom he is an affectionate and caring father. He is courteous and affable to everyone, even the nasty Kalliah and pompous Gowda. He is utterly incorruptible. And in India's twenty-fifth year of independence, he looks back on life under the British with some nostalgia, apparently valuing what he sees as moral rectitude in government more highly than patriotism. Tabara has spent all his working life in the civil service and now, very close to retirement, he is still a lowly clerk, despite the much prized certificate of appreciation which was given to him in the pre-Independence days. Given that so much of the ladder of success would seem to consist of corrupt stratagems, Tabara has not climbed it.

His confinement to the lower echelons would seem to have made him unprepared for his own nightmare experience in trying to get access to his pension entitlements and to clear his reputation from the scandal over the 360 rupees. In this he has to deal with another form of bullying—systemic, codified, defined and labelled—from his bureaucratic superiors. Not all of them are crass like Kalliah, although some of them are indeed quite crude, but most of them are heartless like Gowda, lacking in understanding and unwilling to be of help lest their own security be threatened in some way.

The sub-district revenue office is a scene of apparently orderly disorder. Outside, the cloister is constantly crowded, mostly with complainants, while inside, clerks are all sitting at their desks doing what would at least seem to be their work, but everywhere there are piles of shabby, dusty and tattered files, causing one to wonder what is in them and what importance it might have. One especially wonders how any particular file appropriate to anyone in the crowd outside could be retrieved in such advanced chaos. The overall visual effect is quite dispiriting and touches on absurdity when the camera focusses on a huge pile of files with the arms of the head clerk seen on either side, as though in some surrealistic way the man has been subsumed by paper.

Both the head clerk and the *tehsildar*[1] are civil to Tabara, though at first it is pointed out to him that the head clerk's entry door to the *tehsildar's* office is not to be used by him, and Tabara is directed to the more general entrance. It is clear, however, that the lives of the *tehsildar* and the head clerk would be made easier if Tabara were to simply admit that he has filched the 360 rupees, pay the money back,

[1] The head of the sub-district revenue office.

and clear his name before taking a well-earned retirement. That would be sensible because it would be expedient. However, Tabara knows he has not filched the money, and there is no chance of his submitting to such a confession. The ever-reliable clerical objection that 'there's nothing in writing' is the stumbling-block. In time, both the head clerk and the *tehsildar* show greater kindness to Tabara, but each, in protecting his own back, will go only so far in actually helping. The *tehsildar's* first solution is to send Tabara back to Gowda, to try to reach a reasoned settlement with him. Gowda, pleading that he is no longer the planters' president, sends him to Kalliah with the same aim and evoking the same effect. It is manifestly obvious that buck-passing is a major bureaucratic strategy. There is a sequence in which Tabara, supported by the firebrand activist Bantyappa, is sent from one desk to another, eventually ending up at the one they had started from. Later, when he goes off in quest of certificates to 'straighten out' his employment register, Tabara meets well-practised buck-passers and prevaricators, some of them rude, some even quite aggressive. He is ridiculed, treated with contempt, and turned away. It is all frustrating and most disheartening. Tabara is helped to some extent by the good doctor attending to his wife, but the help he receives from Bantyappa is shortlived once the activist's reputation as an extremist is highlighted and Tabara comes to be threatened with the incurrence of guilt by association. The fact that this nightmare borders on the absurd is made clear by the mirth of an onlooker observing Tabara's desperation in trying to find the missing receipt in a vast garbage dump. In seeking his string of certificates, Kasaravalli has Tabara approach each office by way of a steep set of steps or a staircase, suggesting the uphill battle that he is waging, and the repetitive dialogue presented as voiceover highlights the mechanical and impersonal nature of his quest. Eventually the documentation is complete and the file 'can start to move,' which in effect means nothing. When the question 'how long will it take?' is raised, the camera focusses on the almost stupefied faces of four elderly men waiting patiently outside in the corridor, as they may well have been doing for years.

The story of Tabara's mission to clear his name and ensure the timely payment of his pension is modified by another narrative element, vital in its importance though not as extensively treated. This strand also emanates out of a purely random event. There is a scene of the lovely serenity of river and lush jungle, in which Babu's attention is attracted to some blasting in the distance, where a new road is being forged out of a hill. He hurries to his foster-mother, who is picking coffee beans nearby, and persuades her to go with him to watch it from a better vantage point; lovingly, she agrees to accompany him. However, they get too close to the blast and Appi is hit in the leg by some flying stone, so initiating the injury and worsening the illness that will eventually claim her.

The deterioration in her health is closely linked to her husband's worsening penury. It may be that the good Dr Souza is as lenient with his billing as he is generous with his time, but medicines cost more money than Tabara can afford, and the daily injection for the leg threatened by gangrene soon becomes irregular. While Tabara has retired but is still not in receipt of his pension, there is further vacillation and deferral of action when the removal of his wife to hospital is required. Tabara is shown in the depths of despair when it is made known that she will have to have the leg amputated, even approaching the butcher, Yusuf, to ask him if he could do the amputation. There is a moment of black humour when Yusuf asks if Tabara wants to make a curry of his wife's leg, and laughs uproariously at his own joke. However, the humble Muslim butcher is not a heartless planter or bureaucrat, and he is quickly moved by the pain evident on Tabara's face. He puts down his work and takes Tabara to Gowda to try to persuade the wealthy man to provide some help. Gowda, after some nasty reference to Tabara's association with Bantyappa, undertakes to meet the costs of the patient's removal to Bangalore for her operation, but by the time she gets there, it is all too late. Tabara loses his wife, and on the same day he also loses Babu who, fascinated by the big city to the point of distraction, becomes separated from Tabara and gets lost in the crowd. Tabara now has nothing, all because of a string of events that were randomly let loose by the simple transfer of Tabara and Krishnappa to each other's jobs.

The boorishness of the planters and the various forms of resistance encountered in the bureaucracy have their counterparts in several characters in addition to Tabara and his small family. Krishnappa's first appearance in the film sees him bringing conciliatory gifts to Tabara, believing himself at fault for having placed his friend in a position from which he himself had good reason to escape. He remains a kind and staunchly supportive friend throughout, particularly when Tabara's wife has to be taken to Bangalore. Dr Souza is also very supportive and, had Tabara been able to afford the pharmaceutical side of the treatment, would probably have been quite effectual as well. He is an affable man, ever trying to hearten with good cheer and a positive outlook. In expressing his surprise that Tabara's wife has diabetes, he refers to the ailment as being popularly regarded as a disease of the wealthy. Rather than recognise the irony of this in relation to Tabara and his wife, he suggests that it must be an omen for imminent wealth. Indeed, wealth does come to Tabara, but too late to be of any use to his wife. Bantyappa's reputation as a mischief-maker or rabble-rouser is probably an aspersion emanating from people whom the activist has given cause for discomfort. His strong *pro bono* support of Tabara is motivated clearly by moral outrage at what he sees as obvious injustice. It is indeed an irony that social values are such that it should be harmful to Tabara to be associated with such a strong moral voice. And then, coming from the lower end of the social spectrum, there is Yusuf, the butcher with a touch of vulgar humour, mortified that he might have hurt Tabara's feelings and determined to atone for his indiscretion. What all four have in common is a strong moral sense, but morality is no weapon for the kind of beast that Tabara has to slay.

The penury into which Tabara falls is, of course, due to the combination of his retirement, loss of his last month's salary, and the delay in processing his entitlements. Nevertheless, it is reasonable to assume that he has always lived in straitened circumstances, as is suggested by his very humble home, his wife's employment as a coffee picker, and the fact that Babu does odd jobs rather than attend school. Yet, despite their deprivation, the family seems to be happy, their contentment emanating out of their evident love for one another. There is a touching scene between Tabara and his wife when Tabara gets home from his retirement party—a very low-key affair, but for Tabara quite a memorable one, in which he is garlanded and presented with a box of fruit. He tells Appi how much he wished that she had been there, gives the fruit to her, and remarks that he has been garlanded only twice in his life—at his wedding and on his retirement. He makes the very touching observation that 'In all my life, I have never been able to give you anything,' and gives her the simple garland, which she regards as beautiful, and the fruit, which she wants to save for Babu. There is a short expression of familiarity as Tabara feeds her a piece of fruit, and she becomes coy at the prospect of Babu seeing them. (Of course he does, and is delighted at his foster-parents' affection for one another.) The two then recall their wedding day and enjoy a giggle together as they remember having their photograph taken, something that has probably never been done since. As his wife's illness worsens, Tabara becomes more and more solicitous about her, while he also becomes more and more helpless in his inability to generate any improvement in her health. All the while, she bears her deterioration stoically.

Tabara tells us that he and his wife had no children of their own, and he jokingly adds that he never had the time to do anything about it (which, given his dedication to his work, probably carries an element of truth). Hence they adopted an orphan, Babu, an exceptionally good-natured boy. He is devoted to his foster parents, yet ironically he is central to three instances of arbitrariness which lead to the suffering of both of them. In the first, already mentioned, he genuinely wants to share with his mother his excitement at the explosive roadworks and she, to please him, lets herself be persuaded. What ought to have been mother and son enjoying an unusual event turns out to have a drawn-out tragic consequence, in the injury to Appi's leg and its degeneration to gangrene. Later, there is a seemingly pointless sequence in which Babu undertakes to fetch a packet of cigarettes for a road-worker. His self-esteem swells with the worker's money in hand and after the purchase, with such a symbol of manliness as a packet of cigarettes in his shirt-pocket, placed for all the other boys to see. Here again, Babu is being distracted by the making of the road, for while he is strutting about in a fantasy of virility, Appi has a fall and calls to him. Had he been with her, his presence might have prevented her accident, he may have been able to fetch the doctor or even administer some basic first aid, but quite inadvertently he is negligent of her. After her death, he is distracted again, this time seduced by the excitement of the big and bustling modern city, and he becomes separated, permanently it would seem, from Tabara. Obviously this is a tragedy for Tabara, who loses both his wife and son on the same day, but it is also cruelly ironic that such a force for good as Babu should, albeit unwittingly, be the cause of this suffering. The randomness of life can be tantalisingly aberrant.

The film has an extraordinary ending. While it might have been natural to expect it to end with Tabara, broken and dejected, joining the four patient old men sitting in the cloister outside the *tehsildar's* office, Kasaravalli has Tabara achieving a kind of triumph. At last the red tape would seem to have been cut and Tabara's pension is ready to be made available to him. But this is not the triumph. The triumph lies in Tabara's categorical rejection of it. After all he has been through, Tabara does not take kindly to the sanctimonious suggestion that he contribute some of it to the fund to celebrate India's twenty-fifth anniversary of Independence, smelling a rat of corruption at work. He, whose every utterance to men of a higher station has been mealy-mouthed, now explodes in fearsome anger, telling 'such dirty bastards' to keep it all.

The sequence opens with the *tehsildar* mentioning to the head clerk the distress that the whole Tabara affair has caused him, what with the pressure for 'notes, memos, explanations, clarifications,' and instructs the head clerk to have Tabara sent for right away. Tabara arrives to be informed that his money has come. But why now? Has it been available for some time? What is the connection between the availability of the money and the *tehsildar's* stress over 'notes, memos, explanations and clarifications'? There is a clear suggestion that processes have not been particularly transparent. However, the *tehsildar,* who thought his headaches would go away by giving Tabara his money and extracting from him a substantial contribution to the Jubilee Fund, now has a bigger headache than ever in explaining away Tabara's extraordinary rejection of his entitlement.

The presentation here starts off realistically and gradually takes on a highly stylised nature without losing the underlying realism that gives it meaning and credibility. There is an anticipation of Tabara's defiance in his decision to wear a traditional *lungi* and shirt instead of the service uniform which he has worn throughout the film. Then he insists on entering the *tehsildar's* office by way of the 'public' door, which he was originally directed to use, despite the now fawning persuasion of the head clerk to use his more 'private' door.

Tabara's arrival at the sub-district revenue office arouses some warm feeling, some of it genuine, such as the peon's friendly greeting (though the same peon will physically escort him from the building a little later), but much of it is in puerile anticipation of a bit of fun at 'mad' Tabara's expense. Tabara enters the outer office seemingly dazed and unaware of his surroundings, perhaps being reminded of all the unpleasantness during his previous visits to this place. The daze soon turns to rage with the raising of the issue of the Jubilee Fund, and Tabara is keen to detach himself from such a celebration, referring to it as '*your* celebration.' In British India Tabara's meritorious work was acknowledged; in independent India it has been taken for granted, and even exploited by corrupt and self-serving men. In his cascade of anger he has to be physically restrained and taken out. It is here that the presentation becomes notably stylised. Dialogue is absent and the pace slows considerably. The discomfort of the head clerk and the junior clerks is made apparent by their hiding behind stacks of files or a typewriter or a paper, as Tabara is slowly led out. As he comes out onto the cloister, all the men waiting there turn to him and many make to follow him, all the time watching him in silent amazement, or awe, or admiration. Tabara's defiant face is central to the camera's focus, except for a close-up, left to right pan shot of the faces of the clerks, looking up from their desks and out through the barred window.

There is a final shot of the four impassive, patient old men, and then the camera returns for the last time to a close-up of Tabara's face. A placid, conforming, obedient man has stood up to his superiors in a grand confrontation, a confrontation that has necessitated a sacrifice, but a sacrifice of something he has never had and which is of no use to him now that he has no one to spend it on. Tabara's revolutionary expression of defiance, contempt, and condemnation makes an underling at least momentarily a hero.

A notable feature of Girish Kasaravalli's work is that each film is significantly different from the others. Here, close to the beginning of his career, this quest for difference is seen most clearly; *Ghatashraddha* and *Tabarana Kathe* are worlds apart. Yet there are important similarities that will be found with the other films, too. Visually *Tabarana Kathe* typically bespeaks an eloquent camera, capable of communicating eloquently without too much recourse to dialogue. The shots of Bangalore, for example, have considerable impact, given the striking contrast they assert to Tabara's sub-district world, but they also enable an immediate visual appreciation of Babu's excitement, as well as establishing the bustling city as a haystack in which Babu might be a lost needle. The shots of the sub-district region are well-balanced in their variety—the clutter and confusion of the *tehsil* office, the raucous boisterousness of the planters' club—while the exterior shots of the serenity of jungle and stream and the industrial ugliness of the road-building offer appropriate contrasts. Other interiors, such as Gowda's house and Dr Souza's clinic, are presented with an intelligent care for detail, yet Tabara's cottage is deliberately vague. Its minimal décor of course corroborates his penury, but what is especially notable about it is its obvious isolation from the broader context of the sub-district town that dominates Tabara's life. This lack of spatial connection, or detachment from context, suggests a fundamentally nebulous relationship between Tabara and the town or, by extension, Tabara and the world. Given his warm feelings for British times, he would also seem to be out of temporal relationship with it. In short, the film's visual design tends to highlight Tabara as a misfit.

The film, as its title tells us, is the story of Tabara, but Tabara is hardly a man of such significance that a story about him would excite much interest. Nevertheless, while Tabara as an *agent* is of little appeal, apart from his being a goodly man, Tabara as a *victim* is indeed of considerable concern. In engaging with the story of the things that are done to Tabara, we are witnesses to not only the workings of a particular sub-district revenue office but what seems to be becoming a bureaucratised culture. The bureaucracy is set up to serve society, but in the process it might be seen to be strangling, stultifying and contorting society. To perfect the social machine, procedures and protocols are developed and established, along with rules and regulations. This mechanism, with its immense complexity, is supposed to ensure the good of society, but it is also vulnerable to those who would seek their own personal advantage by searching for loopholes, ambiguities and inconsistencies in it. As Gandhi showed in the Non-Cooperation and Civil Disobedience Movements, a vast political complexity can be attacked from outside simply by ignoring it, and so the coffee planters, perversely acknowledging the Mahatma, refuse to pay their tax, while the protocol followed by Tabara in simply doing his duty bears the seeds of his own—and the system's—undoing. The heaps of tattered and dusty files suggest, cinematically, the worthlessness of the bureaucratic machine, while the suffering of Tabara points to an appalling lack of compassion in contemporary society. The implicit moral criticism in the film, in its revelations of selfishness and callousness, is complemented by occasional flashes of social criticism, such as Gowda's arrogance to Tabara in his home and in the *tehsildar's* office, or the offering of tea to Bantyappa but not to Tabara. In the perverse employment of what Kalliah calls 'civil disobedience,' in Tabara's fond remembrance of the British years, and in the virtual extortion of funds for the Jubilee celebrations, there is even a suggestion that the worth of Indian independence itself should be reassessed.

In its essential simplicity, *Tabarana Kathe* is indeed a powerful film. Its sustained gentleness does not compromise the strength of its revelation, and the bloody-mindedness of the many could never eclipse the director's unshakeable belief in fundamental human values. After all, Tabara has a triumph of sorts, witnessed by many other deprived men entrapped in the bureaucratic tangle, men who might take some heart from Tabara's example of principled outrage. The little person, muffled in confrontation with an antagonistic and subjectifying power, is to be found in one form or another in all of Girish Kasaravalli's films. None is more touching than the humble Tabara, so cruelly dismissed as 'mad.'

3

As Usual, I End up Getting the Blame

Bannada Vesha ('The Mask,' 1988) embraces, in various ways, an orbit of experience ranging from childhood to advanced age, from the lowest levels of human society to the realm of the gods. Conceptually the film is vast and complex, but its actuality is defined and relatively straightforward. Its philosophy obliges us to think far beyond the limits of the mundane, but its narrative is simple, localised and particularised. The integrity of the film is founded on a conflation of the theatrical with the ordinary and the everyday, and a conflation of both with the world of gods and spirits. To simplify, it is a film about Shambhu, whose world is the lower-caste world of village and fields; but he also walks in the world of the theatre, where he sings, dances and acts in a world of gods. One of the film's basic concerns is the question of defining a man, an actor and a deity. In India, especially in the popular culture, such definition is at best loose, in that people who work as actors are often identified as the more memorable characters they have played. A film star aspiring to be a politician should be confident of many votes if he has played the role of Ram or Krishna, for example, for the new representative of the people would not be a mere politician, but a veritable divinity.

Bannada Vesha has two contexts: the particular context is a folk theatre troupe, and the more general context is the rural community which supports it. The theatre troupe is a *yakshagana*[1] company,

---

[1] Kannada folk-theatre, comprising dialogue, music and dance, with highly stylised presentation. These performances often run throughout the night.

devoted to performing 'discourses' on tales or issues from local—as distinct from mainstream or orthodox—Hindu tradition. There is a hierarchy within the troupe, one that is perhaps loosely analogous to the stratified structure of the Hindu caste society in which it is set, albeit without the categorical rigidity of the caste system. Nevertheless, notions of seniority and superiority within the troupe give rise to tensions, inflected by negative emotions such as envy, contempt, resentment and vindictiveness. As might be expected in a theatrical troupe, at least some of the characters are motivated by egos inflated with vanity and self-absorption.

The film opens with the company having their siesta. Bhagwat, the leader and mentor of the troupe, wants them up and about, getting made up for the evening performance, and he would depute Shambhu to wake them, but first Bhagwat must wake up Shambhu. It is here that we see a prominent characteristic of Shambhu, one which makes him lovable to some and vexing to others. It is most likely that Shambhu is already awake, pretending to be asleep while Bhagwat tries to rouse him, for he suddenly sits up and bursts into some loud exclamation, alarming and acutely unsettling the manager. He is a practical joker who enjoys his own jokes immensely, and he proceeds to creatively startle his colleagues out of their peaceful sleep. It is this that allows Kasaravalli to set up the ongoing conflict between Shambhu and Sheshappa that will play a central role in the narrative.

Sheshappa is a leading actor whose magisterial manner impresses many, but not Shambhu. His superiority to Shambhu is manifest theatrically and socially, and the contempt in which he holds the younger man is unconcealed. Shambhu audaciously presumes to waken Sheshappa by tickling his nose with a feather—not any old feather, but a peacock's feather. Sheshappa, however, is not moved by this subtle allusion to the vehicle of one of the sons of Shiva,[2] and petulantly snatches the feather and snaps it into pieces.

[2] In Hindu mythology, Karttikeya, the son of Shiva and Parvati, is transported on the back of a peacock.

The childishness of the gesture is plain, but then Sheshappa moves up to a level of nastiness, referring to Shambhu as a 'lowly clown taking on the airs of a leading actor,' and throwing a pot of water in his face.

Much of Shambhu's feeling of being treated unjustly emanates out of the discomfort Sheshappa seems to inflict on him. Bhagwat, worried that the silly incident might develop to the extent of Sheshappa spoiling the evening's performance, insists on Shambhu's apologising. Of course, if Sheshappa is the venerable leading actor that he sees himself as being, spoiling the show would be the last thing on his mind. Nevertheless, Bhagwat has perceived a serious impropriety, and an apology must be offered. With the apology, Shambhu's humiliation before Sheshappa is complete; however, his vengefulness will not dissipate, so during the performance Maabala and he quite shamefully undermine Sheshappa's role.

Shambhu asserts that he is being victimised: 'As usual I end up getting the blame.' As his friend and colleague Maabala puts it, Sheshappa took the episode out of reasonable proportion, but as Bhagwat sees it, Sheshappa is an elder and a leading player, and must be treated with respect. Shambhu sees no call to respect the one who insults him and the other 'small fry,' leading Bhagwat to accuse him of envy. Shambhu turns this back, asserting that it is Sheshappa and even Bhagwat who are envious of him.

The point of this apparently petty episode is two-fold: to establish the underlying tension between Shambhu and Sheshappa, a tension that will remain relevant for much of the film, and to provide a link to Shambhu's past and so clarify how Shambhu sees himself. Indeed, figures of repute such as Sheshappa are closely associated in Shambhu's mind with the men of authority who made his childhood such an unhappy experience.

There are numerous flashbacks throughout the film, appearing so unobtrusively, or with such little distinction, as to suggest a conflation of the present with the past, and of course it would not be at all unreasonable to assert that Shambhu is indeed carrying with him much of the baggage of his earlier life. There is even an apparent conflation in these flashbacks of Shambhu and Maabala as little boys and some of the present episodes featuring Shambhu's nephew, Shankara, who is of a similar age to that of the childhood depictions of Shambhu.

The purpose of the flashbacks is to show Shambhu being bullied, seemingly unjustly, by both adults and classmates on account of his low caste and for being, allegedly, a liar and a thief. His schooldays were made even harder by having to work in the fields in place of his chronically ill father, therefore missing many days of school and evoking the mockery of the other boys for his comparative backwardness.

The continuity is in no way modified to indicate that at any stage, what may follow is a flashback, perhaps suggesting that Indian concepts of time do not necessarily imply change. We see Shambhu and Maabala walking around the temple that will now be the centre of their *yakshagana* work, remembering how the notion of 'god' inspired nothing but fear in them when they were little boys. 'God' was associated not with love but with intimidation and retribution. The boy Shambhu is dragged to a temple to swear by God that he will not steal betel nut again. Despite the boy's protestations that he has stolen nothing, his subservient father, fearful of his social superiors, begs him to swear such an oath.

Then, at the end of a scene where Shambhu, his mother and Shankara have been looking for their lost cow, the next flashback sequence is introduced with no obvious change in the jungle setting, where two little boys, looking at first glance like Shambhu's nephew Shankara, excitedly burst onto the scene. One is the young Maabala, inviting the young Shambhu to play Krishna to his villain Sishupala. They play the episode creditably, with their improvised costumes and intelligible script, but then they realise they are missing the most important prop—Krishna's *chakra* or discus that is used as a weapon to behead Sishupala. They decide to make one out of areca palm from the landlord's farm. They do no damage, but simply pick up dried palm leaves from the ground; however, one of the landlord's men sees them and jumps to the conclusion that they are stealing betel nut. There is something quite charming about a pair of simple rustic boys knowing and enacting a story from the great epic literature of India, and this makes the man's vigilance notably distasteful.

The next flashback sequence sees a man—the landlord or one of his henchmen—walking along a road; in a clearing beside it, the little boy Shambhu is rehearsing a dance. The man grabs hold of the boy and, without any evidence whatsoever, accuses him of stealing betel nut. He then marches him off to the schoolmaster. The kindly schoolmaster advises him to be like Krishna in his beneficence (despite the god being a notorious thief of dairy products!), and join a troupe where he may act his ideals. Perhaps to the complainant's disappointment, the schoolmaster does not punish Shambhu, though the other boys catch him on the road, tearing at his shirt and calling him a thief. His weak and submissive father expresses his fear that, due to his son, a curse will fall upon their house.

The last flashback sequence shows the boy in tears, refusing to go to school and face the insults and bullying of the other boys, especially because of his inability to keep up with them in class, due to his frequent absences filling in for his sick father in the fields. His father, breathing dangerously heavily, tries to explain that such things are sent by God to test us and that Shambhu should be brave, relying on God's protection, and learn to bear insults. Shambhu goes back to school, but as we see in the grown man, he may bear slights, but does not recognise his obligation to accept them (as his father would). In short, the father's feeble fatalism has not been visited upon the son. The young man's pride might render him liable to accusations of bumptiousness, even arrogance, but pride nevertheless is preferable to submissiveness and it is indeed a redeeming feature of Shambhu.

Herein lies a significant change from Shambhu the boy to Shambhu the man. It is apparent in each of the flashback sequences that the boy is apprehended and punished on no evidence at all. There is not one shot showing betel nut in his possession, and in the sequence that involves the schoolmaster, the boy is manifestly guilty of nothing other than playing truant from school. As he says later in his life, the constant harassment is due to his lowly social status, something that his father accepts as his predetermined lot in life and something to which the boy must not raise any objection, in fear of being punished further for disrespect or arrogance. When, in the opening scene in the actors' dressing room, allegations are laid against Shambhu by Sheshappa and Bhagwat, there is no timidity on his part. Even the apology to Sheshappa is more politic than one offered out of fear, or even respect.

Except for one, the narrative turning points are all minor, more like ripples on the surface of the very simple story. The one critical juncture in the narrative is the change in the troupe's administration and the new direction incumbent in that. This is evident in the context of a tour of a 'one-time splendid' temple, whose new manager Bhimbhatta has grand ambitions to restore it to its former glory. As the members of the troupe, led by Bhimbhatta, wander about the temple, we note the formal religiosity of Sheshappa, whose obvious reverence is seen in marked contrast to the flippancy of Shambhu and Maabala. Bhimbhatta has attached himself to Sheshappa, and we might expect that he has much to offer the veteran actor. However, it is his expressed aim to foreground the local religious tradition that gives rise to Sheshappa's question about the local gods. He is irretrievably lost to the grand plan when Bhimbhatta tells him that in local lore, the spirit Junjutti is even more prevalent than the presiding local deity, Kapaleshwara. Sheshappa is no longer interested. He will not stoop to playing a mere spirit, no matter how popular that role might be. He will not join the new troupe.

It is difficult to imagine an actor turning down any leading role, but here there is a suggestion that for Sheshappa, at least, the connection between himself and the roles he plays is extremely close, so that the difference between playing a character and *assuming* that character is greatly minimised. That such minimisation is to be noted in the perceptions of the common rural people might well be expected; it is interesting to note that the experienced actor has similar perceptions. However, Sheshappa's departure provides an opening for Shambhu, who is now to play Junjutti.

There are really only two spatial contexts in the film: the temple and whatever space in it is used as a theatre, and the rural realm of lush fields, plantations and jungle, along with village houses with their thatched roofs. As an adjunct to the rural scene is a long shot given several times of a broad, mostly rocky landscape with a high hill standing prominently in the central background. This scenery will be seen to carry something of a metaphorical connotation.

The visual focus moves now from the temple sphere to the rural. With his recent promotion in his acting career, Shambhu goes home for a few days, looking forward to sharing his good news with his mother. We find him arriving at a simple but well-appointed house, followed by a shift to the dense luxuriance, where his mother is searching for their lost cow. She is indeed happy with this unexpected visit from her son, but what is of particular interest here is the contrast she incidentally draws between her life and his, or the world of reality and that of meta-reality. At first, she is not particularly interested in hearing his news—'Let it wait until tonight'—for, quite rightly, it is of greater importance to her to find the lost cow. She refers to his world as a fairyland with mythical cities, and hers as one of daily drudgery that begins at dawn. She mentions his makeup and costumes, contrasting them with the workaday clothes of the villagers, and it is this that gives rise to Shambhu comparing his present condition with his experience of the village. 'I'd have gone mad without grease-paint,' he says, describing it as a shield protecting him from the effects of his constant ill-treatment as a boy on account of his birth and caste, treatment which 'made me feel I should not have been born.' His mother tries to console him with the observation that had they had some land, or were of a higher caste, no one would have bothered him—but that is exactly the point he is making. He sees his salvation in *yakshagana,* for no one can harass him again as he is now the spirit Junjutti. His mother is a little disappointed that he has the role of only a spirit and not a god, though he promises her that next year he will achieve such an elevation. She declares her wish to see him play Krishna, and then goes off to resume her search for the cow.

In preparing the script for the new discourse, Bhagwat listens to Bhimbhatta elucidate the mythology of Junjutti. He refers to a time when the demon Sharabhasura tyrannised the earth, a waywardness that eventually obliged the gods to petition Shiva to rid them of this menace. To appease the gods, Shiva sent his devotee Junjutti into the world and he destroyed the demon, restoring peace and true religion to mankind and to the gods. Junjutti was then established in the region of the Kapaleshwara temple, and Bhagwat is asked to include some demonstration of how Junjutti, even in present times, has retained his power and piety in this region. What is of significance here is the link asserted by Bhimbhatta that brings the temple, the *yakshagana* troupe and the local people all under one umbrella, and this syncretising is indeed at the heart of the film.

The one-time childhood inseparables, Shambhu and Maabala, are given the rival roles of Junjutti and Sharabhasura. Apparently Bhimbhatta's account of Junjutti has been taken greatly to heart by Shambhu, whose nervousness before the performance is quite evident. It is not entirely clear whether the cause of his nerves is the gravity of the role he is to play and its profound religious significance, or simply the fact that he now has to prove himself worthy as a leading actor; however, there is more circumstantial evidence for the latter. So far, Shambhu has shown no attachment to religion, but his theatrical ambition has been manifest.

Apparently the show is a grand success. According to Bhimbhatta, this is corroborated by the obvious increase in piety, resulting in considerably more people coming to the temple along with their offerings. Bhimbhatta sees the *yakshagana* discourse as God's work, which must be judged according to religious criteria. Bhagwat, however, is more artistically critical, asserting that the show is theatrically not up to the mark. Bhimbhatta might well see this as neither here nor there, given that the work is a religious enterprise, bearing results that have a religious significance. Bhagwat argues that the dancing is not up to standard, and that Maabala is a better dancer than Shambhu. Bhimbhatta points to the obvious audience acclaim of Shambhu, but Bhagwat is disdainful of this, asserting that an audience is taken in by flashiness and colour, and does not have much critical judgement. Simply, Shambhu's dancing is not 'classical' enough, and with such a vague and subjective criticism, we might tend to suspect that Bhagwat, the once fawning supporter of Sheshappa, is pursuing a personal agenda. When Bhagwat meets Bhimbhatta on his own ground, asking for the logic in the demon dancing better than the emissary of the great lord, Bhimbhatta must reassess. Bhagwat suggests giving the role of Junjutti to Maabala and something else to Shambhu. A temporary compromise is reached with Bhimbhatta's insistence on giving Shambhu ten more days.

In those ten days, Shambhu does a few things to his own discredit, exposing some flaws in his character which, without actually condemning him, do evince a broader and less sympathetic understanding of him. We have noted evidence of his playful mischievousness, which some consider funny but which also causes offence. There seems to be good reason to suspect that his disrespect of Sheshappa is not just playfulness but emanates from the chip he has had on his shoulder since his childhood days. This insecurity expresses itself in other situations. We see him self-absorbed, even worried, as the troupe moves along the road. He seems to be insecure about himself as an actor. At first, we might think that his nerves are the ordinary butterflies experienced by all who have to stand centre-stage sometime in their lives, but his open craving for tobacco suggests that the problem runs deeper. This suggestion is corroborated by his apparently instant addiction to the more powerful 'tobacco from the town,' his over-indulgence in which prompts his colleagues to suggest that he has been taken over by Junjutti. His inclination to malice is evident in his delivering new lines of his own, especially designed as an attack on Sheshappa, who joins the audience one night and swoons under the verbal assault from the stage, and then in Shambhu's smile when everyone else looks reverentially at the old man's body. In his continual and inadvertent undoing of himself, he strikes his lowest point when he falls out with his closest friend since childhood, Maabala. His doubts about his own ability, earlier brought to the fore perhaps by Sheshappa and kept current by Bhagwat's not-so-secret desire to have him replaced, are exacerbated by the notion—undoubtedly exaggerated by himself—that Maabala is plotting to replace him. There are angry words and then Shambhu, venting his bitterness, also asserts his physical strength over Maabala, symbolically keeping him in submission, as it were. A friendship has been ruptured and Shambhu has risked losing a staunch supporter.

As it turns out, there is no change in the casting. As determined by the natural season, the present *yakshagana* schedule comes to an end and the company goes into recess, during which time Shambhu continues in the role of Junjutti, even away from the stage, as Bhimbhatta uses this opportunity to go from door to door, soliciting donations for the company. These are made sometimes in cash, but mostly in kind—rice, lentils, maybe vegetables. He invites Shambhu to go with him, and having introduced him to each householder as Junjutti, he is gratified to note that the contributions are significantly more substantial than they had been in previous years. It is evident that the locals see Shambhu not as Shambhu the actor but as Junjutti the spirit, who has perhaps assumed the form of Shambhu the actor.

Here Shambhu shows himself as being more down-to-earth than the others, especially Sheshappa, for rather than rejoice in his elevation to the realm of the divine, he expresses serious concern that his talent as an actor is being simply glossed over. It is almost akin to being held to be irrelevant. At this point we might remember his boyhood association of God with intimidation and retribution, and acknowledge the fear that this might have distilled in him; hence, it should not be surprising that divine association is not something to which he readily aspires. The weight of his concern becomes fully pronounced when he returns home as Shambhu and is received as Junjutti, a divine spirit who may risk pollution in the home, even that of his mother. Shankara, his little nephew, has been made well aware of the potential danger in touching his uncle, who is dismayed when the little boy struggles vehemently to avoid the man's embrace. It is quite probable that Shambhu is being reminded here, in a most unexpected way, of traditional callous prejudices regarding caste status and physical contact, which are upheld by men who also presume to play God.

It is noteworthy that Shambhu's contrived imprecations have such a profound effect on Sheshappa. The contempt of the older man for the younger could not have been made more evident, so on one level it is surprising that Shambhu should have such a profound psychosomatic effect on Sheshappa. However, Sheshappa's own intense religiosity has also been made plain, and it is not unreasonable to suppose that he, more than the average member of the audience, might be susceptible to the curses of a 'divine being,' even one in the material form of Shambhu. His susceptibility gratifies Shambhu's spite, but the conflation of actor and role by Shambhu's mother and nephew threatens his very identity.

Two minor incidents are discomforting to Shambhu. The first is a shot or two of him heartily at play with a group of village boys. Perhaps he is enjoying something that never really characterised his own childhood; nevertheless, the fun comes to an abrupt end as he notices Bhagwat watching him. The implication is that Junjutti would not behave in such a way and by doing so himself, Shambhu is making manifest his own unworthiness for such a role. Later, when he returns to the temple after enjoying a cup of coffee with some acquaintance in an eatery, Bhimbhatta berates him for being seen in public doing worldly things, so rendering himself vulnerable to loss of respect, or even disapproval.

Thus, it is apparent that Junjutti is becoming a weight around Shambhu's neck. He seeks reassurance from Bhimbhatta about the value of his performance, but Bhimbhatta strongly asserts that the performance as such is nothing; what is of value is the power behind it. The actor cannot be credited with even a revelatory role, for divine power is made manifest only by God himself, the value of the actor being negligible. Indeed, the gullible public adore the role, not the actor playing it. Shambhu knows he is not Junjutti, and Bhimbhatta is telling him that an actor is nothing. Given that, and the fact that his own mother and nephew are frightened of polluting him with their touch, it is no wonder that he is indeed perplexed.

The perplexity is shown symbolically. We see the intense physical struggle of Shambhu, scaling on all fours the wet and slippery surface of the rocky face of a high hill, ignoring the advice of some distant observer who tells him that it is dangerous and that he should take a safer path. It is a simple metaphor for Shambhu's own life and his struggles to overcome seemingly insurmountable difficulties. Hence, his reaching the top might be seen as a triumph, but it only leads to a question which he addresses to his own echo: 'Who are you?'

The film draws toward its narrative conclusion away from contentions about gods and identity. A competition is set up between Bhagwat's troupe and some other, a competition that Bhagwat is desperately keen to win. Both troupes perform the same discourse together, stereoscopically, as it were. There is great confidence among Bhagwat's troupe, the performers accepting his challenges of bigger and better things and performing to their utmost. Only Shambhu expresses any doubt—'Their performance is authentic, while ours is only showy.' It is Shambhu who, doing his best to make his knee-spins truly spectacular, brings everything undone by coming down with a severe knee injury. A cut to a shot of the clouds lifting above the high mountain in the distance heralds the new and final turn in the narrative.

Shambhu, with a staff in one hand and assisted by Shankara, is leaving the temple. He fondly greets Maabala and informs Bhimbhatta that he has injured his kneecap and cannot dance for another six months. Bhimbhatta pays him his dues and wishes him well. Shambhu goes out of the temple with obvious difficulty.

Once again, he climbs the rocky face of the high hill. We might well expect him to bemoan his ill fortune, but instead he jokes heartily with Shankara, first at having wanted to dance and now being unable to walk, and then at the idea of creating theatrical discourse out of mythology. He asks Shankara what is on his mind, and he replies that he is wondering what Granny is doing. This respect for the mundane pleases Shambhu, and he sets out for home with his beloved nephew. The last shots are of his mother calling to him and Shankara. When they eventually reach her, Shambhu will be disencumbered of Junjutti.

The film is presented in the garb of conventional realism, despite the exotic nature of its subject matter and its ambience. The *yakshagana* sequences are naturally highly stylised, but they are realistic presentations of *yakshagana* nevertheless, although we might note the exquisite contrast between the realism of the stylised and the realism of the mundane. There is also one memorable junction where the two converge, and that is the naturalistic representation of the audience in the *yakshagana* performances. The entranced adults, the innocent laughter of the children, and the young boys preferring some rough-and-tumble outside to the discourse within are all reminiscent of the similarly depicted circus audiences in Govindan Aravindan's masterpiece, *Thampu* ('The Circus Tent,' 1978). Memory, and what might well be the subconscious, are presented as realistic flashback sequences, designed to show the growth of emotion and attitude over time.

It is uncertain what kind of future Shambhu might have had as an actor. Consonant with his own personal integrity is the fact that ultimately, he finds himself back amid the humble workaday world of the village. There is much in this visually rich film to assert simplicity as appealing, such as the beating of a drum on a hilltop to announce the coming of the *yakshagana* troupe, or its being publicised by means of a loudspeaker mounted on the back of a truck; the mischief of the boys in the audience is spontaneous, as are the glimpses of rustic life seen, for example, in the manager's fundraising visits. Long, high and panoramic shots assert the authority of the ancient landscape, while the mysterious mixing of artifice and religion in the actors' dressing room, or in the course of performance, excites the imagination.

In *Bannada Vesha,* Kasaravalli draws together several narrative realms. Embraced by the emblematic mask are home and village, theatre and temple, man and god, past and present. It is a masterly process of absorption, where distinctions are gradually dissolved and one realm becomes seemingly subsumed in another. Here the notion of mask is interesting. In the traditional era of the history of world theatre, the mask was conventionally used to signify and to distinguish—king from citizen, hero from villain, sage from fool, god from man, and god from god. While this is true of the *yakshagana* troupe, in the broader context of *Bannada Vesha,* there is also the implication of the melding of the distinctions under the umbrella mask, merging the past into the present, the theatre into the temple, the mundane into the divine. But here the mask is a transforming agent, metamorphosing the actor into character. The ultimate ramification of all of this is loss of individual identity, an ideal in classical Hinduism and Buddhism, for example, but frightening to someone as worldly as Shambhu. Thus, the disputation between the worldly Shambhu and the godly Bhimbhatta represents the contradistinction between the way of the unknowable eternal truth and the way of the knowable ephemeral reality. Shambhu is very much a flawed character, too rooted in the here and now to be amenable to melding with the eternal. His most prominently endearing feature is his ordinariness, especially as it makes him want to be an actor rather than a god. It is ironic, then, that injuring his leg is not a sign of tragedy but of liberation, enabling his escape from the entrapment that came to threaten his very integrity. The mask has been removed.

4

A House is a Stairway to Heaven

Mane ('The House,' 1989) is a social parable, confronting us with some simple but significant moral issues. The film develops the notion of conflict between the private and the social, concerning itself on the one hand with the extent to which we ought to engage harmoniously with neighbours and, on the other, with the extent to which we might reasonably exclude ourselves from the lives of others. We are also led to assess the notion that the gains of some might well entail the losses of others, so evoking the possibility of a moral obligation to sacrifice some of our own benefits to the needs of our neighbours.

Central to the narrative are Rajanna and Gita, a newly married couple, who have made the move from a quiet village to the bustling city. This relocation itself might suggest the aspirational nature of the young couple, a characteristic highlighted by their ideas for a home, ideas that are central to the film and that make sense of its title.

The opening scene contains some elements that suggest mystery and confusion: a suspended, swinging cradle and the cry of an unseen baby; an elderly gentleman with the marks of religious orthodoxy on his forehead, going about his business as, apparently, a dealer in gold and silver; and his customer, with the same marks of orthodoxy, who says nothing at all throughout. The dealer is also the landlord of a small *chawl* or housing complex, and Rajanna has come to see him for the fourth time, seeking a house to rent. He tells the landlord that he has escaped the drudgery of rural toil to seek happiness in the city, in his case as a floor assistant at S&W, a multinational manufacturer of bulldozers, the suggestiveness of which will be appreciated as the film progresses. Rajanna's persistence does not greatly impress his prospective landlord, who suggests that 40 times would have been more appropriate than four, for 'a house is not just four walls.' He quotes from somewhere, 'A house is not just a home, it is the path to enlightenment ... a stairway to heaven.' (The irony in these words will soon become apparent.) He then declares that the house is unavailable. However, after the fade to black, we see Gita, and then Rajanna, inspecting the house, with the landlord saying, 'Had I known who you were, I'd have given you the key straightaway.'

This statement serves to introduce another important element in the narrative, the character of Aunty, for a little later, in response to Gita's question, Rajanna explains that he prevailed over the landlord by taking recourse to 'Aunty's handiwork,' which he clarifies as name-dropping and deceit. He then tells Gita that Aunty is much spoken about (and, we shall see, much maligned) and that it would be well to keep away from her. Apart from the underlying self-righteousness, there is also a double-standard being introduced here, for while Rajanna might deplore his aunt's less-than-wholesome reputation, he is not averse to using her to his advantage on several occasions. Here, then, is an early indication of Rajanna's illiberality, a shortcoming that will become more and more pronounced. When Rajanna issues his caution about his aunt, it is also important to note the close-up of Gita's face, expressing an element of concern and possibly disappointment, a reaction which might indicate the first sign of a growing breach in their marriage.

That there might be anything at all unpleasant about Rajanna seems highly unlikely at the beginning of the film, and indeed for some way into it. He is a playful, clowning character, genuinely amusing and sometimes very funny. Yet there can be a negative element in even his joking, such as in his captious comments about the owner, the old lady who lives opposite, and another neighbour who is a seemingly obsessive body-builder.

The house is very small—apparently two rooms with a bathroom and kitchen, and unfurnished except for an imposing yet ugly cast-iron bedstead. Neither Rajanna nor Gita likes it, and so they decide to dispense with it. However, it is so heavy that they cannot move it and, even if they could, it would not fit through the door. There might be a lesson in this, that some things—or people, or ideas, or forms of behaviour—are not easily obviated and are perhaps best left as they are. So, rather than move the bed, they prudently accept it as it is and lie comfortably on it. However, it will be seen that Rajanna is unable to apply this lesson more broadly.

As they lie on their immense bed, Rajanna marvels at their new-found freedom from what must have been for them a stultifying life in an extended family in the village. Gita speaks of her dream to have a house of their own, no matter how small, with flowers growing in the courtyard, and Rajanna even goes so far as to yearn for 'lilting music coming in waves from afar,' as a popular film song of the 1970s described it. While their dream is obviously remote from their reality, they both happily acknowledge that at least they do have privacy, peace and quiet—or so they think.

Lying comfortably on the bed does not mean sleeping well on it, for we are now introduced to the basic element of conflict in the narrative. Abutting their kitchen is a shed which, at bed-time, comes to life with a constant industrial-sounding clangour. The noise goes on throughout the night, and is made by people vaguely referred to as 'the shed people.' Who they are and what they are doing remains a mystery, as the focus continues to remain almost entirely on Rajanna and Gita, their inability to sleep, and their desire to be rid of this cacophonous curse.

Indian cities must be as noisy as any in the world, although the noise is not typically nocturnal; however, while the neighbours acknowledge a problem, it is not apparently so serious an inconvenience to them as to warrant their involvement in any action to evict the noise-makers. One day, when the shed people have gone to wherever they go in the daytime, the landlord is seen putting a lock and chain on the door of the shed in an apparent gesture of sympathy towards his new tenants, but in the night, the lock is easily broken, the noise resumes, and the landlord is unmoved to do anything more about it.

According to the body-builder the landlord is unscrupulously mercenary, having cunningly wangled the ownership of the *chawl* from the old widow—the one who lives opposite Rajanna and Gita—who once owned the whole complex. For all his quoting of scripture and his outward marks of piety, he is at heart a hard-nosed money-maker. The old woman—referred to as 'Granny'—has lost her property to this man and her son to America, and spends her time making votive bundles and hoping that her son will return. The body-builder, it seems, is aware of everything while remaining judiciously detached from it.

The last of the central characters to be introduced is Rajanna's aunt, known simply as 'Aunty.' We first meet her when she comes to visit Gita one morning. She is a handsome and elegantly dressed lady. Finding Gita asleep on a chair (having been kept awake all night by the shed people), she sits down quietly and watches her affectionately for a few moments. Initially, she does not give the impression of someone who is best avoided, as Rajanna has described her. She does make a couple of innocent jokes, with mild marital allusions, but that she is a woman of loose morals is clearly refuted when she mentions that some men equate 'single woman' with 'easy woman,' and explains that she lost her job because of her moral stance in rejecting her boss's invitation to his hotel room. She has come to see Gita to ask her to go with her to the temple where, as she tells us, she finds 'peace of mind.' Indeed, in the sequence in the temple, she reveals something of a soul in torment. She talks of dying from within, of feeling hollow inside, and of her fear of an unseen hand beckoning to her from the darkness. She gives an impression of a growing despair without, at this stage, any explanation other than what might be inferred from her reference to her lecherous former boss and her expression of profound antipathy for her ex-husband. During this account of her despondency, two little boys are chasing each other around the temple and one of them bumps into her, bringing to the ground her tray of offerings, including some red *kumkuma* or vermilion powder. Gita wonders whether the spoiling of the *kumkuma* has upset her and Aunty replies that what did in fact upset her is the little boys' enjoyment of their ice-candies turning to disappointment, when the confection too went to the ground in the collision. We may be developing sympathy for Aunty on account of her troubled soul, and we might well be warmed by her affectionate and generous spirit. Nevertheless, Rajanna will insist that Gita does not associate with her, arguing that 'the shed people may ruin our sleep, but she'll ruin our lives.'

Indeed, their lives are already being made vulnerable by several things, and Aunty is not one of them. Perhaps they have come to the city with too much bucolic innocence, unable to cope with the trials of urban life. Rajanna gets upset when his reasonable plea to the shed people to stop the racket is greeted with a suggestion to go and see a movie, even with the offer to pay for his ticket. On one occasion, to get away from the noise and to ease their ill feeling, Rajanna and Gita go out for a walk and experience a slight wave of nostalgia for the village, remembering which trees would be in flower now and how beautiful their fragrance would be. Then the idyllic illusion is shattered by a drunken man who pulls his car up near them, offering Rajanna money for Gita, whom he takes to be a prostitute. They return home feeling worse than they had when they went out, with Gita in tearful distress.

While the other residents of the compound seem to be able to tolerate the shed people, Kasaravalli is careful to demonstrate that the disturbance they are causing is indeed real and is not blown out of proportion by two rather precious young people from the country. The noise is loud enough to make walls vibrate and cause steel tumblers to fall from shelves. The owner becomes used to Rajanna using his phone to call the factory and notify them of his imminent lateness due to sleep deprivation. On one such occasion, there is trouble with the phone, and so he is obliged to go out to the public booth nearby. To the frazzled Rajanna, a simple experience assumes elements of nightmare. A high shot shows him entering a network of very narrow alleys on his way to the phone booth. It may seem odd that at this time of the day, in a densely populated part of a big city, there is no one other than Rajanna to be seen. Then a handcart piled high with 44-gallon yellow drums comes into view, taking up the whole width of the alley and yet miraculously moving easily through it. Rajanna heads home, only to be seemingly chased by this pile of drums on wheels, with two pairs of human legs visible behind it. At last he finds refuge in his home and goes to the window in front of the hideous cast-iron bedstead to see the pile of drums rolling off the cart, just in front of his house.

As an upright citizen, Rajanna decides to go through proper channels, writing a letter to the Municipal Corporation. Granny will not sign it, resolutely declaring that she will 'sign no more papers.' She also advises Rajanna that he lacks tolerance and can hardly expect the rest of the world to fall in behind him. The body-builder is sympathetic, but simply sees no point in approaching the Corporation. His advice to Rajanna is simply to toughen up and to not let it worry him.

There follows a scene which, visually at least, brings to mind the surrealism of a similar scene in Satyajit Ray's *Pratidwandi*.[1] At the municipal offices, Rajanna enters a waiting room to find a long row of young men, all dressed similarly and each holding what looks like a petition, waiting patiently. Rajanna is not prepared to be as patient and apparently bribes the doorman, in order to be given access to the appropriate official before any of the others. Before entering the building, he confronts momentarily a very noisy demonstration and now there are more shots of that demonstration, but from behind closed windows, so making it absurdly silent and perhaps visually corroborating the body-builder's questioning of the value of trying to engage with the Corporation. There are also two sequences of shots of the gardener watering the flower beds, one a point-of-view shot as seen by Rajanna looking down from an upper-floor window and the other at ground level, both highlighting the seemingly alien serenity of the world of the humble gardener. Rajanna sits at one end of a vast table facing an official at the other end, the physical distance separating them suggesting the social and political gulf that prevails between them. The official reconstructs what Rajanna sees as actuality, telling him that he bought the house knowing about the noise problem and so has only himself to blame. His advice is nicely ironic: 'If you want peace and quiet, why don't you go to some village?'

---

[2] 'The Adversary,' 1970.

Despite the Corporation officially rebuffing Rajanna (as the owner had once rebuffed his application for a house), Rajanna is later heartened by a phone call from Gita, telling him that a Corporation man had come to take some action. However, when Rajanna comes home with a celebratory bag of sweets, he finds that the shed enterprise is going on as noisily as ever. His dismay with the shed people and the Corporation, together with the obsessive in him being offended on discovering one or two hairs from Gita's head under the bed, cause him to take out his frustration on his wife. Their marriage, which started out in such childlike happiness, is now becoming increasingly strained. There is still much laughter and tenderness, but that is gradually being eclipsed by the doubt and suspicion born of Rajanna's frustration with the shed people and his insecurity about his aunt.

Perceptive to the menacing emanation of stress, Gita suggests that they take their problems just this once to Aunty, but Rajanna is adamant that they should have nothing at all to do with her. There is a cut to black, and then we see Rajanna and Gita coming through the front gate of Aunty's house. This is an interesting sequence with regard to character. At the outset, Rajanna repeats his discomfort in absorbing the dirty looks of the neighbours on account of Aunty's reputation, something that he is exaggerating if not wholly imagining. His duplicity is evident in seeking her help on the one hand, while carping about her alleged moral frailty on the other. The duplicity is given concrete symbolism by the bag of mangoes he presents to her, telling her that he has brought them from their village; her cursory inspection of one of the mangoes proves this to be a very clumsy lie. By contrast, there is nothing at all duplicitous about Aunty, who welcomes them effusively and does not try in any way to cover up the presence of a man in her house. Subdued suspicions of lechery are expressed about him, even by Gita (who perhaps is still affected by her unpleasant experience with the drunken motorist), but the salient fact is that the man is a police inspector who not only wears a mantle of rectitude but bears the power of the law. While pointing out that the law is not really able to do anything about such a phenomenon as the shed people and their mysterious enterprise, he comes up with the compromise that the shed people be persuaded to pursue their cacophonous work during the day and allow silence to reign at night.

The police do their work with an efficiency that involves a somewhat ruthless severity. The men are dragged out of the shed, leaving a woman and her small child to fend for themselves. Gita, at home alone, has to suffer the subtle reproach of neighbours and others at this cruelty. The owner wonders why people have to be so selfish, and Granny expresses her dismay at such treatment being meted out to a man with small children by people to whom 'God has been so good.' What had been a simple dispute over seemingly unwarranted noise has now taken on a new dimension. Its evolving complexity is highlighted by the toddler coming out of the shed to fetch his ball; Gita picks it up and kindly offers it to the child, who is obviously reluctant to approach her. A hand reaches out from behind the door and snatches the child away, and the door actually and figuratively closes on Gita.

Rajanna is happy with his new-found silence, even trying to cajole Gita to be happy and carefree, but she is starting to become withdrawn. Her earlier effervescence has evidently dissipated as she confronts unforeseen complications in what really ought to be a simple and straightforward life. And without the shed people to bother him, Rajanna confesses to boredom and restlessness. The joke he tells, which in itself is quite funny, falls flat, as do his gestures of affection.

Even though the shed people have been sent on their way, Rajanna's dream of domestic tranquillity does not materialise. One monster is not exactly replaced by another, but what develops is unforeseen and by no means conducive to Rajanna's peace of mind. The industrial noise, with its grating, screeching and rasping, its harsh flashes of oxyacetylene light and its enterprise cloaked in mystery, is suddenly seen to have been replaced by another noise, one that is softer, not so obtrusive, open to all, and designed to bring pleasure. A video game parlour has been set up and is now open for business. Dings, twangs and bongs, squeaks, rattles and buzzes rend the evening with an unrelenting frenzy, while the flashing of coloured lights gives form to an obligatory manufactured gaiety. The place is popular and crowded with people intent on engaging with the colourful machines, with their animated cartoon-like life and the programmed challenges they offer. However, the shed menace has not been replaced by a parlour menace. In fact, there is no menace here at all—the noise level is controlled, the crowd and their activities are orderly, and there is a young, well-educated manager to keep a supervisory eye on all that goes on.

There are two points worth drawing from this element in the film. The first is poetic. We have an audio-visual presentation of a technologically generated madness. It is not exactly a chaos, for despite appearances, it is all programmed and unquestioningly obedient to the flicks of switches and pressure on buttons. But the notion of life lived at the flick of a switch is just as surrealistic as the experience of being pursued through back alleys by a handcart laden with yellow 44-gallon drums, the technological superiority of the former notwithstanding. The second point is narrative. The owner of the new video-game parlour happens to be the nephew of the inspector and so, in satisfying a request to please Aunty by doing a favour for her nephew and his wife, he also found a propitious opportunity to shower some avuncular largesse in order to foster his own familial interests. That in itself is of no consequence to the film. What is of interest is the ramification of the inspector's interest in the gaming parlour, for it brings him and Aunty into closer and more frequent proximity to Rajanna and Gita, especially Gita, while Rajanna is at work during the daytime.

While Rajanna's personal defects lie within himself, it is the proximity of Aunty to their marital life that puts these shortcomings on display. The 'problem' with Aunty is her reputation as a 'loose' woman, but we are given no reason to believe that she actually warrants such a reputation. Some would object that her maintaining a non-marital relationship with the police inspector is disreputable, but should the man not expect censure for the same reason? Social opprobrium seems to be much more readily imposed upon women than on men. In a scene set in a Christian cemetery, Aunty speaks to Gita of the pain she has suffered on account of having been a deserted wife. Initially, she did what was socially acceptable in marrying a man chosen for her by others, presumably her father and brothers. He took her to the city and, when supporting her became an inconvenience to him, simply abandoned her. Rather than bring down scandal on his own head, his selfish violation of his responsibility placed his wife in an invidious position. She might have returned forlorn to the village and sought support there, and even then she would not have been immune to gossip (after all, why would a man leave a good woman?). She did what, by rights, should have earned her respect and admiration, asserting her independence and self-sufficiency. However, a strong and independent woman is not desirable in traditional society (which tolerates men like the drunken motorist, who pay women for sexual services), for such a woman, in seeming to be assuming equality with men, is like Prometheus vying with the gods. It is a key feature of traditional society that a girl belongs to her father, a woman belongs to her husband, and a widow belongs to her sons. An independent woman is her own person, and that goes against the traditional grain. Aunty makes this point in regard to property. When Gita reminds her that her brother offered to give her a house, she smiles resignedly and points out that it would never have been her own house, for a house always belongs to a father or father-in-law, or a brother or an uncle. To accept her brother's offer would have meant letting herself be tied down and being dependent on him. 'At least now I have the satisfaction of living in my own house.'

The implications of home ownership are important. There is a significant symbolic aspect to it. We might recall the *chawl* owner's words to Rajanna: 'a house is not just a home, it is the path to enlightenment ... the stairway to heaven.' Perhaps this is a rather elaborate way of making the simple point that ownership of one's home implies ownership of one's life. We might note that old Granny's quality of life declined as her property was gradually subsumed by the present landlord. Their lack of total control over their home is illustrated in the fact that Rajanna and Gita must live with the stress created by the shed people. And ultimately, we shall see that destruction of home is accompanied by destruction of life.

As the film approaches its final stages, both Rajanna and Gita become more and more withdrawn, increasingly detached from one another and seemingly introspective. Minimisation of self is implied in the minimisation of relationships, and both Aunty and Rajanna sense within themselves a growing hollowness. Gita certainly senses a dream slipping away from her, the dream of a happy marriage in a home of their own. It is fair to suggest that Rajanna's apparent introspection is more of a petulance, a little boy sulking, because Gita will not defer to his attempt to restrict and stifle her happy friendship with Aunty, a friendship which is more an act of kindness on her part for an older woman who has unjustly suffered, rather than a relationship that is personally rewarding to herself. Her introspection is less selfish, more directed at the partnership, and she sees a major inconsistency in Rajanna's character to be at the core of what threatens their marital happiness. She quite reasonably accuses Rajanna of duplicity, pointing to his disdain for Aunty and the inspector on the one hand and, on the other, his readiness to use them in his own interests. He even uses Gita similarly when the noise becomes unbearable and he sends her to seek the inspector's help, even knowing that she would feel uncomfortable with him. While the reality of Rajanna's self-centredness is clear, his own realisation of it and his childlike and emotionally supplicant burying of his head in his wife's lap suggest hope for his maturity and for the future of the marriage.

And yet the final episode of the film sees the same duplicity at work, and Rajanna's lesson is not fully learnt until this episode has been played out to its horrible conclusion. If the film had been a story of moral triumph, it would have been played out by Rajanna and Gita, hand in hand, facing their problems in a spirit of compromise and readiness, to sacrifice in return for whatever gain might be won. However, this social parable is not a minor epic, in which a little man can become a hero overnight. Rajanna is by nature a little man and whether he can grow at all will remain controversial, even after the final titles have rolled.

Rather than positively confront his besetting demons, Rajanna opts for escape, intending to do so with the aid of—amazingly—the shed people. His duplicity is still buoyant, and he will now make use of those to whom he expressed so much acrimony. Apparently, one of the men had once assured him that they could find a place for him should he want to move, and so he goes to the landlord seeking their present whereabouts so that he might ask them, presumably, to lead him to a house with a swing, flowers in the courtyard, and lilting music coming from afar. Self-absorbed, he goes off to meet them, quite oblivious of the difficulties under which other people are obliged to live.

The place is apparently on the outskirts of the city, and Rajanna is directed to it by a humble man rolling a yellow 44-gallon drum up a hill. There is a slightly Sisyphean suggestion in this, especially when he momentarily loses control of the drum and it threatens to roll all the way back down the hill, but he recovers it soon enough and directs Rajanna to where he wants to go. While the allusion to Sisyphus might connote a suggestion of futility, the yellow 44-gallon drum connects us to Rajanna's surrealist experience of being pursued by a handcart laden with such drums, as well as with the shed people, outside whose shed the drums were dumped.

Rajanna seems a little perplexed as he looks in the direction in which he has been pointed, having expected to find a house—maybe even one with flowers and a swing and lilting music. What he sees, however, is a large crowd of onlookers held back by police, encircling an area in which a huge bulldozer is at work, and numerous people running about in some sort of panic. In fact, what is happening is a slum clearance project at work. The people had apparently refused to leave when their eviction notices were served, and now the bulldozer has been sent in to get them out and to flatten and clear away their humble homes, just as the police and the gaming parlour manager had done previously at the *chawl*. A simple yet striking visual symbol highlights Rajanna's connection to both assaults as the bulldozer turns to face the camera and the machine's logo comes into close-up: S&W, the firm in which Rajanna is employed.

Rajanna is visibly shocked by what he sees here, maybe even moved by a sense of guilt. But the last dramatic moment of the film is brought about by a sudden change in the natural light—not so much to indicate a time lapse as perhaps to suggest the appropriateness of darkness to what is happening. One of the shed people is quite distraught, running about calling to the little boy who was earlier involved in the incident with the ball and Gita. These people have lost their home, such as it might have been, and probably their child. An optimist might claim that he has got lost in the crowd in the commotion, but a less optimistic realist might point to the impersonal and ruthless advance of the great S&W machine and imagine his little body ploughed into the ground with the rubble which once was a home. It is possible that now a degree of enlightenment has come to Rajanna. It does not really matter, for life has gone on in its complex and irresistible way, and there can be no going back. How Rajanna goes forward after this is no longer a matter for this film.

On the surface, *Mane* might appear to be a light social comedy, with patches of 'dramatic relief' and a bit of sadness thrown in for entertainment leavening. However, there are a number of signs indicating that such a description would be seriously inadequate. 'Light social comedy' generally carries a verisimilitude to the social *mores* that it aims to represent, and so too does *Mane*. However, interwoven with the social realism in *Mane* are elements of exaggeration, notions that may be plausible but highly unlikely, embellishments that seem to be heavy-handed and even slightly out of place. We see disharmony where the fluency of the narrative progression is fractured in several contradictory turnarounds: at the beginning of the film, the owner declares categorically that the accommodation is unavailable, there is a cut to black, and then we see him handing over the key to Rajanna; Gita declares that she will not sleep in such a monstrosity of a bed, and then is seen sleeping on it; she tells Aunty that she cannot go to the temple with her and then is seen going to the temple with her; the Corporation official tells Rajanna that he has no case and so nothing will be done, and then there is a phone call from Gita telling Rajanna, at work, that an official from the Corporation has come (as it turns out, to fish for a bribe); and Rajanna tells Gita that under no circumstances will they seek help from Aunty, and in the next shot we see them both at

Aunty's front door. The point is that the logic of life is frequently to be found in a labyrinth of unreason, subjectivity, and inconsistency.

It often seems that within accepted social realism there are occasional experiences that do not seem to belong, though they are entirely plausible. For example, while it is a fact that men, sometimes affected by drink, cruise the streets of a big city in their cars seeking to pick up women, it seems almost surrealistic if it involves oneself. The seeming unreality of Gita's experience of being mistaken for a streetwalker is given visual emphasis by the lighting, which highlights her and Rajanna, less so the drunken motorist, and blacks out all background, taking Gita and Rajanna completely out of any social context and lending intensification to a particular subjectivity.

Social realism is aided by rationality, whereby mysteries are solved and questions are answered. In *Mane,* the mysteries deliberately minimise the film's social realism. Some of the characters are presented as incomplete pictures in a jigsaw puzzle, so distinguishing them markedly from Rajanna and Gita and Aunty, who are presented fully enough within the conventions of social realism. The landlord's business dealings and his past enterprises are not much more than hinted at and are perhaps obscured somewhat by his outward indications of religious orthodoxy. One may wonder what the body-builder does, apart from ministering to his muscles and flying kites. The greatest mystery is thrown up by the shed people. What do they do, and where do they go in the daytime? Then there is the suspended cradle in the room of the landlord, the yellow 44-gallon drums, the highly stylised sequence in and from the Corporation waiting room, and the larger than life Corporation official and his exaggerated officiousness. Ultimately, the video-game parlour is presented as an umbrella image of the disorderliness of order, a seeming mystery in itself, but one which, fundamentally, is carefully and intelligently programmed to rule over the whims and presumed intelligence of its customers. Self-absorption—in money-making or body-building, or seeking excitement in entertainment technology, for example—is rampant in our world, which is teeming with unanswered questions and unexplained mysteries. Perhaps the propensity toward self-absorption, such as when we might try to modify our social environment to suit our own interests, militates against the satisfactory answering of questions and explanation of mysteries. Maybe there would be more simplicity with less selfishness. *Mane* is very much a metaphor for the snowballing lust for prosperity, a lust which is satisfied in some, while for many it is never gratified. For those whose humanity is encompassing, this is a troubling metaphor and is underlined by Gita's telling line, 'What they've lost is greater than what we've gained.'

5

I've Used up all the Stories I Had

The title of Salman Rushdie's *Haroun and the Sea of Stories* is instructive in its use of 'sea' as a collective noun for 'stories.' The sea is vast, especially if 'the seven seas' and all the others are viewed, rightly, as one, and indeed the number of stories that may be told is infinite. But just as the seas flow into and mix with one another, stories—arising out of the human experience, conditioned by the human mind and given form by human creativity—often overlap and blend with, or bear resemblance to, one another. Stories beget stories; a story about something can give rise to another story about something else. It might also be said that a story is never finished, for there is often much to be imagined after the final full-stop. And all stories embrace a number of subordinate stories, actually smaller but potentially bigger, each in turn giving rise to, well, oceans of stories. A story may be a pleasant diversion, but like any work of literature, it is also a document of the human condition.

Kraurya ("The Tale of a Story Teller,' 1995) is, as a film, such a complex document, embracing the story of Rangamma and the village children, of Rangamma and her son and social peers, of Murthy and his family, of Murthy and Rangamma, of Murthy's brother, and many other stories, sometimes intertwined or sometimes running concurrently with one another. When, in the realm of experience, we enact what might well become our own stories, we create our own worlds in which that action may take place, erecting, perhaps unwittingly, barriers separating one world from another—his from hers, mine from yours, theirs from ours—and in the process elevating the individual self and its particular interests in vain while failing to even recognise, let alone embrace, the reality and the potential of a greater entity. An examination of the building of walls provides much of the rationale of *Kraurya*.

In the pre-title sequence there is a subtle yet very clear illustration of compartmentalising as a basis for story-telling. This introduction opens with a shot of a train in the distance, running from the left of the screen to the right. There is a brief survey of the raised countryside looking down on a village, across an area strewn with boulders and large rocks. Here a group of boys are playing cricket in a clearing among the rocks when a little girl comes and calls out to the boys, telling them that tall-tale Granny is about to tell a story, and the boys rush off to her house to hear it. We follow one of them, Murthy, as he rushes into his house, quickly informs his mother where he is going, and rushes out. We note the massive pile of rocks marking one border of the village. Inside the old woman's house, the children are served a little snack by Uncle Vasu, who we learn is the old lady's adult son. The old lady tells an utterly improbable story of a trip to the moon, and pulls a loose tooth from the mouth of a little girl. It all sounds quite inconsequential.

If, however, we describe this introduction a little more slowly, we will notice some significant symbols and suggestions emerge. The prominence of the rock-strewn landscape offers a random formation of an enclosure, which might suggest a separation of the boys' world as a distinct realm. The shots of the end of the town, hard up against the natural barrier of a huge pile—a hill, indeed—of rocks, also suggest its separation and distinction from the rest of the world. While the rock-strewn hills might suggest barriers and separation, the distant train (and later the bus) suggests the opposite, an opportunity for communication, for weakening an urban-rural dichotomy, for cultural and social synthesis, but it is an opportunity, not a symptom. The train also indirectly suggests the unhurried perception of time here—Murthy knows he is late for school because of the arrival of a certain train. A girl is sent as a messenger to the boys, suggesting another distinction—that boys and girls play separately—but also an integration, as the boys leave their game instantly and rush to join the girls in anticipation of the delight that Granny's stories always bring. On the way to her house, there are indications that at least some of the adult population do not share their children's love of the old woman, as Murthy is stopped by his mother just long enough for her to warn him that his father will be displeased. Another separation of worlds has opened up, distinguishing the world of children from the world of adults. But just for the moment, this is fleeting.

The 'story' of the story-teller and her audience is at once a tale of happiness. The children are delighted in expectation of what is to come; Vasu's token attempts to keep order are part of the fun, and the old woman seems well and truly in her element with her joyful admirers. The story she tells about her self-piloted trip to the moon in her grandfather's aeroplane is, of course, sheer nonsense. Yet, given some minor suspension of disbelief, much of it is plausible enough to hold the children's interest. They laugh at the exaggerated improbability but their imaginations are excited, nevertheless. While sophisticated adults might scoff, innocent children are led to wonder. And while Granny's story does not merit belief—if ever, indeed, it was meant to—we must remember that many aspects of actuality are often very difficult to accept too.

All this is by way of introduction. The opening titles roll and then a crucial narrative element directs the course of the 'umbrella' story of *Kraurya*. This is more unexpected than anything in Granny's trip-to-the moon tale, and in some ways it is harder to believe and reconcile oneself to. By chance, Murthy discovers the drowned body of Vasu in the tank of the temple.

Storytellers and filmmakers often leave certain things unaccounted for. Perhaps some reasons are irrelevant to the story's greater purpose, as would seem to be the case here. Whether Vasu died by mischance or by suicide is not clear. If it were suicide, there is no explanatory indication. His death may be inexplicable, but it is a fact, nevertheless, a fact that gives rise to other facts, central to which is the irrevocable change in Granny's life and, by extension, the lives of Murthy and his family. The brief story of Vasu has come to an end, bringing into existence a number of new stories, just as the little girl's tooth, pulled from her mouth by Granny, has made way for a new and larger one.

The subsequent narrative crisis, or turning-point, is the visit paid to Rajanna, Murthy's father, by a group of leaders of the village. Their point is simple: religious law insists that Rangamma—or Granny—may not live in her house for a year after the death of her son for fear of a curse falling upon her, or even upon the entire village. It is apparent that Rangamma has two distant relatives to whom she might turn for shelter. One is a watchmaker, whose exact whereabouts in Bangalore might take very long to ascertain; the other is Rajanna. The leaders implore him to take Rangamma in, at least until the watchmaker can be found, and thus avoid offending religion and inviting a curse upon the village. And so begins the story of Rajanna.

Ill-feeling between Rangamma and Rajanna—the reasons are beside the point—had evolved years earlier. Without forgiveness or any element of magnanimity, the acrimony hardened and became a simple, continuing actuality. Rajanna is adamant that he will not offer hospitality to Rangamma, for reasons that are feeble. He tries to show himself as a struggler, up to his ears in debt, hardly at all helped by his older son, who lives and works in Bangalore. In fact, the cost of maintaining the old woman would be negligible. Rajanna, indeed, is simply niggardly, as suggested by his insistence that Murthy make do with a broken sandal for another six months. Then he tries to argue that the misadventure of her son's death would bring the inconvenience of the police and their questions. The misgivings of his wife Parvathi—minor and intolerant as they are—concerning the old woman's scruples about ritual purity would seem to carry more weight. Rajanna is simply parsimonious, bloody-minded and territorial, but Parvathi persuades him that they can hardly go against the collective opinion of the village, and so Rangamma is given a dark room to share with Rajanna's baskets of silkworms. She is, as she puts it, 'an unwilling guest in an unwelcoming house.'

Again we are reminded of the gulf between the adult world and the world of children. While Rajanna does an act of kindness, albeit coupled with a weighty grudge, Murthy is overjoyed and his older sister Sita is happy too. A new story is now introduced to mingle for a short time with Rajanna's story, and to start an engagement with Rangamma's story.

Subanna, the elder son, comes home for a brief visit, hoping to obtain funds to realise his dream of purchasing a soap agency and so become a financial success. We first see Subanna as a loving brother to Murthy, for whom he has brought a simple present—a pair of heavy-rimmed plastic glasses with an exaggerated false nose. This provides a lot of mirth for Murthy and Granny and amuses Sita and Parvathi, but it invokes the anger of Rajanna, who sees the twenty-five rupees spent on it as reprehensible profligacy. His spiteful pettiness has him deliberately break the harmless toy. There is obviously an acute tension between Subanna and his father. Subanna finds support in his mother, but necessarily behind his father's back. He starts to get on well with Rangamma, but when she delays his catching the bus to return to Bangalore, prosecuting some scheme or other, he quite insensitively describes her to his mother as a 'real pain.' In fact, she is delaying him while she gathers together the ten thousand rupees that he needs to purchase his agency. And thus begins the Subanna branch of Rangamma's story.

The story begins with a moral imperative. Rangamma informs Subanna that the money has a notable source, as it was merited by her late husband for being a fighter for India's Independence. There is a reference to a spinning-wheel and the characteristic cap worn by followers of the Indian National Congress, and there is mention of Rangamma's own hard work and frugality as well. So she charges him with the responsibility of spending the money only on business necessities and not on personal pleasures. Finally, she insists that it is an interest-free loan to be paid back as and when he starts earning money. A significant point of interest in the Subanna–Rangamma story will be the genuineness or otherwise of Subanna's willingness to uphold the moral requirement of Rangamma's generosity.

The Subanna–Rajanna story then takes a twist that causes an even greater twist to the Rangamma–Rajanna story. Subanna writes to his father, informing him that he has purchased his agency but is so busy that he cannot cook for himself and so has to eat out, thus creating expenses that preclude his sending the current month's two hundred and fifty rupees to his father. This means that Rajanna will not be able to meet the monthly instalment of five hundred rupees to pay back a loan he had taken out. Suddenly, Rajanna views Rangamma in a less unfriendly light.

Aware that her money is the sole measure of her value to her temporary host family, Rangamma flatly yet diplomatically refuses Parvathi's request to help Rajanna in his aberrant emergency. While the relationship between Rangamma and Rajanna and his wife has somewhat thawed after her generosity to Subanna, animosity flares again with her distancing herself from Rajanna's need. It is here that the Rajanna–Rangamma story comes to an end as the Subanna–Rangamma story flows out of it and, for a while, remains prominent. The cause of the redirection is simple. Rajanna and Parvathi contrive to send Rangamma to Bangalore, arguing that if Subanna does not have time to cook then Rangamma could cook for him, enabling him to continue sending his monthly monetary contributions. And as a bonus, Rajanna and Parvathi would be rid of the encumbrance of the old woman.

So Murthy takes Granny to Bangalore where, we might expect, Subanna would cordially welcome his benefactor. However, the smile drops from his face as soon as he sees her, and he refers to her bitterly as 'the old hag' while venting his irritation to Murthy. There is no warmth in his merely formal courtesy. Clearly, he sees Rangamma as an obstacle to his new life, and she just as clearly sees that he has been enjoying the money she lent him, as well as putting the rest of it to good use. (Rangamma, it must be said, does jump to conclusions. She sees the pictures of an advertising model and assumes them to be photographs of a girlfriend, and she regards Subanna's smart clothes as an indulgence rather than a basic requirement of a businessman.) Nevertheless, Subanna has no residual gratitude to Rangamma for the great favour she has done him, if indeed there was any at all to start with. In fact, he is callous toward her and resentful of her presence. He wants Rangamma gone as soon as possible and contrives a lie, telling her that he is being sent to Bombay for two months of training. However, before he arranges their transport back to the village on a truck, there is an insertion of the brief story of Padmanabhiah, the watch-shop man whom the village leaders had mentioned to Rajanna when they came to solicit his help in accommodating Rangamma for a year. This is necessitated by Rangamma's flat refusal to return to the village and be obligated to Rajanna for another six months. Subanna makes a tactless joke about Padmanabhiah probably being dead, which prompts a violent reaction from Rangamma. As her relationship with Subanna has obviously soured, she would seem to be pinning all her hope on this man, who had been a comrade of Rangamma's husband in the days of the freedom movement.

With the help of a neighbour of Subanna, they find a watch-shop whose proprietor knew Padmanabhiah and his family; he informs Rangamma that Padmanabhiah is indeed no more. Of course, those heady days of decades ago are still fresh in Rangamma's memory, and she is incredulous at the watchmaker's words. To make his point that everyone ages and dies, he offers Rangamma a mirror, so that she may behold the actuality of her own senescence. This is both a dramatic and crucial moment in the film. As the shop assistant reminds the proprietor, an orthodox widow will customarily not look in a mirror. Rangamma violates that custom and is plainly disturbed by what she sees. Struck by the reality of her age and the likely imminence of her own passing, she says little more than to tell Murthy to take her home and she then slips into sleep, soon becoming apparently comatose. Murthy, perhaps confused and frustrated, expresses an angry concern for himself on account of Granny spoiling his holiday. A little later come the last words we hear from her, 'I've used up all the stories I had,' suggesting that her own story is approaching its end.

As we see Murthy and Rangamma in the back of a truck loaded with goats, the Subanna–Rangamma story also ends, running into the final story of the film, which is Murthy's story. While Murthy is central to this narrative, he is anything but its hero, finding himself as still a little boy in a world which he does not have the experience to negotiate. While he is in the truck and the truck is headed for home, he is relatively at ease, albeit greatly worried about the condition of his Granny. However, his story briefly yet tellingly overlaps with the somewhat sordid story of the workers who are also in the back of the truck. They squabble over some dispute concerning money and then come to blows, rolling over the backs of the animals as they grapple with one another, with one of them falling heavily on the frail and sleeping Rangamma. At night the truck comes to a road-stop where the contractor, genuinely frightened of the consequences of an old woman dying on his truck, off-loads Murthy and Rangamma, gives Murthy some money, and tells him to find a bus. It is night in a strange place and Murthy has the responsibility for an unconscious old woman; he is quite clearly out of his depth. When he goes to the toilet, Rangamma rolls off a raised platform they had been sitting on and, as we might guess, her condition worsens. A policeman comes and, by some negative psychological association, frightens Murthy, despite his kindness. The boy's fear intensifies when they are taken to the police station and Murthy is overwhelmed by a terror of the unknown and his place in it—or at least how the formidable policemen there might determine his place in it. In fear of the police station and its officers, of a Granny who won't wake up, of a strange place at night, and of his own inability to cope with the circumstances in which he has been suddenly plunged, he takes the opportunity to slip out and run away. With this, the umbrella story of *Kraurya* comes to an end.

Beyond the final titles Murthy's story will, of course, continue, as will Rajanna and Parvathi's and that of the self-centred and callous Subanna. It is difficult to see the latter two stories developing into much, for a story of a self-centred soap salesman or one about a misanthrope and his biddable wife are not likely to be the stuff of entertaining literature or cinema, at least without the inclusion and interweaving of a number of much more colourful and engaging stories. The continuing story of Murthy, however, does appeal to the imagination, given that when his story is brought to an end by the sound of a train's whistle in the dark distance and the rolling of the closing titles, he is an uncertain entity. He is of course his parents' son and his brother's brother, and so he carries something of a handicap into his formative years. On the other hand, he enjoys some advantages, prominent among which is his love of stories, suggesting that his mind is not cast in a rut but has some elasticity and capacity for intellectual and moral endeavour. He has also had the opportunity to learn much from Rangamma—not just her stories from the epics (which he would be most unlikely to hear from his parents and brother), but her anecdotes about her past, her husband the freedom fighter, and the treasures that she has stored in her locked box. As he matures, these impressions may well offer meaning to him and even shed some explanatory light on the moral vacuum in which his father lives. Of course, he may well be accused of cruelty to Rangamma, having abandoned her and run away in what were probably the last moments of her life. However, he has not been directed by self-interest so much, as his father and brother might have been, but by simple fear of the unknown. It might even be suggested that Murthy is fleeing from the callous society of the world's Rajannas and Subannas, the goat-traders, and even the police, in whose environment he feels threatened to the point of being terrified. Murthy is a little boy who is quite unschooled in the world in which he now finds himself alone. It is easy to be optimistic about Murthy's future, but it is just as easy to be sceptical—after all, society often wields a much greater influence on its young than we might like, and it keeps a harsh school for those not easily prone to its ways.

'Society' is an easy and inclusive term that is often vulnerable to vague interpretation. Perhaps it is better understood by looking at some of its components. In *Kraurya,* there are several 'sub-societies' or social realms to which we might ascribe significance. Two broad divisions are the adult world and the world of children. The adult world is very often fragmented into particular interest groups, but generally it is a world marked by independence, self-reliance, authority and responsibility; it is also a world where self, ambition and power might flourish. Conversely, a child's world is largely one of mutuality and cooperation, such as the boys gathering to play cricket or all the children coming together to enjoy Granny's stories. But when it comes into orbit with the adult world, it is also one of dependence, mostly on parents and older siblings, as well as deference and respect, particularly to teachers or men who are familiar with watch-shops, or truck drivers or the police. There is really no fluidity in the world of Rajanna; for example, his values are set in stone and his life is generally predictable. His world is a tribute to self-interest and aggressive self-preservation. There might perhaps have been some fluidity in Subanna's world. He genuinely enjoys Murthy's pleasure in his gift and the crazy fun that he and Rangamma have with it. However, his callous selfishness in Bangalore shows him in a different light, and hence it seems clear how that fluidity would eventually become stultified. On the other hand, the world of children is in constant development, taking form as the individual acknowledges, interprets and reacts to the experiences that come his or her way. It is thus that we would hope Murthy might grow, keeping hold of the legacy of Rangamma.

Rangamma is shown to have a foot in both worlds. Given her age, she obviously belongs to the adult world, but given her natural disposition, she also fits comfortably into the world of children. There are times when she is evidently unhappy, such as on the death of Vasu, her first days in Rajanna's house, when she is at Subanna's place, or when she is in the watch-shop learning of the death of Padmanabhiah. In all such cases her unhappiness is brought on by adults—adult interests and adult realities. However, when her world is lit up by the innocence and joy of the young, such as in the two story sessions or when she is alone with Murthy, her true happiness is evident.

The mix of stories in *Kraurya* are not at all crafted with the traditional beginning, middle, and end. There are starting-points rather than actual beginnings, and nothing seems to come to a conclusion. Even the death of Rangamma, while imminent, is not manifest. Like life itself, *Kraurya* takes its own time, creating impressions, showing experiences, and suggesting directions. In this sense, it is as realistic as any of Kasaravalli's films.

Kraurya champions the two powerless extremities of life—childhood and old age—and examines them for the moral values they embrace. The children in the film, particularly as represented by Murthy, evince an innocence that highlights by contrast the artfulness of adults, especially Murthy's parents. There are in fact two instances where Murthy's innocence might suggest a maturity beyond his years. One is in the subway in Bangalore where he is desperately concerned that Rangamma should not appear like one of the beggars she is sitting near, and the other is his concern for purity in opting for cupped hands rather than the public mug in bringing water for Rangamma at the police station. It is also significant that children's pleasures are shared, while adults are often seen to be grasping and exclusive in their interests. Murthy has a sense of moral responsibility to the elderly and relatively helpless Rangamma and his care and concern for her are quite palpable, especially after being charged with escorting her to Bangalore. On the other hand, Rajanna, Parvathi, and Subanna all see the old woman as a burden to be suffered as they try to devise a way of getting rid of her.

Age is represented in the film only by Rangamma. Clearly, she has more in common with the children than she has with the adults of their parents' generation, but it cannot be said that she represents the same moral values. The innocence that is natural to children lives on perhaps in Rangamma, but she is by no means without guile, especially in her handling of Parvathi and Rajanna's thirst for money. She does indeed share her pleasures, especially with the children, but much of her happiness is internalised, deriving from memory, the concrete symbol of which is her box of treasures. Of course, Murthy's sense of moral responsibility toward her is genuinely reciprocated. To all the children she would show kindness without motive and set to them an example of what those like her late husband fought for so selflessly.

Kraurya is made up of an ensemble of stories, each emanating out of another, working parallel to each other, overlapping with one another, suggesting a rather complex film that arranges a marriage between cinema and the craft of storytelling. However, the central narrative is indeed very simple, as are its offshoots. It is a film more about attitudes and personalities than complexities of action, and it is certainly a perceptive and sometimes disturbing human document.

6

He Has Done Great Injustice to the Women of this House

Tai Saheba[1] ('Lady of the Manor,' 1997) is significant for two reasons, quite apart from the fact that it won Girish Kasaravalli his third National Award for Best Film.[2] It is the first of several films that examine the meaning and value of Indian independence, and it is also the first of several to focus on a remarkably strong and exemplary woman. Previous films recognised notably worthy women, but in this and some subsequent films, the woman in focus is much more prominent.

During the freedom movement, Mahatma Gandhi had insisted that Independence—or *swaraj*—would not be an end in itself but rather the means to an even greater end. A mere change in those who hold the reins of power would not ensure independence for those who had traditionally lived in thraldom, such as the Untouchables and other low castes, the legions of poor, and the countless thousands of illiterate or ill-educated people. Also in pressing need of *swaraj* were women—of all communities, classes, and castes. Tai Saheba's own personal crusade to liberate women from at least some of their

---

[1] There are several spellings of the transliterated title. Kasaravalli's preference, and the one given in the official certification, is the one that is given here. *Tai* in Marathi means 'sister,' while in Kannada *Thayi* means 'mother.' The setting of the film is the northern part of Karnataka, where the influence of Marathi culture is very strong, hence *Tai*. *Saheba* is an epithet of respect, the feminine of *saheb*.

[2] The previous two were *Ghatashraddha* and *Tabarana Kathe*. *Tai Saheba* would be followed by *Dweepa*.

shackles, set in the context of her husband's passion for the movement to 'free' India, provides the subject matter for this remarkable work. Temporally, the film is set mostly between the assassination of Mahatma Gandhi in 1948 and the death of Jawaharlal Nehru in 1964; spatially, it is set in the manor of a wealthy landlord in the princely state of Mysore; and its philosophical environment is pre-modern, a socio-political value system where feudalism lingers in many different ways. The film is conventionally realistic in style, much of it set inside the manor house of the Inamdar family where the décor, dominated by shadows and hues of brown and red, suggests antiquity, a bygone era and, by extension, a way of life that is no longer relevant.

There is a tidy connection between the beginning of the film and its end, both sequences focussing on the evening ritual of the lighting of the lamps. At the beginning, Tai Saheba is waiting for her husband to return from jail; at the end, she is awaiting her own arrest and incarceration. In between, the film proceeds with deference to chronology. Given that much of it is a response to history, albeit sometimes personal or particular, title cards are used to indicate the year in which the ensuing narrative takes place. A number of key historical events are given specific reference or focus. The film opens, for example, in the latter days of the Quit India Movement; Partition is mentioned, the declaration of Independence comes and is celebrated, and the assassination of Mahatma Gandhi is deplored.[3] The integration of the princely states into the new nation has significance to the narrative of the film, as has the Land Reforms Act of 1961. The death of Nehru marks the end of the direct connection with the Gandhian era in Indian history.

In the film's opening sequence, the ritual of the lighting of evening lamps is being performed; central to it is the apparent piety of Tai Saheba, who goes on to read aloud from scripture and to allude to her frugality when asked by her servant, Radhakka, what

[3] Significant reference is made to the perverse few who actually celebrated the murder.

she would like for dinner, preferring leftovers from lunch rather than something cooked especially for her. Her religiosity might indicate a devout and morally upright woman—an indication that will be corroborated as the film progresses—but it also suggests the continuance of tradition in the world in which the film moves. In fact, throughout the film we will note the prominence of religious tradition, noting also the tension between it and social and political actuality.

There is an immediate illustration of this. While Tai Saheba is still at her devotions, she learns from Venkob Rao, the steward of the estate, that her husband Balakrishna Inamdar, known as Appa Saheb, has been released from jail (he is obviously a political prisoner of the British) and that Venkob is taking the cart to bring him home. We will see that Appa Saheb is a devout patriot, imbued with at least some Gandhian values and attentive to the protocols of religion. He is also an unabashed womaniser. Venkob Rao learns that he will, in fact, spend the night with his 'keep' or kept woman, Chandri, and will come home in the morning. It is because Chandri has just given birth to a daughter that he has been given temporary release. Once his duty of compassion to his mistress has been performed and the priest consulted about the baby's horoscope, he must return to prison and serve out the rest of his term. We soon learn that Tai Saheba—or Narmada—is his second wife, as the first, Akka Saheba (the sister of Venkob Rao), had become an ascetic and taken up residence in a temple. Theoretically, then, Appa Saheb is responsible for three women.

In pre-modern times the harem had its established place in the palaces of both Hindu and Muslim rulers, many of whom had a multiplicity of co-wives or concubines, to say nothing of singers and dancing girls and other delights of erotic confectionary. It should be of no surprise that even in the twentieth century wealthy landlords' enjoyment of the favours of more than one woman was not seen as untoward. Indeed, one could say that keeping at least one woman was almost expected of them. Hence, Appa Saheb has no cause to keep secrets and nothing is kept under wraps. While Narmada's feelings on the matter are of little or no concern to him, they do become fundamental to the narrative, as it is driven by her for the greater part of the film.

There is an incipient tension in all this. A major reason for Narmada's feelings not being of much, if any, concern to her husband is that she probably never raised them with him, on account of her knowing her place. The traditional view of a husband having virtually divine status and his wife existing merely to serve his every need was prevalent in the world of Tai Saheba. We might note the disappointment on her face when she is given the news that he has gone to Chandri and will not be home until the morning, yet we might also note that she never articulates that disappointment. When he comes home, she politely inquires after the health of mother and child and offers, 'I heard Chandri had a girl this time too,' to which the only reply is a somewhat indignant look. She takes this up by asking: 'Are you upset at what I said?' To some, the implication might be clear, that a girl-child is worthless and Chandri has produced two. However, Narmada's remark is more likely to be a simple observation. The question comes with the realisation that Appa Saheb would certainly have wanted a boy, there being no issue from his first or second marriage. Narmada would have been sympathetic to this. The tension now evolving in her mind is between her implicit and unswerving dedication to her husband and her nascent awareness of sexist injustice.

It is important to note that Narmada bears no ill-will toward Chandri. Inwardly she might wish that her husband would renounce his mistress and sleep only with his wife, but that would be wishing for the impossible. Society may look down on a kept woman, but a man's right to keep her is not an issue. In Narmada's mind there is no question of blame. Appa Saheb is only doing what is accepted and Chandri merely accepts his favours. There may be material advantage for her in this liaison, but there is also a degree of ill-repute and the difficulty of being a single mother of two. Indeed, Narmada genuinely feels sympathy for her; later she will offer her hospitality and eventually the two of them will form a firm friendship.

It is not made clear why the first wife renounced the world to become an ascetic. Actually, her renunciation is by no means a cast-iron one, as she keeps abreast of news of the world—or, particularly, her former family—and receives visits at the temple from Narmada; but despite Narmada's pleas, she will not return to the manor, even for a brief time. She offers no threat to Narmada's marriage for with her renunciation, she presumably renounced her own marriage. Narmada's relations with her continue to be warm and cordial.

The first wife is a recluse and the second is a fringe-dweller in the world of her husband. While catching up on domestic goings on from Akka Saheba, Narmada learns that she, being shut up in the monastery all day, is unaware of so much that is going on. Indeed, a little earlier, Appa Saheb actually berated Narmada for her isolation, calling her selfish for being interested only in the home, while the whole nation was eagerly anticipating independence. There is a touch of irony in this, for while Appa Saheb is a devout patriot, he shares nothing of his freedom fighting experience with his wife. Indeed, one might wonder if he shares anything with her at all, for in his society the life of a man and the life of a woman are separate and distinct in almost every way; hence, Narmada gently complains to Akka Saheb that their husband never consults either of them about anything. Appa Saheb's public life and his private world are also separate and distinct, and his women, most notably Narmada, are kept largely out of both of them.

A great moment in Appa Saheb's life is the historic 'stroke of the midnight hour' on 15 August 1947 when, with all his tenant farmers and labourers present, he raises the Indian tricolour and salutes the newly independent country. Narmada's role in this has been, along with Radhakka, to prepare innumerable sweets for the celebration, which the two women watch from a room that assures their privacy, while giving them visual access to the ceremony. The tenants would seem to have no idea of what is going on, one even suggesting that Appa Saheb may be out of his mind, and it is evident that Narmada and Radhakka, too, have not been given any preparation that might enable them to truly appreciate the momentous occasion.

Given his sympathy to the cause of independence as well as his willingness to significantly suffer for it, it cannot be said that Appa

Saheb is typical of his class. We have seen him released from jail; from conversations with Narmada, it is apparent that he has served a number of jail terms in the cause of India's freedom. Some months later, at the end of January 1948, he is seen by a group of Congress activists to be distributing sweets to his tenants on the occasion of a family celebration. He is unaware of the news that has just rocked India and the world concerning the assassination of Mahatma Gandhi, nor does he know of the ultra-right wing Brahmans in Pune and Kolhapur who are distributing sweets in celebration of the killing. The young activists, not knowing Appa Saheb, identify his celebration with those of the extremist Brahmans, and rush in and attack him and his guests. Appa Saheb suffers a beating before taking in the devastating news of Gandhi's death. Sometime after this Appa Saheb takes up another cause in the process of *swaraj*. Grateful that the nation is now independent, he is disturbed that many of its people are not wholly free, as they remain under the privileged rule of princely dominion. However, before he can launch his protest movement, he is again arrested, this time by the agents of the Maharaja of Mysore. When he comes home after his sentence, it is clear that he has been badly treated, and his right leg will remain seriously maimed.

Most of this forms the bulk of the significant historical context that embraces the fictional narrative, the major turning-point of which is intimated to Narmada by Akka Saheba at the temple. Appa Saheb, she informs her, wants to adopt the youngest son of Venkob Rao. Narmada's surprise can be explained by the fact that her husband has not mentioned a word of his intention to her. (He later confesses that 'it had never occurred [to him] to seek a woman's counsel on the matter.') Appa Saheb has no children by either of his wives and he has two daughters by his mistress; thus, he has no heir in the traditional sense. The wish for an heir is probably the reason for his decision to adopt Venkob Rao's youngest son, Nanu, although he tells Narmada, perhaps a little patronisingly, that his intention is to give her an interest. It is easy to understand Venkob Rao's complicity in the arrangement, for as long as he continues as the

Inamdars' steward, he will have frequent access to his son; of greater significance is the fact that his son will inherit the Inamdars' estate.

While Narmada takes to the little boy as naturally as if he were her own, establishing with him a relationship of great affection, Nanu never really seems to bond at all with his new father. For the most part, Appa Saheb is simply absent. There is one occasion when the little boy is playing 'blind man' with Narmada and does not see Appa Saheb come in. He bumps into him, bringing a formal smile to Appa Saheb, but the close-up of Nanu's face reveals anything but happiness. In a later sequence, when the boy is approaching adulthood, he is able to articulate his disdain for his adoptive father and, indeed, for his natural one.

Soon after Nanu has been taken under Narmada's wing, there is a scene in which she finds him alone, sobbing and missing his mother. She cossets him and distracts him from his melancholy by introducing him to some intensely fragrant perfume. The camera shows quite clearly the delight on the boy's face as he experiences the pleasure of this wonderful new aroma, which will now be a regular part of his personal grooming. While this may be pleasing to Nanu, we see three examples of it being a hazard to him. When he is still little, his brothers will not play with him because of his strange smell. When the daughters of Chandri play hide-and-seek with him, he is easy to discover, as his smell gives him away. And some years later, his physical intimacy with Chandri's daughter Manjari is betrayed to Narmada by the smell of the perfume on her. There might also be a much more symbolic significance in the boy's fondness for perfume, conventionally deemed as feminine, which would make a simple semiotic connection with the boy's alacrity in taking up cudgels on behalf of oppressed women and against exploitative men. His profound and well-argued compassion for the women in his life would certainly seem to be more innate than learned; once he starts articulating that compassion, it becomes evident that Tai Saheba has had an influence over him beyond whatever she might have intended.

Appa Saheb, as an idea, will be prominent right through to the end of the film, though his physical presence fades with his relevance and Nanu comes to occupy more of the foreground. After his term in jail for his proposed agitation against princely rule, the erstwhile activist seems to find himself more and more alone. There is now no cause for him to engage with and his fellow landlords, well aware of where their own advantages lie, desert him. A somewhat pathetic scene sees him picking flowers for worship, noticeably aged and still crippled from his jail injuries. He is not quite a retired activist for one last call of a Gandhian ideal will stir him, but off-screen and mysteriously. Before then, Tai Saheba will become an activist of sorts, too.

The relationship between Tai Saheba and Nanu has to overcome some significant challenges. The first is Nanu's taking to drink, seemingly brought about by a growing depression infused with a surfeit of boredom. It becomes evident that Nanu loses respect for his two fathers—Venkob Rao and Appa Saheb—particularly on the issue of the treatment of women. His close observation during his formative years of Tai Saheba's marriage, his curiosity about where his adoptive father goes at night, his sympathy for Chandri, and disgust at his natural father's covert attendance at a girlie show all serve to lower, in his eyes, the prominent men in his life. His growing affection for Manjari makes him determined that she should not become like her mother, or either of the official wives of Appa Saheb. But the world in which he is obliged to live is run by men like his two fathers, and this awareness deflates his optimism to the point that, in one scene, we see him sitting in the warehouse of the jaggery middleman in utter dejection. Believing that he is doing him a favour, one of the traders takes him to a liquor den and thereafter, much of what we see of Nanu is of a young man somewhat the worse for drink. This saddens Tai Saheba greatly, but she makes no concrete endeavour to persuade him to give it up; perhaps she trusts that in time he will do so of his own volition.

Another significant challenge concerns Nanu's growing love for Manjari. Earlier in the film it was reported to Tai Saheba that Nanu had been fighting with boys of the town, and the skirmish was caused by Nanu's taking offence at Manjari being teased for being the daughter of a kept woman. He is frank in asserting Appa Saheb's culpability, for it was he who madè Chandri a kept woman in the first place. To the injustice meted out to Chandri, Nanu adds that which is suffered by Akka Saheba and Tai Saheba as well. 'Appa Saheb has done great injustice to the women of this house.' Narmada knows this. Her later resolve that no girl should have to be another Tai Saheba or Chandri is a tacit acknowledgement of Appa Saheb's guilt, as is her offering of hospitality and, in time, friendship to Chandri on the grounds of her having suffered, but she—unlike Nanu—is able to balance that guilt with virtues that the young man cannot see, or even care about. Her nobility consists in the magnanimity of her heart and in her readiness to maximise rather than minimise people. On this occasion her reaction to Nanu's criticism of her husband is to try to set it aside, aiming to encourage Nanu to find positive things to say about a man with such a fine reputation. Nevertheless, the argument has been clearly won by Nanu. It is of course a hollow victory, for in achieving it he has hurt his beloved Tai Saheba, and for this he is filled with remorse.

Nanu's relationship with Manjari grows to the point where he declares his desire to marry her. At first Narmada's reaction is conventional, arguing that no such marriage can ever take place because it is incestuous, Manjari being Nanu's younger sister. Nanu argues quite reasonably that there is no blood relationship between them; the only relationship is inferred from the contractual relationship pertaining to his adoption. Narmada tries to counter this by asserting that while there is no blood relationship, there is indeed a moral relationship. Her reasoning here is weak, but instead of exploiting it with a rational argument, Nanu resorts to an emotional attack on the moral turpitude and hypocrisy of Appa Saheb. What he says is quite true, but like his previous reproach it is also very hurtful, and Tai Saheba beats him ruthlessly for it. The umbrage she takes, however, is not personal but an offence taken on behalf of her husband. The fact that she cannot rationally defend him intensifies her frustration and anger. It is the one cross moment they have ever experienced together and it has the potential to shatter their relationship. Nevertheless, despite her unwavering devotion to her husband, Narmada recognises the truth of what Nanu has said; despite his contempt for his adoptive father, Nanu recognises the spite he has inflicted on his beloved Tai Saheba. A subconscious mutual forgiveness is clearly implied.

Narmada's opposition to the marriage is based on a principle with which the law is in accordance. His natural father, Venkob Rao, is adamantly opposed to it, but moral argument is not particularly relevant to Venkob's thinking. He stresses to Nanu the girl's lowly status as the daughter of a kept woman and counsels his son to maintain a liaison with her as long as she pleases him, but to let his father choose a respectable wife for him. Nanu immediately recognises the moral bankruptcy in his father's proposal, which is quite consonant with traditional attitudes, and threatens to expose him for the hypocrite he is by broadcasting Venkob's patronage of the 'pay-as-you-enjoy' girlie show. Later Venkob will go ahead with what he considers to be right for the son he gave away in adoption by calling in a priest for pre-marital horoscope discussions. On this occasion opposition to his intentions is voiced most strongly by Tai Saheba, who has come to be convinced of the sincerity of the love between Nanu and Manjari. She realises that any arranged wife would become another Tai Saheba, and that Manjari would become another Chandri.

It might be suggested that part of Nanu's drinking problem comes from boredom, arising out of having little to do that is of any consequence. As an exercise in grooming for a possible managerial future, Venkob Rao introduces him to a major part of Balakrishna Inamdar's enterprise: the jaggery trade. Here, Nanu finds a niche where he can be happy. He has no design for wealth, and he is truly grateful for being paid even a modest wage in the jaggery market. His associates are simple, unpretentious men who show no inclination at all to exploit people weaker than them. We see him joking and skylarking with fellow traders (perhaps a trifle overplayed) and his happiness is obvious, for doing useful work has enhanced his self-esteem. While Venkob Rao is displeased that he is living beneath his proper station, Tai Saheba expresses her satisfaction that she has never seen him as happy as this.

Quite remote from happiness, however, is Appa Saheb, who entered the film as part of the march of history, not without an element of triumph and a gust of optimism. He will now fade out of the film, limping to keep pace with history, defeated and cheated on a major plank in the Gandhian platform.

One of the great catch-cries of the freedom movement had been 'Land to the tillers!,' and the worth of that ideal was at the root of the agitation for land reform throughout the 1950s. In Mysore, Basappa Danappa Jatti was the chairman of the Land Reforms Committee which did the groundwork for the Mysore Land Reforms Act, under which the tenancy system and the tradition of absentee landlordism would be abolished. The obvious social justice in this was not seen, however, by many landlords and their stewards. The spirit of the law abolishing the tenancy system was aimed at enabling a more general and equitable share in land ownership, meaning that the wealthy would become somewhat less wealthy.

Venkob Rao, fearing a diminution of his son's inheritance, sets about beating and evicting tenants from Balakrishna Inamdar's land. Appa Saheb reacts angrily to his steward's actions, going among his tenants and encouraging them to seek and establish their entitlements under the new law. Then he disappears. At first Venkob Rao half seriously tells Narmada that he has become an ascetic, but then he offers the more plausible explanation that he has been arrested and jailed for communist activism. A round of the jails by Narmada and Chandri, however, finds no trace of him. At the first jail they go to, an obviously thorough search of the register is made before declaring that Appa Saheb is not there. The visit to the second jail arouses suspicion—a guard is asked if Balakrishna Inamdar is imprisoned there; the guard hangs his head in seemingly instinctive discomfort and asks another, 'Is he here?,' to which the reply comes without any consultation of a register, 'No!.' The visible demeanour of the first guard and the spontaneous, peremptory reply of the other offer circumstantial support for the credible suspicion, first voiced by Nanu, presumably on the basis of rumours he has heard about town, that Appa Saheb has been liquidated by fellow landlords with the connivance of Venkob Rao.

Appa Saheb has been forced out of the narrative and Venkob, now that his nest has been feathered as well as it might be, fades out of it too. The notion of the relationship between Nanu and Manjari, and their freedom, dominates the remainder of the film, with the visual focus on Narmada and Chandri.

Nanu has declared his disdain for the legacy for which he was given in adoption a decade or more earlier. The new land laws have played a role in diminishing it—at least as far as the efforts of the unscrupulous Venkob Rao have allowed—but Nanu can be happy only if he can break free of a world founded on values that he cannot accept. He sees clearly through the double standards of both his fathers and categorically rejects the life they would have him lead. His idea of happiness is apparently doing simple but honest work, while being married to Manjari.

With her husband presumably dead, the notion of loyalty to him is no longer as pressing as it was, and Narmada devotes herself to the freedom of Nanu and Manjari. Never having been able to enjoy personal freedom herself, Narmada has lived her life in devotion to her husband and her adopted son. With her husband now gone, she is left with the son and is prepared to devote the remainder of her life to his freedom and happiness. All her life has been a sacrifice in the interests of others, and this last service will be no different.

In order to render this beneficence, Narmada must grapple with the law. The view that she expressed to Nanu about his relationship with Manjari is a view supported in law, which holds that Nanu and Manjari are legally brother and sister. If the adoption had not been carried out in the first place, there would be no objection to Nanu marrying Manjari. The situation is made more difficult by the law not allowing the annulment of an adoption. The suggestion that Manjari be given in adoption is scotched immediately as there is no provision in law for adopting a girl. The sexist force of the law is further evidenced in Chandri being unrecognised as Appa Saheb's wife, despite having served his physical needs and borne his two children.

One last element is put into the historical framework with reference to the death of Nehru when the two women find their lawyer absent from his office. Another lawyer is there—clever, but clearly lacking in integrity—who snatches the chance to take on Tai Saheba's case while her own counsel is mourning the death of India's first Prime Minister. The new lawyer advises legal cunning or twisting the truth, without actually uttering the word 'perjury.' He has Narmada sign an affidavit which claims that the adoption of Nanu took place in British times and that a religious ceremony joined Chandri with Balakrishna, thus giving her the right to inheritance. One major problem pointed out by Chandri is that Appa Saheb's being beaten by confused Congress activists on the day of the adoption quite clearly places it five months after the end of British rule. When a possible allegation of perjury is mooted, the lawyer casually assures them that it can be dealt with when the time comes (he will have his fee by then, we may well assume), and by the time the case does actually come to court and judgment is pronounced, Nanu should be a father.

Narmada is patently unmoved by the matter of perjury and she must, therefore, be held morally accountable. She knowingly and deliberately breaks the law. Many, of course, would agree that she acts in defiance of an archaic law to give freedom to two young people caught in a tangle of definition. Her excuse, or reason, does not absolve her of her offence, not does she expect absolution. She is fully convinced that Venkob Rao will perform one last act of treachery, which will result in a jail sentence for her. However, she is quite willing to sacrifice her own freedom to ensure that of Nanu and Manjari. She tells Chandri, 'Appa Saheb used to say that one must go to jail to get freedom. To free Nanu, I am ready even to go to jail.'

Nanu is brought home drunk, perhaps for the last time. Narmada tells him of his freedom and a brief sequence of simple and touching sentiment sets the course for the next stage in Nanu's life. As an expression of his gratitude, she suggests that he might call her 'Mother.' Like a little boy, a smile overwhelming his face, he curls up on the floor beside her, rests his head on her breast, and lovingly puts his arms around her.

It is a happy ending, but to be realistic, it must come at a cost. The last title card reads, 'Yet another twilight.' We see Tai Saheba and Radhakka engaged in the ritual of the lamps, just as they had been some two decades ago at the beginning of the film. Tai Saheba tells Radhakka that she is expecting someone, and in deference to the guest, Radhakka turns on all the electric lights. Tai Saheba sits on the floor and the camera pulls back into a long high shot, focussing on the widow in the midst of the erstwhile grand manor house that is now dated and out of place, its anomalousness suggested in previous external shots of the physical disrepair of the exterior of the house. This last shot is held as we hear a voiceover announcing himself as police. Tai Saheba's achievement is about to be fulfilled.

Tai Saheba is not about historical change but it is, indeed, set against the background of historical change. In the time span of the film there is significant, indeed, radical change—the Quit India Movement, the dissolution of the princely states, wholesale land reforms—and two remarkable passings: the assassination of Gandhi and the death of Nehru. Appa Saheb gets caught up in most of these and, through him, the narrative is affected by them, but what is particularly remarkable about the role of history in this film is its foregrounding of people whom history seems not to reach. In the new India many things were changing and many changes were far-reaching, but at the same time much remained the same. One of the greatest changes needed was—and perhaps still is—the liberation of the female mind. Prompted by love and devotion more than by history, Tai Saheba makes a profound commitment to that liberation.

7

You're Just the Means—God is the Force

The most visually beautiful of all Girish Kasaravalli's films is *Dweepa* ('The Island,' 2001). It is set amid hills in an extensively dammed region of a mighty river where the human population is negligible and nature is predominant. The lush green of the land and its forests, beside the vast expanse of silvery water with its glassy surface, creates a geographical context that is both spectacular and socio-economically revealing. The tranquillity of the region in sunlight, its exciting transformation in constant heavy rain, shots combining both fire and water, and the harmonious simplicity of human habitation are some elements of the film's visual appeal. It might be a superb setting for a romance, but *Dweepa*'s narrative is by no means a romantic one. Rather, the film relates closely to globalisation in its concern with the growing phenomenon of big dams in the 1990s and at the turn of the present century. However, the focus throughout is on the human concerns of a small family and their particular cultural refuge in the face of the threat posed by the march of progress.

A number of binary conflicts provide the narrative with content and much of its structure. The most fundamental of these is the conflict between technological and industrial development on the one hand, and the traditional human way of life and means of production on the other. The economic controversy of big dams is not specifically addressed; one might well imagine that such a controversy would carry little cinematic potential, with or without an overdose of polemical dialogue. However, we are prompted to think about the moral implications without any philosophical imposition from the director. A fundamental fact regarding the creation of big dams is that vast areas of land become submerged, depriving huge populations of their homes and livelihood, to say nothing of the seeming intangibles like human relations, religious practices and popular or local cultural traditions. In short, human sentiment is trampled and dignity and self-worth are bruised and fractured. We may be led to wonder whether or not this is a reasonable price to pay for whatever is promised by progress.

In the narrative of *Dweepa* things initially go smoothly for the developers and their agencies and the state and local government functionaries. As the planned flooding goes ahead, more and more people are facing what they are led to believe is reality, accepting government compensation for their property and relocating. However, one family—a father, son and his wife—remain adamant that they will not leave. Interestingly, they are not landowners with valuable property. The elderly father is a priest of a regional *nema* or spirit cult, the son is his acolyte, and the young woman is wife to one and housekeeper to both. As the film depicts them, they form one party to the fundamental dispute, while local government officials form the other.

As the threat of eviction—or worse—looms, other conflicts develop. At the heart of it all there is simmering conflict within the family. The father, Duggappa, is utterly intransigent in resistance to change; Nagi, the one seemingly modern person of the three, tries to assess their plight rationally; and the son, Ganapa, a somewhat feckless and ineffective man, hovers vaguely between the two, but generally finds it comfortable to defer to his father. Nagi's own father, as well as others from their region who have moved to the town, try to persuade them of the benefits of relocation but are unsuccessful to the point where an element of acrimony threatens the relationship between father and daughter. The most significant of the lesser conflicts is between Ganapa and Krishna, a young man who goes to stay with them in order to help them through impending difficulty, and a consequence of this conflict is, by extension, a growing tension between Ganapa and Nagi, a conflict which will reach beyond the final titles.

The opening segment of the film, including the opening titles, is visually superb. A few of its elements—a mass of water, a vast blue sky, small forested islands and the surrounding forested hills—give it its striking simplicity. However, apart from the purely aesthetic effect, two important ideas are established here. The first is water as the underlying reality of the film. The dominance of the vast body of water taking up so much of the screen is more than a passing picture; it is the fundamental concept on which all the ideas and narrative elements are based. The other important idea is the notion of harmony. The manifestation of natural harmony is visually obvious, while the human presence immediately seems felicitous—a young woman paddling a dugout across the waters, having foraged for vegetables in parts that have been abandoned close to the water. This notion of human harmony with nature, as distinct from human dominance over nature, is at the core of *Dweepa*'s philosophy. However, that notion is under threat. Very soon, after the last of the opening titles, an element of tension threatens the apparent tranquillity. A man is seen riding a bicycle along the bank, and then there is a shot of a depth gauge in the water; the man, Chaniya, a messenger of the Relief Department, takes note of the depth, observing to Nagi, whom he recognises, that the level of water is rising and that at the current rate their house should be submerged with the coming monsoon. Soon police will be coming in to evict those reluctant to move. His advice is simple: she should convince Ganapa to accept the compensation offered by the government and relocate. He also stresses the urgency of the situation. Her plea—that their own region, Sita's Peak, cannot be flooded as her father-in-law says it is sacred—simply prompts derision.

However, Duggappa's belief in the sacredness of Sita's Peak is not simply an expression of superstition from an ignorant old man. The brief introduction of Duggappa suggests a cultural reality that is quite profound. Duggappa's intimate connection with the land is indicated by his close inspection of animal marks in the earth and his concern that they may be evidence of a tiger's presence. He then binds his natural attachment to the physical with a connection to the metaphysical in his capacity as a *nema* celebrant. We see him dressed in an ornate costume, surrounded by many elements that might also be found in orthodox Hindu rituals, performing what seems to be some sort of shamanic dance. What is significant here is not so much the ritual or the principles on which it is based but the faith which it inspires in its adherents, in this case a small group of people who are about to relocate.

The seemingly animistic cult in which Duggappa celebrates his faith binds his spirit to what he believes to be the spirit of the natural world in which he lives. Thus, a very special significance is assumed on behalf of the land that is threatened by human progress. It would seem, however, that for the majority of people a fear of destructive floods is greater than their faith in the natural spirit's ability to withstand that threat, and so their relocation is accompanied by little that is more traumatic than a temporary melancholy. Nevertheless, for Duggappa and his son, faith in the spirit is so earnest that their future, as it is seen by officials of a modern, secular society, is indeed precarious.

Nagi manages to persuade Ganapa to heed Chaniya's advice and visit the Relief Office to ascertain their situation. There is a reprise of the opening, nature-affirming section, but this time we see a pensive and somewhat worried Ganapa paddling across the dam, while the view of the dugout plying the vast waters is followed by a lovely panoramic shot of lush pasture land—albeit dominated by electricity pylons and cables, serving as a gentle reminder of the nature-progress tension. Ganapa exchanges his dugout for a bus, and then is seen in the government office.

Fundamental to Ganapa's case is the implicit importance of *nema*, and so he begins by showing the official a number of photographs of his father—'a highly sought after *nema* practitioner'—performing his ritual in various contexts associated with the dam development. Underlying his argument is the observation that the development represents a conflict with the spiritual, and that his father has the authority and the power to see that the spiritual prevails. To the assistant at an adjacent desk, *nema* is of no concern at all as it bears no relevance to the situation, but what is irrelevant to Ganapa is the bureaucratic process of measuring land, asserting a formula and paying appropriate compensation. To him, that which is being threatened with extinction is not property but a certain quality of life, comprising, as he puts it, honour and respect. How can the loss of such qualitative things be compensated?

Ganapa seems to excite a degree of impatience in the assistant clerk who, in simple bureaucratic fashion, sees all problems, including the essentially human ones, with clerical reference. His senior betrays a slight degree of amusement, yet treats Ganapa with courteous tolerance. The patently obvious fact is that Ganapa is absurdly out-of-place in a government office. His concerns are abstractions, which bureaucrats are not trained to deal with; his relationship with his natural environment would rarely be recognised by clerks and their seniors, let alone understood; his faith in the metaphysical is quite inconsequential in government service, where even orthodox religion is best kept concealed. Sita's Peak, an insignificant step along the way of development, is the world to Ganapa and his father, whose quality of life is simple, unprofitable, and economically unproductive. To modern, secular minds, it is dispensable.

It is very important that Kasaravalli has enabled at least a subjective element of support for this humble quality of life to be established at this early stage in the film, for the defence of it is the substance of most of the rest of *Dweepa*. The defence is mounted when a government team comes to Sita's Peak to measure and assess, with a view to compensating Duggappa and his son and daughter-in-law. Now the notion of *ownership* becomes vital to the dispute. Duggappa tries to authenticate his claim by appealing to subjectivities, which impress the officials only so far as they find them amusing. Duggappa is dismayed to find that the Sita's Peak memorial and the *nema* shrine, two things to which he has the closest attachment, are public or government property, and he cannot lay claim to them. It is observed that he is confusing faith with fact, that what makes a fact is not faith but an entry in government records. To Duggappa and his son, the presence of Rama and Sita here during their exile is a continuing actuality; to the government official, the great epic *Ramayana* in which that exile is recounted is merely a 'fairy story' that does nothing to substantiate Duggappa's claims. Duggappa's inability to engage with the Relief Office lies in his failure to understand the difference between *owning* and *having access*. Realising the futility of trying to communicate with officialdom, Duggappa defiantly resolves to stay, while friends and neighbours continue to leave.

The departure of one upper-caste family brings a stroke of luck to Ganapa. The owner suggests that should the water level rise to Ganapa's house, he should move to their house, which is higher up; that way Ganapa and his wife and father will be safe and the house will have a caretaker. Moreover, Ganapa would be welcome to take whatever excess crops he might care to reap. Caste proprieties are significant here, for although Ganapa and his father have an established religious importance in the region, they are nevertheless of a lower caste, while the departing family are high-caste Brahmans. Hence, Ganapa and his family might seek sanctuary in their house, but would be obliged to avoid the kitchen and the prayer room, in order not to bring defilement upon their benefactors. This is of passing interest. However, this brief section allows the focus to come onto Nagi. In conversation with the lady of the departing family she admits that she is happy at the thought of their village being flooded, for that might force them to give up 'this *nema* business' and take on a more productive occupation. Thus, Kasaravalli has set the basis for a demarcation in personal philosophy between Ganapa and his wife.

The narrative offers a further illustration of the refractoriness of Duggappa. Apparently catching sight of Chaniya arriving at their place with two police officers, he dashes to another room and locks himself in. The police have come to forcibly evict the three, and while Nagi is content to go and Ganapa sees no alternative, Duggappa has to be cajoled to come out of his hiding-place. Try as he may, Ganapa cannot get him to unlock the door. However, one of the policemen merely informs him that they are taking Nagi and Ganapa, so the father, realising his utter helplessness without them, opens the door. He struggles furiously but is no match for the two strong policemen, and he is next seen in their dugout, being taken to the mainland. A further expression of defiance is to snatch the *lathi* of one of the officers and throw it into the water, but it is merely a petulant gesture, inconsequential and pointless. At Nagi's father's house he refuses to eat and, it would seem, to talk. And then, without a word or a sign, he disappears.

Obviously, the old man has returned to his home on the island, and Nagi agrees with Ganapa that they have no alternative but to go after him. Her father expresses serious concern for their safety in such isolation, especially if Duggappa's health becomes a problem or a wild animal should come upon them, or if the water comes up to a dangerous level. This concern allows Kasaravalli to set in motion the major turning-point in the narrative. Sharing her husband's concern, but also resigned to Nagi and Ganapa's determination to return to the island, Nagi's mother proposes that someone should go with them to be of assistance should things get difficult. She suggests one Krishna, a young man whom Nagi knows as vibrant and joyful, and the suggestion is appealing to her. Krishna would come with some mystery in his baggage, having been to Bombay to make his fortune and come back after suffering some grave disappointment, which he will not talk about. There is no narrative significance in this, as it transpires, but the actuality of the memory will add a dimension of interest to Krishna's character as the film plays out.

So life resumes on their island, but it is now lonely with so many gone elsewhere and lacking in joy without the festivities that would normally accompany this season of rains and planting new crops. But then, like a summer storm, Krishna bursts into their lives. He has come by bicycle, which he rides as though it is a clown's prop, whooping and laughing, theatrical in his delivery of largely immaterial dialogue. The young man's vibrancy and vivacity are obvious, and there is a clear cinematic suggestion that life in this deserted and threatened part of the world is about to experience a significant change. He goes out in the rain to greet Ganapa, who is working in the field, and soon appears as a possible annoyance to the latter with his assurance of bringing in labourers and generally seeing to it that Ganapa's life will be a lot easier because of him. It is all simply the ebullient and naïve enthusiasm of a young man who is still a boy, but the close shot of the look on Ganapa's face suggests that he is not likely to accept it in good faith. The shots of Krishna eagerly darting around, sliding down an embankment and sprawling in the mud, indicative of his vitality, might also suggest his ineptitude.

The featured shots of water—close-up shots of water forming globules and dropping from plants, of a hillside waterfall, of butterflies flitting about in the damp soil—enhance the underlying reality of water discussed earlier and evoke the natural loveliness of the rainy season, contrasting somewhat to the sequence of Ganapa working the soil in the rain. Indeed, both sides of the contrast serve to remind us of the threat that water poses to the lives of these humble people. We may also remember Chaniya's warning that by the end of the monsoon their house may well be submerged.

It does not take long for the incipient conflict between Ganapa and Krishna to become manifest. Ganapa may well feel aggrieved that his authority has been snubbed by Krishna's bringing in workers to plant the new crop. He might also resent his resources being tampered with by Krishna doing a 'package deal,' offering the workers 500 rupees, and meals and tea. But what sparks off the first expression of conflict is something seemingly trivial. Krishna, playing with his camera, gets the idea that Duggappa might be an appropriate subject for a photograph, depicting the face of the hungry in order to generate sympathy and, in turn, more generous compensation. Duggappa happily engages in what he sees as fun, and Nagi thinks it is harmless enough, especially as it might get them more money. But Ganapa senses in Krishna's publicity stunt a lowering of their dignity in its aim to attract charity born of sympathy. He offends Krishna, winning no support from either Duggappa or Nagi. Nagi fears that Krishna might take umbrage enough to leave them, prompting Ganapa's heartfelt 'Then let him go. The world won't end if he leaves.'

There are now two parallel themes: the continuing theme concerning the rising water level and the recently introduced theme of the tension between Ganapa and Krishna. Krishna happily rides off on his bicycle to get away from the sullen Ganapa for a while and discovers too late that the road he is riding along suddenly runs under water. He falls off, gets soaked and damages the bike, returning home to report his bad luck to Nagi. She realises that all the roads must indeed be flooded, making their land an island in fact and not just in name. Nagi now is seen as being caught in the throes of both themes: she is profoundly worried about the rising water level—more so than her husband and father-in-law would seem to be—and she must also bear the strain of Ganapa's negativity and growing nastiness toward Krishna. The heavier the rain gets, the more the four of them are confined indoors, while symbolically the waterfall outside the cottage gets stronger and its previously clear water has now become muddied. And very soon the water level comes right up to their walls.

As the rain becomes torrential, three points of view have to be considered. The first is that of Duggappa, who has to come to terms with a shattered faith. It had always been his belief that Sita's Peak could not be submerged, but now he is being proven wrong. Such a realisation has the potential to be devastating to this intellectually limited old man, and while it might be easy for some to dismiss him for his arcane beliefs, his way of coming to terms with this new challenge will be vital to the narrative. Ganapa tends to do nothing, arguing that the rains will recede in a week as will the water. Krishna, however, argues that the water is dam water and will not recede; they should, in that case, move to Heramba Hegde's deserted house on higher ground and buy some time for themselves. Nagi is determined to go, even Duggappa allows himself to be coaxed by Krishna to go, and so Ganapa has no choice. But his resentment of Krishna deepens.

Since their return to the island from Nagi's father's house, the camera has kept us constantly aware of the reality of rain and its effects, especially the rising water level. Even the internal shots are dominated by rain, framed by open doorways or windows, or streaming down through leaks in the roof. Even now at the Hegdes' house—a big, well-built, dry home—the rain is still present, pelting down into the courtyard. Krishna revels in it, convincing Ganapa even more of his fatuousness.

It is when Krishna, with genuinely good intention, asks to be given some big job by which he might be of help to Ganapa, that the older man pits one male will against another, ensuring that Krishna will either back down or fail. He asks him to bring the cow and her calf up to their new house. Krishna agrees willingly before he realises that since there is no road, he will have to swim with them across the waters. There is a nasty element in Ganapa's challenge, while there is sincere goodwill in Krishna's acceptance of it. Krishna seems to manage the task to start with, but there is no obliging the animals to be biddable, and with the cow swimming one way and the calf another, Krishna is caught in the middle, struggling not only to keep control over the animals but to keep himself from drowning. Ganapa finds it highly amusing; Nagi, appalled at his malice, paddles the dugout to bring Krishna back to safety. Later, she comforts him with hot tea. While this is going on, Ganapa plays his drum with a beam of satisfaction on his face, but when a certain degree of familiarity is apparent in Nagi's rubbing the young man's chest with eucalyptus oil, the smile dissolves, the drum is hung up, and Ganapa goes to bed.

The argument that ensues reveals that Ganapa is peeved about his worth in the household being minimised, while the outsider enjoys undue appreciation from Nagi. 'Who is it who has lived all his life here? Who knows everything about the rains, about landslides, snakes, medicinal herbs? It is me, no one else but me. But he makes you feel that he is our saviour.' Nagi declares that Krishna should stay until their compensation comes through. To Ganapa, that is more than too long, and he expresses his displeasure by moving his bed away from hers. There is a chasm between him and Krishna, there is now a gap between him and Nagi, and there remains for a breach to develop between Nagi and Krishna.

A jump cut brings Ganapa back to the Relief Office, where he is informed that the government will not move the shrine as it has no archaeological significance. It is suggested that the government might have acted favourably had Ganapa and his father sought the support of others who have now left the region; however, when opinion was sought of them, they no longer held strong views about it, having quickly settled into their new lives in a new environment. Some even described Ganapa and Duggappa as mad. However, Ganapa sadly raises a significant moral question, 'Is it right that the lives of some should be ruined for the benefit of some others?' It is a much bigger question than he might imagine, and he gets no answer to it, though many in the audience should find it significant. Defeated, Ganapa takes the new application form for a 25,000-rupee compensation increase. There is then a brief, pathetic scene of Ganapa paddling back at twilight, offering a prayer of entreaty to the river as mother.

Ganapa now sees compensation as the only way out of the ominous challenge that they face. With his lifelong faith in the invincibility of Sita's Peak now virtually brought to nothing, Duggappa decides to observe night-long *nema*. Ganapa rows him to the shrine, to which they would have walked not long before. There are shots of his meticulous makeup and costume preparation, and then he sends Ganapa home, intending to spend the night alone in the water-threatened shrine.

Back in the house, Nagi, Krishna and Ganapa are seen in stifling closeness, weighed under a silent tension that is almost palpable, a tension that is exacerbated by the sound of raindrops falling into tin dishes which the playful Krishna is moving around for his amusement. The tension is momentarily released when Ganapa gets up and angrily kicks the dishes away. This prompts a jump-cut to the veranda the next morning, with both men sitting at either end with their backs to one another. Neither even acknowledges Nagi's brief delight at the sight of a peacock. Amid this heavy self-absorption, Nagi suddenly realises that Duggappa has not returned. Ganapa refuses to fetch him, giving rise to Nagi's allegation that he is suspicious of her being left alone with Krishna, and Krishna will not go, wanting to be left out of what is essentially a family matter. As she does everything else, Nagi takes the dugout and sets out to bring back the old man.

The shrine is now more than half submerged and only the remnants of costume and elements of ritual are seen floating about. Nagi probes some flotsam and, it seems, sees the body of Duggappa. Another jump-cut takes us to the desolate scene of the rain continuing to fall and thunder continuing to sound, even as the flames of the raging fire take the last of the remains of the old man. Overcome more by grief than the rain, Ganapa and Nagi are impervious to the earnest ministrations of Krishna, who is trying to provide them with umbrellas. Krishna's kindness is not wanted; the wind and the water take away one umbrella, while the other is held by the mud. As though coming from somewhere else, an impassioned yet helpless cry comes from Nagi; Ganapa seems to see rather than hear the cry, and it means nothing to him. Now Ganapa becomes even more withdrawn. Added to his aversion to Krishna's presence is the fact that he has to come to terms with the very significant loss of his father.

A tiger is now introduced, almost as a focal character, into the narrative. It is heard and evidence of its presence is observed, but it is never actually seen, even though it remains central to most of the remaining proceedings. It first appears as a challenge to Nagi when she wants to go looking for the cow. Krishna warns her against doing that, for fear of the tiger; Ganapa corroborates the essence of his warning. Nevertheless, Nagi coolly and bravely takes a chopper and sets out through the jungle in search of the cow. It is an extremely tense scene, especially given the denseness of the vegetation and the near impossibility of seeing for any significant distance at all. There is shock when a face is seen through gaps in the foliage, a shock that quickly turns to relief as the face is recognised to be Ganapa's. There is a strong hint here that the relationship is still viable, as with a slight smile, Nagi acknowledges Ganapa's concern for her, and a smile from him shows his appreciation of that. However, it is only a hint and a possibility. Quite realistically, Ganapa again withdraws into himself, detaching himself from Nagi as he leaves everything regarding the threat of flood and tiger to her.

The narrative role of Krishna now takes an unexpected turn. A cut to a shot of him trying to remove leeches from his legs prompts Nagi to wonder how he got them, and she expresses the suspicion that he had been spying on Ganapa and her. 'Some kind of distrust is brewing among us. Each one mistrusts the other.' For her this is intolerable, and she tells Krishna to go back home. He refuses at first, confessing that he will be laughed at again as a failure, alluding to his Bombay experience. In a moment of slight self-pity he sees himself as having been denied much needed support, first in Bombay and now by Nagi. He is shattered to realise that Nagi is really no different, in his eyes, from anyone else on whom he might have depended. She expresses her understanding of this, but also realises that he must go. He tries to argue that he is needed with them, given that the water is rising steadily and the tiger is on the prowl, but Nagi remains resolute; when she changes her tune, it is too late.

The lengthiness of this scene emphasises the dramatic and categorical break that has been effected by Nagi's moral stand. Krishna has taken their dugout, leaving them even more inexorably confined, and has left his bicycle, as an ironic indication of uselessness. Nagi expresses her anger and frustration at all of this while Ganapa is utterly impassive, watching her in sinister silence.

Despite the unbearable stress that Nagi is being put under, she is genuinely solicitous about her husband's mental and emotional state, and implores him to share his pain with her. He puts it simply, 'Neither the government cares for us, nor do our own people. There's no meaning in carrying on with my life anymore.' Indeed, it seems that the death of his father has sapped all his hope and that he is headed toward despair.

Closer attention is given to the tiger. Patches of red on the vegetation, the string of bells presumably from the cow's neck, and sounds of the tiger's roar are clear suggestions that it has invaded their lives. Nagi faces the truth: 'I think the tiger has killed our cow.' Preparations are then made to defend the house, boarding up doorways and windows and, later, setting fires around it. This is a narrative element that has now been set in motion, while the Krishna element reaches its sad resolution.

Ganapa makes a show of pulling palings off the doors and throwing them on the fire, then lying down to sleep in a gesture of come-what-may. It is of no concern to him that the shed collapses, trapping the calf in the rubble. He nonchalantly pulls the blanket over his head as Nagi frees the calf by herself. The shed debris clogs the guttering and again Ganapa is unmoved, content to leave it to Nagi to clear away. As she works, we hear the ominous roar of the beast. She appeals to Ganapa again, and again he ignores her. He ignores her plea to help with the setting of fires, so she sets them herself. And she offers him the drum to beat and, significantly, ends up beating it herself. It is not that Ganapa is pathologically lazy. Perhaps his apparent obliviousness comes from the dissolving of what he sees as the curse of Krishna by the boy's departure; perhaps his strange faith is working toward what, in fact, will be expressed by him at the closing of the film.

There is a cut to a new day, with a clear sky and a new sound, which turns out to be the sound of the overflowing dam. Nagi rejoices that 'Nothing will now be submerged. Now we can cultivate the land and live in harmony with it, with the hill and with the river.' Ganapa, too, is happy again, but his words are cause for Nagi's consternation.

> Didn't I tell you that grit and determination can see us through any crisis? We survived, even on this island.
>
> I also told you that if the government forsakes us, even if our friends leave us in the lurch, the Spirit will be there to save us. We must be grateful to him.

She offers a look of slight bewilderment and an amused smile.

> But my effort was nothing small either. Wasn't it I who saved the family?
>
> It is all the grace of the Spirit.
>
> But wasn't it I who struggled all night to keep away the gushing water and the tiger?
>
> No.
>
> Who struggled to save our crumbling house? Wasn't it me?
>
> You think you have done all that? You are just the means—God is the force.

It is a conventional theological argument, asserting the omnipotence of God and the helpless dependence of people. It would seem that Ganapa's faith in the grace of God, and the power of that grace to work through human deeds, had given him assurance throughout the trials of the previous night, whereas it is perfectly plain to Nagi that, notwithstanding someone's decision to open the floodgates and bring down the water level, they still might well have been devoured by the tiger, had it not been for her epic struggle. And so his happy invitation to go and see how the seedlings have survived is a positive expression. However, she sits, deflated and alone. What has really been her role in what they have experienced? What will her role be in whatever the future has in store for them?

8

You Have Such a Good Husband and You Complain against Him

In *Hasina* (2004), Girish Kasaravalli takes the Muslim community as his subject for the first time, although at the root of the drama is a problem that is not characteristically Muslim but universal, wherever education in human biology is taught minimally, if at all, and wherever sexism prevails. The film deals with the victimisation of women, again something which is not characteristically Muslim; it is focal to *Ghatashraddha* and is variously significant in *Mane, Tai Saheba* and *Nayi Nerulu*. Moreover, children are focal in *Avshesh, Ghatashraddha* and *Kraurya,* and in all of these films they are directed and perform exceptionally well, yet no performance is as profoundly memorable as the presentation of the three little girls in *Hasina.*

The narrative dynamics are basically confrontational, actuated on the one hand by adversarial binaries and, on the other, complementary relationships containing elements of mutual support. Disputation seeks to resolve itself in various ways: to some little extent by reason or committed appeal to justice, but to a large extent by political manoeuvrings, authoritarian directives and outright bullying.

Fundamental to the narrative is the fact that Hasina, the mother of three girls, is expecting what an illegal medical prognosis reveals to be a fourth daughter. Yakub, her husband, knows nothing about the Y chromosome and its exclusive possession by males, nor, apparently, does he know anyone who does, and therefore blames Hasina for her perfidious failure to give him a son. His mother would argue that Hasina is incapable of bearing sons, a natural and certain indication of her inferiority. On such pitiful ignorance and infantile reasoning, Yakub justifies his desertion of his wife and goes home to mother.

Yakub is a brutish bully. He is self-centred and, despite his age, behaves like a spoiled and temperamental boy. He is conniving and untrustworthy. In short, he is an ugly character, and his ugliness permeates the film. His nastiness is so profound that his presence is felt even when he is out of the frame, in that the effects of his actions are either apparent or under discussion. The focus of the film is Hasina, who gives the work its title, but it is a Hasina who is conditioned by Yakub. She is mistreated by Yakub, thrown into tragic circumstances by him, and ultimately she rises above Yakub. She may also be said to have inspired other women to rise up against other Yakubs.

Yet Kasaravalli does provide us with a glimpse of a potentially somewhat good Yakub. The opening scene offers context for a flashback, one that is relatively recent as it is during Hasina's present pregnancy. It is the time of the Muharram festival, and in the evening, Yakub takes his family to a fair in his gaily decorated auto-rickshaw. He is effusive with good humour, lovingly carrying the smallest girl in his arms, and buys trinkets for the children and *jalebis* to satisfy the craving of the sweet-toothed Hasina. However, the family joyousness is tempered somewhat by him constantly referring to the son that Hasina surely must be carrying. Its repetition becomes slightly ominous in Yakub's purchase of a prayer cap for his son; again, his relentless desire is seen in a close shot of him in prayer at a *dargah* or tomb of some holy man. Subsequent events will indicate that none of this is to establish Yakub's piety but to underline the intensity of his wish for a son. It is important that this be established in order to construct a credible basis for Yakub's brutishness. It is also reasonable to suggest that Yakub wants to achieve equality with other men who happen to be the fathers of sons, and who are, in his mind, superior.

Yakub takes the extraordinary step of arranging an ultrasound examination for Hasina. One wonders why he should do this, given that the examination is quite expensive, especially for an auto-rickshaw driver, apart from the fact that it is illegal. It would seem that the birth of a son—or an ego-extension—is so important to Yakub that he has to have confirmation of its imminence. This desire has reached the point of being an obsession. What is confirmed is, in fact, the opposite of what Yakub's heart and small mind are set on, and his natural reaction is to see himself as an innocent victim of Hasina's perfidy and to blame her for what, in his eyes, is a vicious offence. He drives the auto home recklessly, causing the obviously pregnant Hasina to be tossed around in the back seat. At home he beats her cruelly and locks her in the house before he walks out on her and the children, petulantly throwing away the key and causing physical stress and injury to the blind Munni in her efforts to find it. Yakub's violence toward his wife and his callousness to his daughters are shameful in the extreme, and his irascibility shows him to be a man of stunted maturity, one who runs home to mother when things do not go the way he wants them to. Kasaravalli has made the loving father and husband at the fair very plausibly, yet with great narrative economy, metamorphose into an object of disgust.

Yakub's abhorrent nature is further exposed by the focus given to Hasina and the three children and the underlying realisation that their plight has been caused and continues to be maintained by him. The opening scene needs to be observed and then recalled to be fully appreciated. On first viewing we note the provincial context of the film and that the time is early morning. Smoke from morning fires drifts about like mist. The camera then focusses on the mosque of this small town where, from a minaret, the muezzin is chanting the call to the *fajr* prayer. As though in response to this call, the door of a very humble cottage opens and a woman appears. Her face is badly masked with a large, ugly wound on her forehead and, it seems, a split lip. She is carrying a baby in her right arm and holding with her left hand a girl who appears to be blind; running along behind them is a third girl. They hurry down the hill and are then seen crossing the grounds of the mosque to take up a position on its plinth. From the way she walks and the manner in which she ushers the children, there is obviously something resolute about this woman.

It is highly significant that the mosque be made central to this opening scene—and it will remain central, by focus or by implication, throughout the film—for it forms the political, social, and moral centre of the film. Hasina sees it as her source of hope, the well-spring of the justice she inexorably seeks. It is the authority by which most of the characters seek to justify their actions. It is seen even as a refuge by Yakub, albeit perversely, and it becomes, through Hasina, a rallying-point for reform demanded by the women of the community.

Some men are already at the mosque, some of them sweeping and tidying. One elderly gentleman greets Hasina, and she tells him that she has come to see the *muthavalli*, or the president of the congregation, and that she has no intention of taking the children and waiting somewhere else. Soon after, the *muthavalli*, Khan Saheb, does arrive, and we see from his demeanour a touch of aggression, of hot-headed intolerance. He strides up to Hasina and, unlike the kindly old gentleman a few moments earlier, launches into an attack on her, berating her with words like 'tantrum' and 'shameful.' She simply reiterates her request for justice, which he pompously declares not to be something 'available over the counter,' but something which takes time, given that the *jamaat* (in this case, an assembly of the congregation) would have to be called, and Yakub would have to be summoned. It is hard to imagine what would be so time-consuming about these two simple procedures, but Khan Saheb is all bluster, and soon assures Hasina that he will call the *jamaat* and Yakub 'today.' Hasina again refuses to accept his direction to go home, resolving to stay where she is until he has carried out his promise. To save at least some face, he peevishly directs her to 'go and sit in a corner, then.'

(The *muthavalli*'s authoritarian nature, especially when standing over a humble woman, gives a hint of a gender conflict that will develop gradually, burgeoning into a feminist victory of sorts and culminating in a major double comedown by the proud man.)

The film's opening, then, sets out the basis for the narrative's argument, and the subsequent flashback sequence gives explanatory substance to it. What Kasaravalli sets out to do next is to examine Yakub's contemptibility from another angle. We have seen him disgrace himself by his own actions, particularly beating his wife and deserting her and the children. Now we get a more detailed look at what it means for those children to be fatherless. First of all, three children and their pregnant mother are deprived of a breadwinner. Yakub is under no obligation to pay maintenance to Hasina, and he lacks the necessary sense of honour that would persuade him to take up that responsibility of his own accord. Second, the eldest girl, Munni, is blind and attends a special school. When Hasina is employed in a domestic industry, rolling incense sticks, the girls help her, and Munni is taken out of school to increase the output and income. However, there is also hope for Munni, in that a visit to the doctor reveals that she does actually have partial sight, which could be greatly enhanced by an operation; without the operation, that partial sight would deteriorate to nothing. The cost of the operation, for a single mother supporting her children on the rolling of incense sticks, is prohibitive. Nevertheless, Hasina is determined to raise the money and save her daughter's sight. Yakub has no interest in helping her.

The director's treatment of the children is masterly. Given the circumstances of this fatherless family, there is immense opportunity for sentimentalism, an opportunity which Kasaravalli most creditably avoids. However, while tear-jerking is never his object, there are some warmly touching moments. In the opening confrontation with Khan Saheb, we might note Shabbu's subtle holding on to her mother's arm as though to suggest protection, and Munni's reassuring hand on her shoulder. Then there is Munni's optimistic question, 'Am I pretty, Mummy?'. It is a sad question because the little girl cannot see into a mirror to form her own opinion, but it is also a question that many members of the audience would want to answer: that all things taken into account—her loving and kindly nature, both at home and at school, her propensity to warm-hearted laughter, and her courageous acceptance of her disability and natural determination to live in spite of it—she is far beyond 'pretty.' And then there is the time when Hasina is too late in getting to the pump before the water supply is cut off for the day, only to find Shabbu with a couple of large containers, sitting waiting for her, a reassuring grin on her sweet face. Yakub's wilful neglect of these children is indeed heinous. Moreover, it is made even worse as he attempts to tutor Shabbu in dishonesty, bribing her with ice-candy to lie in his cowardly interests. Yakub's neglect of his girls, especially Munni, contrasts markedly with Hasina's passion to raise the necessary money for Munni's operation. To supplement the money earned from rolling incense sticks, she applies for domestic work in the home of a 'modern' woman, Julekha.

This personal depiction of female liberation is interesting when seen in comparison with the nature and values of other women in the film. In the first instance, we are shown two aspects of the female nature: one that tends to sympathise with and even admire Hasina, and one that would condemn her. Word gets to three neighbours, all tied to domestic drudgery, that Hasina and her children are sitting outside the mosque again. Two of the women note her doggedness, one expressing the view that she is being treated unjustly. The strongest voice comes from the more conservative of the three, who brands Hasina foolish and actually the cause of her husband's desertion. Had she looked after him better, he would not have left her. This, of course, is a canard, as Hasina's domestic efficiency has not been brought into question, while there is no awareness of the beatings on account of her carrying a female foetus. However, what is significant here is the implied submissiveness that many women pride themselves on in their familial relations, a submissiveness that egotistical men and bullies like Yakub are ever ready to exploit.

However, Julekha is far removed from this sadly typical woman of accepted dependence. Initially she also seems somewhat removed from conventional feminism too. We first see her in her opulent flat, perhaps a trifle over-dressed, over-ornamented and obviously made up, getting ready to go to a friend's wedding. Of course, all women will dress well for a wedding, but it seems significant that the initial impression Kasaravalli gives of her should show her as a little self-pampering, a little too concerned with her appearance. She shows merely cursory interest in Hasina, maintaining a notable detachment from a social inferior. When asked, Hasina says she would like a wage of 650 rupees a month. Julekha seems outraged and offers 200. There is a degree of haggling over what must be a paltry sum to someone wealthy enough to live in such an apartment, but a title card tells us that eventually they settled for 500. Hasina came down 50, Julekha went up 400. Thus it was not so much about money but self-assertion. Julekha would seem to thrive on dominance, a facet of personality that makes her appear uncongenial and standoffish.

This scene is immediately followed by one sometime later with Hasina cleaning the floor and obviously feeling aches and pains. We meet a much softer, more agreeable Julekha here. We also learn that she walked out on her marriage soon after it was celebrated, giving us another indication of her strong will and assertiveness. She is indignant to hear of Yakub's desertion of his family and the reason for it, while her mother reminds us, somewhat ironically, that in Islam bringing up girls well and marrying them off earns as much grace as the Haj pilgrimage. Here there is a recognition of a special fondness for girl children, but there is also an admission that their purpose lies in being given for the pleasure and service of men. Nevertheless, Julekha is genuine in her condemnation of Yakub and advises Hasina to present a petition to the *muthavalli*, who must then call a meeting of the *jamaat* and summon Yakub, who will be reprimanded and directed to resume his proper paternal duties. Hasina is amazed. 'I didn't know that it was so simple,' she declares, now swept up by optimism. However, it is not at all simple, given the nature of certain men such as the *muthavalli*, as we shall see.

Another prominent woman is the *muthavalli's* wife, a very attractive woman who is concerned that she is losing the best years of her life in pregnancy after pregnancy on top of the constant grind of domestic labours. She wants to have an operation to put an end to the production line of babies, but her conservative and authoritarian husband will not allow it. Eventually she stands up to him and has the operation.

What is significant in her small rebellion is the fact that it is inspired by Hasina and her untiring quest to obtain justice for herself and her girls. She watches Hasina's many visits to their home to try to get the *muthavalli* to consider her petition, and she is also aware of Hasina's daily sit-in at the mosque. Finally, she gives material support to Hasina and the girls, taking food and drink for them at the mosque, and she defies and resists the reactionary woman, an ally of Yakub and his mother, who tries to take the children away.

This support from the wife of the *muthavalli* is the only actual, material support Hasina gets. Everything else is moral support, encouragement, perhaps advice that is sound and rational, but ultimately Hasina is left to fend entirely for herself. The previous *muthavalli*, Hanif *saheb*, a friend of her late father, offers her strong encouragement based, we may suspect, on his disdain for his successor. Both the doctor and the schoolmaster give strong and kindly encouragement out of genuine and loving concern for Munni, but neither is able to give any material support or provide any productive action. However, Hasina relies very heavily on Julekha and is sincere in declaring her immense debt to her. She has indeed given her a good job at marginally less than the amount she herself had asked for. Moreover, she is happy for Hasina to bring the baby, Habiba, with her each day and plays with her while Hasina does her work—happy until the baby wets herself on the floor, evoking disgust and intolerance in Julekha, who then forbids Hasina to bring the little girl again. Of most value, at least potentially, are the petitions she writes for Hasina to present to the *muthavalli* and the outlines of the argument in which she tutors Hasina to support her case. The value is only potential, as the success of the petitions depends on the *muthavalli*'s actually reading and acting on them, and until he does, Julekha's help is merely theoretical. When news comes of Yakub's intended next marriage, Julekha is again free with her advice on how Hasina might stand to gain from the court's directions concerning settlement, but when Hasina innocently rejoices in her assurances, Julekha is shown to be as self-obsessed and full of artifice as we may have already suspected her of being, in stating quite plainly that she can do nothing outside the house, for to be seen in public would minimise her prestige. Again, the illiterate Hasina will have to fend for herself.

This particular conceit of personal status and whatever prestige may attach to it is pertinent to three very different characters in the film. Julekha would seem to live in self-imposed exile, being in the world, but not of it. It is truly a comfortable exile, as is visibly evident in the scenes inside her apartment. The camera is more than adequate to the task of manifesting the contrast between Julekha, who enjoys upper-class status, and Hasina, who has no status at all outside of her own family. Julekha's apartment is comfortably furnished and tastefully decorated; Hasina's home is little more than a shanty, its only luxury being its relative isolation from neighbours. Julekha is fashionably and expensively dressed and ornamented; Hasina, while always presentable, is by no means glamorous. But one is inclined to wonder at the value, the purpose—if any—of Julekha's 'status.' Maybe it keeps her in the 'right' company, such as the friend whose wedding she was getting ready for when Hasina first went to her home, but she holds no position of any significance—prestigious or otherwise—which might warrant some restraint on her public appearances. Fundamentally, she is an egoist.

The *muthavalli* is also concerned with status. Given his position as president of the congregation, his concern is justified, at least to a degree. Its pertinence can be seen in two visual images, both of the *muthavalli* walking down a lane. Apparently it is customary for women to hide themselves from his august presence, and in the first of these scenes that is exactly what they do. His mere passing by sends them hurrying inside. His status is virtually palpable. On the second occasion, after the cataclysmic conclusion to his neglect of Hasina, he is seen to walk down the same lane and not a woman so much as moves a finger; even when his aide angrily points out to them that the *muthavalli* himself is passing by, there is no reaction. His status has been lost. Once or twice he mentions to his colleagues at the mosque his concern that Hasina's agitation could be bad for his status, and when his wife mentions the contraceptive operation, he points out that he cannot allow it on the grounds that his status would be threatened in the eyes of others. Basically the *muthavalli* is a man who relishes a position but not its more pastoral responsibilities and politically difficult demands.

The third character to be concerned with his image is, curiously, Yakub—curious, because he clearly does not warrant any status at all. Yet status is what he appeals to in condemning Hasina for bringing the children to the auto-rickshaw stand in an appeal to get him to come home to them. He berates her verbally and physically for embarrassing him in front of his fellow auto drivers, whereas, in fact, his loss of temper and use of force to get his family out of his rickshaw make him a disgrace in the eyes of the other drivers who, in concern for his wife and children, protect them against him. And so he tries to turn what should have been his shame into an attack on his status. Blame-shifting is an art that Yakub has long practised, it would seem. The fact is, he does not have status, except only among people like his mother and her reactionary women friends and neighbours. He would also like to enjoy status among the men in his workaday world, and that would require being like them—in having a wife who produces sons, perhaps.

In passing, we might also note that Kasaravalli offers us two characters—the schoolmaster and the doctor—who rightly enjoy a certain status and the prestige that accrues to it, purely by virtue of the work that they do and the manner in which they do it. Here are two patently worthy men who make each day a valuable contribution to the betterment of the world. And neither of them, it might well be assumed, could cherish the slightest interest in status and prestige, for neither has the preoccupation with ego to be bothered to cultivate it.

It is ironic that the *muthavalli's* concern for status should be the basis of his losing it. This is because his political security is not assured, given the antipathy toward him by his predecessor, Hanif *saheb*, who still harbours an ambition to be re-elected as *muthavalli*. In short, Khan *saheb's* bluster against Hasina and his prevarication over her petitions are due to his fear of doing something that might give Hanif and his supporters the opportunity to bring some kind of case against him. Hasina meets with Hanif when she is called off the street by his man. Hanif courteously remembers Hasina's late father, and then raises the matter of her complaint against her husband. The matter of the *muthavalli's* inaction is raised, and Hanif describes him as lazy and good-for-nothing. Perhaps this is a welcome reprimand, but when it is immediately followed up by 'When I was *muthavalli*...,' we might wonder if it is not, perhaps, part of an expression of self-projection on Hanif's part. Like Julekha, he is one to make strong assurances, telling Hasina to give her petition to him and that he will see to it that the *muthavalli* gets it and acts on it. Hasina looks greatly heartened, but like Julekha's assurances, nothing will come of this. Hanif is undoubtedly a good man, and his apparent gesture of self-advancement may really be a morally-motivated desire to remove an incompetent leader in the best interests of the community. Nevertheless, the potential insidiousness is communicated with intended effect to Khan *saheb* by none other than Yakub. Expert as he is at twisting reality to suit himself, he frightens Khan *saheb* by saying that Hasina's petition against her husband is, in fact, a petition against the *muthavalli*. It was written by Julekha, a woman separated from her husband—as though this fact disqualifies her from any right to serious consideration—and who is backed by Hanif in a ploy to have himself re-elected. While he accuses the *muthavalli* of naiveté for not being able to see this, it is obvious that Khan *saheb* is, indeed, naïve for listening to someone as malevolent as Yakub.

As well as this political intrigue, the film also has an underlying suggestion of an interest in class. The gap between the well-off and the not-so-well-off is not vast, but it is indeed noticeable. Three homes—those of Julekha, the *muthavalli* and Hanif—give visual representation to comfort, taste, and the wealth from which they emanate. The least attractive home is that of the Khan family, but that is simply due to the clutter made by a number of young children. It is, in fact, a grand old two-storey home. We see only the reception lounge of Hanif's home, which is rather like that of a grand hotel. It is completely open on one side, and is furnished with plush sofas and arm chairs. Mention has already been made of Julekha's delightful apartment. The simple shanty in which Hasina and her children live is in sharp contrast to these homes. The *muthavalli* sitting back in an easy chair on his veranda, Hanif sitting in an armchair in his lovely lounge, and Julekha reading, while her mother just sits in the comfort of their living room, represent a different world from that of the auto drivers, the carpenters, the petty shopkeepers, and the women who are seen outside their houses, washing clothes or sweeping. Basically, however, this may be just a simple depiction of reality, but then we might consider that a little blind girl might see after an operation that will cost 15,000 rupees. It is a huge amount for Hasina, but for others—especially collectively—it is pennies. Yet not even the offer of an interest-free loan is forthcoming. However, there is no moral condemnation to be made here, for the responsibility for his daughter's sight or blindness is, ultimately, Yakub's.

Despite the unrelenting harshness of Yakub and the procrastination of the *muthavalli,* there are notable flashes of kindness in the film. In addition to Julekha, Hanif *saheb* and the *muthavalli's* wife, there are those with a notably gentle side. The teacher at the school for blind children shows great compassion toward Hasina, while giving loving care to Munni and all his other students. He shows, quite clearly, that the education of disabled children demands a special approach, in which kindness and gentleness are vital. Indeed, as he is kind to his students, it is notable that his students show care and kindness to one another. The doctor who examines Munni's head after her fall—indirectly caused by her father—is also very caring and establishes a happy relationship with the little girl, giving her cause to laugh and offering her hope and reassurance. We also note the kindness of the men at the mosque, with the exception of the *muthavalli.* One old man, whom Hasina addresses as Uncle Sharif, is particularly solicitous of the welfare of Hasina and her children.

And, interestingly, there is Zarina, Yakub's intended second wife. When Hasina goes to visit her with Munni, she receives them graciously and with simple hospitality. It seems likely that Zarina also contributes to the fund for Munni's operation. On the way home from their meeting with Zarina, they meet Yakub driving a fare the other way. He stops suddenly on seeing Hasina and Munni, grabs a heavy metal spanner from his toolbox, and chases after them. He challenges Hasina, who tries to assure him that she went to Zarina only to talk about the formalities of the divorce, but Yakub is convinced that she has taken money from her. He forcibly takes money from her pocket, money which she declares is the proceeds of rolling incense sticks, but he does not believe her. She does not push the argument, a reticence that might suggest that the money did indeed come from Zarina. Yakub pockets it, thus denying his daughter the advantage that the money might have given her. Whatever kindness Zarina might have shown is negated by the brutal beating Yakub then gives Hasina.

The ending of the film is an extraordinary mixture of malicious violence, revolutionary defiance, apology and reform. There is no happiness, though there is hope, but it comes out of appalling tragedy. Nothing is concluded, though much is foreseen. There is benefit, but it comes at a terrible cost.

The sun has set and it is time for the *magrib* prayer. Hasina and the children are still in their accustomed place outside the mosque. The little girls are cold, and Shabbu finds a blanket which she wraps around Munni. It is, in fact, a burial shroud, and the poetic significance of this will be realised a little later. The camera pulls back to show the mosque at night, the electric lights coming on, and the silhouettes of Hasina and the girls; out of the dark on the right of the screen come the lights of an auto-rickshaw, blazing like those of some alien beast, the rickshaw wobbling from side to side as it comes over the uneven ground, driven, as we shall soon see, by a drunken Yakub. The *muthavalli* and the men of the mosque go down to him rather than have him enter the mosque in such a state. When drunk, Yakub is even more savage than we have seen him so far. He is full of vitriol, referring to Hasina as a 'slut' and Julekha as 'that filthy bitch.' His abusiveness is a prelude to physical violence and soon he is kicking Hasina. Women's faces suddenly appear, looking out from behind windows or doorways. The men of the mosque have trouble restraining Yakub as he is very strong, quite out of his senses, and angry. His knack for twisting reality is at its best, with his condemnation of Hasina for 'using children to extort money'—it would seem that Yakub is capable of believing whatever he wants. As we have seen before, Munni is always ready to protect her mother, pleading with her father not to hit her. This time the brave little blind girl gets caught in the crossfire, sustaining a kick from her father that is meant for her mother, and it kills her instantly. As she realises that her daughter is dead, Hasina throws her arms into the air, so letting fly the papers containing her accusations and arguments as written by Julekha.

This simple gesture blends into a brief surrealistic sequence that lends, with exquisite compression, intense significance to the horrible realism we have just been witnessing. The papers are carried by the breeze against the background of the night sky, all of them eventually falling to the ground where they are picked up and read by various women who are then seen walking together, in solidarity as it were, toward the mosque and the body of the dead Munni. The symbolism of this is simple. The story of Hasina spreads, and it so moves the women who read it that they are prepared to stand up against what might be seen as a kind of tyranny of authority or tradition. One wonders what would have eventuated had the story been told earlier. It is possible that Hasina's justice might have prevailed, that Yakub might have been held to account and obliged to accept his responsibilities, that Munni would not have been killed, and that she may even have had her operation. But the story was not told, and the *muthavalli* must bear full responsibility for this.

He does, indeed, do the right thing, although with such delay as to make his gesture quite meaningless. He is probably right in saying that God will not forgive him, but it no longer matters. The dispute has been settled forever, not by him, but—as Hasina points out—by Yakub.

Kasaravalli offers no sign of Yakub after his abominable behaviour at the mosque. We may be keen to see retribution delivered with great force and the brute punished and humiliated, but Kasaravalli is not interested in what is essentially negative emotion. Rather, the emphasis is on two women.

The first, naturally, is Hasina. The *muthavalli* assures her that the *jamaat* will be called today (how many times has he said that before!) and that Yakub will be made to pay all that is due to Hasina by virtue of his taking a second wife. Hasina makes two simple points. The first is that she needed the money for Munni's operation, and Munni is now no more. The second is her resolution to bring her girls up on her own, so showing her exceptional strength of character in refusing to accept money from the man who killed one of them.

The second woman is the wife of the *muthavalli*. Having been spurned by the women in the street, who refuse to acknowledge his presence, Khan *saheb* goes home to a wife who is no longer submissive. Her trolley bag is packed and is being pulled by her son. She does not ask her husband, but simply informs him that she is going for the operation and will be back in the evening. She directs him to look after the baby, to keep the front gate shut, and to use the back entrance. She leaves with not a word from him, dumbly staring after her as the gate shuts. The strength that Hasina has shown has been an inspiration to at least one other woman.

Hasina achieves admiration for her resolution, but it is passing admiration at best. Once she and the little girls have stopped sitting in front of the mosque every day, they will be forgotten and no one will be aware of the struggle their lives might well be proving to be as they meld with the vast and anonymous poor. The *muthavalli's* wife, however, may well have taken Hasina's struggle to its next stage. The scene in which she announces her decision on behalf of her body and then leaves the house, bent on her purpose, is directed so very clearly as to leave little doubt that Kasaravalli has faith in an eventual attitudinal change which will see women standing up to men for their rights. Hasina's story is a profoundly moving human interest story, but it also represents a clarion call for the growing empowerment of women.

9

We All Find the Truth We Desire

The mystery of the mundane would seem to be quite profound in *Nayi Neralu* ('In the Shadow of the Dog,' 2005).[1] The arcane daily regimen imprisoning the life of a high-caste widow and the theory of rebirth—two age-old features of Hinduism—are brought together here in circumstances that belie harmony or any degree of happiness. Characters come to be judged not as actual identities, but as perceptions evoked and fashioned by others, centuries earlier.

The all-pervasive authority of perennial religious tradition is established at the opening with a close shot of a large temple. Circumambulating and then entering the temple are an elderly man, dressed in a red *lungi*, his forehead and shoulders adorned with the white marks of devotion, and a young woman who bears no outward signs of piety. Elements of ritual follow, with bell ringing, lamp lighting and offering, and included in this are pleasantries shared between the two—who, we learn, are grandfather and granddaughter—and the priest, eliciting a contrasting element of secular, modern import: an allusion to the fact that the girl is a student in higher education in the city of Mysore. The grandfather also remarks on how close the girl is to her mother. Outside the temple, they meet an elderly friend, Putram Bhatta, who has recently returned from a visit to Bangalore. Some small talk gives the film a temporal context: the reference to Gandhi's followers demonstrating under the slogan

[1] The title is an allusion to the story in the *Mahabharata* of King Yudhishthira's reaching Heaven and his refusal to enter unless his faithful dog is allowed in too.

'Quit India!' places it in, or sometime after, 1942. Putram Bhatta's purpose is much greater than this, however. He provides the one narrative element that will direct the remainder of the film.

On his recent travels, Putram tells us, he met a stranger who, when told Putram was from Krishnapura, asked if he knew one Achchannayya—the name of the grandfather we have known since the beginning. He then mentions that there was a boy in his place, one Visvesvara, claiming to have been Achchannayya's son in a previous life, and then gives what might seem to be supporting evidence, such as knowledge of his parents, his wife, and the fact that she was pregnant when he died. Moreover, the boy is about 20, and Achchannayya's son died some 20 years ago. Achchannayya seems to be troubled by this, whether angry at it for being arrant nonsense or perturbed by its possibilities is not quite clear. Putram suggests meeting the boy to verify the truth or falsity of his claim, but Achchannayya sees no sense in that. As far as he is concerned, his son is long dead and gone.

There is an ambivalence at work here. While an educated man like Achchannayya can know from experience that 'dead men rise up never,' there is still the mystery of the soul, sensed but not known, that would compromise our science and pester us with Putram's ever unanswered question, 'But what if it's true?' Achchannayya strides off home with this question starting to plague his mind.

And so the mystery of rebirth has entered the film, and now the discipline of widowhood is introduced. When the granddaughter, Rajalakshmi or Raji, comes home, she is annoyed to find her mother outside with the barber, having her head shaved. The dialogue makes it clear that this monthly tonsure is at the direction of her grandmother, whom we shall come to see as an extremely conservative and orthodox woman.

Hindu widows—or at least the high-caste ones—would seem to be almost responsible for the deaths of their husbands, given the punishing regimen to which they must submit for the rest of their lives. The monthly tonsure is but one of its elements. She may dress in only a plain red sari without a blouse, and she may not wear ornaments. She may eat only one meal a day, frugal, and without any nicety such as ghee or sweets. She must sleep on the floor. She may not attend rituals or social engagements—a widow's presence at a wedding, for example, is considered worse than bad luck. As we see Venku—as Raji's mother is called—bearing all this, we also see the restraining hand of the authority of the tyrannical mother-in-law. Venku good-naturedly and sincerely submits to all the privations and cruelties of the widow's lot and shows no sign of disobedience, except when her mother-in-law would compromise the prescribed regimen herself.

Meanwhile Achchannayya, if he wanted peace of mind, makes a big mistake in passing on to his wife the details of his meeting with Putram Bhatta. She is convinced that the boy is their lost Ramanna, but the grounds on which that conviction rests are not enunciated. It would seem that she is convinced simply because she wants to be. She insists that Achchannayya visit the boy, and Achchannayya refuses, reasonably arguing that their son is no more, having drowned 20 years ago. 'Now he is mere memory. Let it remain so.' His wife's response is quite unscientific, yet not easily refutable. 'But now his soul is back in another form.' Achchannayya tries to end the argument with the warning that seeing the boy would only increase their misery. Indeed, if he could have realised the full extent of the truth of his words, he would not have given in to his wife's self-pitying exhortations, laced with reference to her suffering. Her emotional bullying prevails, however, and he agrees to go and meet Visvesvara at his cousin's home.

The meeting with the boy reveals little at all, and it is clear that Ramanna's rebirth as Visvesvara is not going to be proven. He is asked a number of questions and his answers to some are true and close to true for others. However, the questions themselves are vague and nothing is pinpointed. While Putram is delighted at his answers and is willing to accept them uncritically, Achchannayya maintains a healthy scepticism. There will be a defining test of his veracity later at the village, when an oracle will indulge himself in ritualistic mumbo-jumbo and declare Visvesvara's claim to be authentic, although there is nothing convincing in this or any other acceptance. Kasaravalli, of course, is not interested in proving or disproving Visvesvara's claim. What is relevant here is what his characters think of it. After all, *Nayi Neralu* is a film that is very much about people's perceptions of others, and it is these that occupy the director's interest.

One significant matter emerges at the home of Visvesvara's cousin, and that is the eccentric nature of the boy. We are told that since the age of 10 he has been talking of his father in a previous life, by the name of Achchannayya, so it would seem that the young boy might well have been attracted by the name, rather than the person. We are also told that his behaviour is such that it makes him something of a local freak show, with people coming from nearby villages to see and be amused by him. As we see more and more of him, he emerges clearly as an oddball, though giving no reason enough to suggest madness.

The film is divided into four sections. The opening and untitled one serves as an introduction. There follow three more sections, each named after one of the three women who is central to that section. The first is titled Nagalakshmi, after the mother-in-law.

While Nagalakshmi simply 'knows' that Visvesvara is Ramanna in another form, his acceptance by others is not as simple. Her long suspended maternal urges now find expression in her new opportunity to cosset her 'son.' We see her sitting close to him on the floor and feeding him. We see her giving him an oil massage, and the playful frolic that goes with it. She tells him to allow the sunshine to do its work, and then she will be back to bathe him. The visuals here might make us feel a little uncomfortable, as we hardly need to be reminded that this 'boy' is 20 years old. While Nagalakshmi happily pampers him, to Venku he is 'the stranger,' from whom she keeps herself secluded. Some effective camerawork makes interesting use of slatted window-shades to emphasise the awareness of each by the other and the choice to remain in separation. When asked about him by Nagalakshmi, Venku asserts that he does not resemble her late husband at all, whom she describes as a man of dignity—a description that cannot fit well with Visvesvara.

There is a series of scenes in which the need to authenticate Visvesvara's claim to be Ramanna in a new form is dealt with, much to the satisfaction of Nagalakshmi—and those who simply want him to be genuine, for whatever subjective reason they might have—but hardly to the satisfaction of a critical audience. Curious local young women gather at the window to enjoy a glimpse of the exotic stranger and curious local men come into the house to meet him. He is hardly interrogated, but rather treated like someone who has returned from a long time abroad, with questions like 'Do you recognise him?' His replies are easily made, even perhaps a little glib; as one girl puts it, 'some of them are grain, some are chaff.'

A letter is sent to Raji in Mysore, causing her lawyer uncle to conclude, as a lawyer might be expected to, that Visvesvara is an imposter pursuing a ruse to obtain Achchannayya's property. Raji, the modern woman (1940s version) and the product of modern education, cannot be party to what is, to her, fictitious at best and criminal at worst. However, fundamental to her opposition to the boy is her concern for her relationship with her grandparents and, particularly, her mother. She sees Visvesvara as a threat to the familial harmony she has enjoyed all her life and is worried by the thought of how far this threatening discordance might go. So her letter to her grandfather does not mince words, concluding with the demand to 'kick him out.'

The final and decisive word on Visvesvara's authenticity belongs to the voice of superstition. An oracle in an entranced state communicating with the gods, or performing a fit of frenzy, accompanied by a cacophony of screeching wind instruments and frenetic drumming, all lit up by flambeaux, decides in favour of Visvesvara. We do not know the basis of his decision, as an oracle is not obliged to justify himself. There can now be no argument, at least as far as public opinion and Nagalakshmi are concerned, that Visvesvara is the new embodiment of Ramanna, who has been dead for 20 years. Achchannayya remains doubtful, but goes along with it all for the sake of marital peace. Raji will never accept it, and Venku does not accept it either.

There are shots of Nagalakshmi's new-found maternal bliss, but something would seem to be missing. Nagalakshmi might wonder why she is the only one enjoying her 'son.' After all, he has a place—a role, one might even say—in the family, besides his relationship with his 'mother,' so why do he and Venku maintain isolation from each other? She asks him and his reply is simple and rational. He cannot have anything to say to her, or share with her, as long as she wears the red sari. In other words, if she is his wife, she cannot be a widow. No woman can be both. And this is perfectly rational.

Whereas the central problem until now had been establishing the identity of Visvesvara—who now, thanks to a popular religious charlatan, is Ramanna in a new form—the new problem is establishing the identity of Venku. If she continues to submit to the widow's regimen, decreed by scripture and tradition and insisted on by her mother-in-law, then she cannot be Visvesvara's wife. And if Visvesvara is indeed the son of Nagalakshmi and Achchannayya, then where is the wife who was pregnant by him when he died? She cannot be a widow unless her husband is dead, and if her husband is dead, so too must the son of Nagalakshmi and Achchannayya be dead, and Visvesvara is a fraud. And this terrible tangle of identity discernment has not even begun to consider the sense in a husband being 20 years younger than his wife—the same age, roughly, as his own daughter. If he is Nagalakshmi's son, then he has to be the husband of Venku, 20 years his senior, and the father of Raji, who is much the same age as himself. And the word of the oracle is still not brought into question.

Sensing the uncertainty of credibility, Nagalakshmi plays into Visvesvara's hands and sets the narrative in a direction from which it cannot turn back. She tries to persuade Venku to forsake her widow's red and wear something to please Visvesvara. She cannot know, however, that the matter of identity—of anyone—is no longer the central issue, and that a more basic, human urge will drive the narrative from now on, so she relentlessly cajoles Venku to change her dress and simply make a 'fleeting appearance' to please Visvesvara. As usual, she gets her way.

When Nagalakshmi parades Venku dressed in a green sari before Visvesvara, his eyes obviously light up, but the two women clearly see something besides joy in that light in his eyes, and Venku, in alarm, makes an urgent retreat. Soon we see her reaching for the familiar security of her red sari, and a little later Nagalakshmi demands the return of the green one. But the damage has been done. Nagalakshmi has given Venku a fleeting taste of life outside a widow's prison. There are some nice shots of Venku rummaging through a box of old clothes and ornaments, and soon she sees herself unshackled once again. There is then a shot of her lying on a mattress on a bed, rather than on the stone floor. Venku's emancipation has clearly begun.

Visvesvara starts to assert his will over Nagalakshmi, insisting that Venku join them for dinner. Nagalakshmi's difficulty here is her contradictory perceptions of Visvesvara as her son and Venku as a widow. Nagalakshmi goes along with indulging Visvesvara, who lavishes Venku with spoonful after spoonful of the hitherto proscribed ghee. A close-up of her face, partly covered in modesty by the end of her sari, reveals her childlike pleasure at Visvesvara's childlike gesture. This is another sign of her emerging transformation.

The childlike nature of what is developing is emphasised in some subsequent scenes. It will be some time before Visvesvara is seen to have stepped over the threshold between boyhood and manhood, and for a time his behaviour is noticeably immature. Venku, however, finds it appealing. While she is sitting under a guttering carrying a stream of water with which she can wash the cooking utensils, she notices an occasional flower floating on the stream. Like an adolescent lover, Visvesvara is sitting above the guttering, sending the flowers down to his beloved. Later, he is lying in the garden eating bananas and is censured by Venku for keeping Nagalakshmi from her meal, waiting, as she is, to serve him. Despite Venku's words being an admonishment, Visvesvara is overjoyed that she freely spoke to him. He expresses his delight in a childish over-reaction, shouting repeatedly that Venku spoke to him and throwing bananas anywhere and everywhere. A little later Visvesvara is beset by a swarm of bees. Venku shouts out instructions to him, then hurries to him. There is a cut to a shot of her lying protectively over him; she gets up, but he reaches out and holds her wrist; she struggles to free herself, but his strength draws her down to him and into his warm embrace. A close shot of her face reveals the positive emotional impact of this simple gesture on a woman who has not been in such proximity to a man for some 20 years. Her hand gently caresses his shoulder.

Achchannayya had expected Visvesvara's cousin to come for him after a fortnight, but that time has long passed. Achchannayya is keen to take him back, as he is concerned at the change he is discerning in Venku—'She is a little too joyous'—and at the fact that 'something is going on between them.' Again Nagalakshmi overrules him.

This 'Nagalakshmi' chapter ends with the monthly visit of the barber. The import of the exchange between Nagalakshmi and Venku is perfectly plain. Venku says she will not see the barber today. Nagalakshmi asks if she will see him next week.

No.

Then when?

Never again.

Venku's resolve is unmistakable, despite the low volume of delivery and her head hung down, and its significance is evident too. Her transformation from widowhood would seem well-advanced, as she is no longer tonsured and is wearing saris of her choice, but what her transformation is *to*, exactly, is something we do not know yet. When even Nagalakshmi agrees that Visvesvara should be sent away, it is Venku who protests. Her mother-in-law, evidently deeming her to be morally unworthy, bans her from cooking and from all domestic rituals.

Raji is dismayed at her mother's affection for Visvesvara or, as she would see it, her infatuation with him. When she sees Venku dressed other than as a widow, she tells her that she looks lovely; but from Raji's point of view, at what cost has this visual loveliness come? To her it is simply the belief in rebirth and the oracle's endorsement of it that explains her mother's infatuation. Venku evades the question of rebirth, but it seems clear that her relationship with Visvesvara has nothing to do with that matter, and this notion is given utterance at the end of the film. Raji, however, has difficulty seeing past it. In applying a metaphysical notion to mundane circumstances, she tries to belittle Visvesvara with the absurdity of father and daughter being the same age, something which he finds simply amusing. She concludes that he is an imposter, and orders him to go. Venku tries to explain that things are not as simple as Raji would see them. 'Each one finds the truth one desires,' she pleads.

Raji's distress reaches a pinnacle in an ugly scene in which Nagalakshmi becomes physically violent with Venku, and Raji steps in between them. It is very unpleasant, revealing the old woman's obsession, and her alacrity for bitterness. It also reveals a touch of compassion in Raji, as she senses the pathos in the false braid that falls from her mother's head. That positive emotion has scorn poured on it by the old woman saying, 'Don't try to justify your clandestine pregnancy.' This sees Raji devastated.

There is still some chance that Visvesvara may go away, as his cousin said he would come and get him after the initial fortnight, and that time has well and truly passed. However, he and his wife do come to take him back, but Achchannayya insists that they take the couple, not just the man. They baulk at this, claiming that they bear no responsibility for Venku. The cousin suggests that he might reconsider, given an offer of land and money from Achchannayya, but the saintly old man sees that there is no love—as he puts it to Raji—for Visvesvara, only for money. He is a truly good man, 'not prepared to play games using Visvesvara as the dice.' But Raji sees this as a wasted opportunity to finally get rid of an undesirable. It is quite clear that Achchannayya is motivated by a genuine concern for the greater moral good, something that is not dictated to him by scripture or custom but by genuine love for his fellows.

Such love is by no means universal. Her neighbour and friend invites Venku to a married women's ritual, but no one will sit with her. The friend's mother-in-law crudely pronounces that Venku has no place there as she is engaged in debauchery. As a widow, she received no invitations, and now she sees that giving up the widow's regimen and accepting Visvesvara has changed nothing. She is accepted neither as a widow nor as a married woman. What is significant here is that who she may be is determined not by herself, but by the perceptions of others.

A similar question of identity and the perceptions of others arises when Achchannayya is called to a meeting of the village elders to explain gossip concerning untoward goings-on in his house, and the consequent threat to the good name of their community. While no one questions the decision of the oracle, they almost drown in their own confusion when querying whether the young man should be accepted as Ramanna or Visvesvara. The conclusion is that he can be Achchannayya's son, but not Venku's husband. Evidently, the individual must live his or her life according to decisions made by others. Venku's words may echo here: *Each one finds the truth one desires.*

The final section is titled 'Venkatalakshmi' and at last, we will observe the narrative from the point of view of the woman who has suffered so stoically at the behest of others throughout the film so far.

The falling out between Venku and her mother-in-law is now virtually complete. Venku expresses to her father-in-law her desire to go away, for she wants complete independence from family and friends as a total stranger in an unknown place. Achchannayya mentions a friend of his who has a house by the sea, and there is a cut to that place.

As the camera is taken along one of the many inlets of what seems to be an estuary region, we are overwhelmed with the idyllic scenery, its beauty in isolation, its water, and its greenery. Clearly, this would seem to be the escape that Venku needs so much.

The couple and their belongings arrive in two boats. Among the group of bearers waiting to help them unload is a very striking and vivacious girl, who is highly amused at Visvesvara's ineptitude in getting out of the boat. It is apparent that he is readily attracted to her, asking her name—it is Sukri—and its meaning, which she does not know. As she passes by Venku, she refers innocently to Visvesvara as her son, and as she carries her load up to the house, the exchange of smiles and silly giggles continues. Visvesvara remarks to Venku—tactlessly, as he is wont to—that she moves like a fawn. 'Can you move like her?' Once it is time to get the house in order, his ineptitude is seen again, sitting around like a dreamer while she does all the work. Narrative indications are clear that life in this seemingly idyllic place is going to have its complications.

Visvesvara's infatuation with Sukri is established in a sequence that sees him returning from the market and needing her to ferry him across the river. She mentions incidentally that she could not afford to buy chillies and he immediately bestows handfuls of his own purchase on her. The silliness of this is underlined by her constant giggling, but she wraps the chillies in her cloth and keeps them, nevertheless. When they get to the other side, he tells her to take him back. There are more giggles. Later he realises that he forgot to give her salt, which she was also unable to buy. He wraps some in a cloth, ties it around his waist and swims across to her hut. There are more giggles when the salt is seen to have dissolved. It is all quite fatuous, but innocent enough. However, there is a sour turn to it when, later that night, we see Visvesvara being escorted home by Sukri's father and a couple of assistants. The man did not like Visvesvara sitting outside his hut while Sukri was alone inside. He told him to go and gave him a push. He stumbled, fell, and hurt himself. The man tells all this to Venku, whose sense of insecurity becomes evident. She seeks reassurance from Visvesvara, and there is a warm and tender embrace, spoiled by his vocal discovery of a grey hair on her head.

We then learn of the death of Nagalakshmi, distraught at the moving away together of Visvesvara and Venku. She lost her appetite for food and drink, went without sleep and eventually succumbed. It has to be said, however, that she brought all of this upon herself. Her preoccupation with customs, rites and regulations, and her obsession with indulging herself with her 'son' are largely responsible for setting so much of this sad narrative in motion. The good Achchannayya might blame himself for it all, for, as he tells Raji, 'I brought him here in the first place.' What the good man neglects to say is that he brought him there at the relentless insistence of Nagalakshmi. Raji, however, is as persistent as ever in blaming Visvesvara for everything, declaring that he took away her mother and caused the death of her grandmother. Ominously, she vows, 'I shall end this matter.'

The scene changes back to the seaside, where the pregnant Venku is seen doing all the manual work while her husband sits day-dreaming. It is then that two policemen arrive, wanting to take Visvesvara away. He comes out with a jug of water for Venku, which he now empties over her head before going in dignity with the policemen. There are two clear implications in this. Following on so closely to Raji's resolve to 'end this matter,' it would seem that she is responsible for the arrival of the police. But the pouring of the water over Venku's head suggests that Visvesvara thinks he has been betrayed by her. In fact, as has been the case all along, his and Venku's lives are constantly being shaped by other people.

That he is not malleable is suggested by the simple dignity with which he goes with the police, and this is reinforced by the fact that his anger will be maintained for the rest of the film. He has made up his mind that he has been betrayed, and will not budge in the slightest from his unforgiving and adamantine antipathy toward those whom he once called family. He spurns them when they come to see him at the jail, and he respectfully rejects his lawyer's offer to get him bail. A little later his daughter will be born, and at the court, he does not even acknowledge her.

Just as adamant in her antipathy is Raji, the one truly responsible for his plight. She is consoled by her lawyer uncle who asks her to be glad that Venku's baby is a girl, since a boy might have complicated claims to inheritance. She insists once again that she has no care for property, nor does she bear the baby any ill will. All she wants is for Visvesvara 'to rot in jail.' If he is locked away, her mother might come back to her. This is all she wants. Another narrative indication is then given by the uncle, pointing out that he would certainly be jailed if the girl, Sukri, were to file a case.

Sukri is a simple village girl, more than likely illiterate and probably terrified of the police. The likelihood of someone like her filing a case against anyone is minimal, so when we see her in court testifying against Visvesvara, it is difficult to suppress the suspicion that she has been suborned. She testifies that Visvesvara came to their house, he held her hand—and then she seems to have trouble remembering her lines. She recovers and says that he dragged her by the hair, bolted the door and 'molested' her. From all that we have seen of Visvesvara, this seems highly unlikely. Visvesvara denies the accusation of molestation, but agrees not to oppose the charges, in order to stop the humiliating interrogation that is being inflicted on Sukri. For his compassion and moral stand, he is given two years' rigorous imprisonment.

Venku is probably right in fearing that the sentence will intensify his anger, and that he will never come back to her and their child. Nevertheless, she resolves to stay there and wait for him. After all, what else can she do?

In a final reference to the fact that control of her life was long ago taken out of her hands, she points out to Raji that Nagalakshmi and the villagers wanted the oracle to 'sanctify my relationship with him,' and that it needed a court to break it. However, 'my experience was enough for me to validate my relationship.' The tragedy of this film lies in the fact that she was never given the right to act solely on her own experience as long as there were people who felt they could run her life better than she could. Ultimately she wants independence and privacy, to be alone with her own perceptions, emotions and values. Her great misfortune is that other people were unable to respect that, self-righteously meddling in her life.

The nature of character and character differentiation are very significant in this film. All of the four family members, plus Visvesvara, have their own personal stakes in the development of this most extraordinary drama. Sometimes some of them work in mutual support, often one or more are pitted against the others. Achchannayya is an immensely moral man, admired for his reason and soberness. He is prudent and judicious, but in his compassion for everyone he cannot take sides and this militates against his ever being meaningfully decisive. This is particularly so when he indulges his wife. Nagalakshmi is a foolish old woman, obsessed with ritual and custom, with outward signs and acts. But she is ignorant, self-centred, and judgemental. In her unceasing endeavours to get her own way, she is uninterested in the concerns of others and intolerant of any view that threatens her own. Venkatalakshmi is her victim, a stoic sufferer and, consequently, a most ill-used woman. Fundamentally, however, she is simply a woman with natural womanly needs and feelings, a fact that no one really seems to care about. In public, she is either a widow or a fallen woman—as a widow, she should not have needs and feelings, and as a fallen woman, she should be ashamed of them and suppress them. Rajalakshmi is deeply loving of her mother and fiercely loyal to her, but her devotion clouds her judgement, lending her to think that she knows what is best for her. She focusses strongly on negative emotions, and while she is educated and intelligent, she lacks maturity, so minimising her understanding of an older woman. And then there is the film's central enigma, Visvesvara. Is he, as Rajalakshmi believes, an imposter? He is probably not clever enough to maintain a guise. He is depicted as very simple, urged on by natural impulses, unable, for example, to discriminate between love for Venkatalakshmi and infatuation with Sukri. His eventual submission to anger is a form of personal pride, perhaps demanding of respect rather than the pity that would be forthcoming for an ill-treated simpleton.

This volatile chemistry of character gives animation to an extraordinary narrative concerning the stifling effects that tradition can impose. *Nayi Neralu* is yet another incisive examination of the treatment of women in Indian society, providing an interesting coupling of the harsh and seemingly pointless regimen imposed on high-caste widows, and a young woman enthusiastically embracing tertiary education. It also aims to provoke some critical understanding of traditional social proscriptions concerning the right to love. Indeed, a study of this chemistry of character will persistently provoke a questioning of the nature of love itself.

10

One Movie, Many Dreams; Many Movies, One Dream

In *Gulabi Talkies* (2008), Girish Kasaravalli again looks at the Muslim community, not as exclusively as in *Hasina* but as a minority in the broader society. There is a concentration of place, which ensures a clear definition of the *mise-en-scene* and clarity of narrative. The setting is largely a small island in what appears to be an estuary area (remarkably similar to that in the latter part of *Nayi Neralu*) and to a lesser extent the small fishing town on the mainland, which is easily reached by boat. The mundanities in *Gulabi Talkies*, much less mysterious than in all the other films, are to do with relational conflict—marital, familial, social, communal, labour and, toward the end, international. Indeed, for a Kasaravalli film, the narrative elements seem unusually many, but integrity is effectively imposed on this broad miscellany by the central character, Gulabi, who gives the film so much of its appeal, over and above any of its narrative developments.

The early sequences of the film provide a sound basis for an understanding of Gulabi. We first see her at the fish market in the town on the mainland. She is dressed in a black *niqab*—as she always will be while away from her island—and is anxious to buy prawns but is deterred by the price. So she is a Muslim in a largely non-Muslim community; her purchase seems to be urgent; and she is not well-off. This skeletal aspect of character is soon fleshed out. Her husband has taken a second wife, by whom he has an endearing little boy, Addu, who is adored by Gulabi. Because it is the child's birthday and he loves prawns, Gulabi is keen to buy some to please him. In the course of her conversation with the fish vendor, we learn that she is also pressed for time, as the evening session at the cinema is fast approaching—Gulabi is an insatiable movie lover.

Perhaps the most significant element in all of this is Gulabi's doting on Addu—the son of another woman for whom her husband left her, a woman who makes perfectly clear her dislike of Gulabi, and even punishes the little boy for having anything to do with her. Gulabi pampers and cossets the child, and even cultivates a conspiracy with him to keep their relationship secret from his parents. While she may be bitter toward her husband, from whom she is not yet divorced, and resentful of his new wife, Gulabi is able to love Addu in complete detachment from any negative feelings that she may have for his parents. Gulabi, in fact, finds it easy to be genial to everyone; yet at the end, when she needs friends to stand up for her, almost no one comes forward. A generally delightful film must end with a bitter taste.

She cannot afford the prawns at the asking price and so must wait until she can have them at a reduced price. She is a midwife, but in a relatively small community babies are not a thriving or even reliable source of income, and so she supplements whatever she gets as a midwife with her earnings as a domestic servant in some of the homes in the town. Her one indulgence is cinema and the dream-world it offers her.

The old net-mender remarks, as he sees her heading for the ferry, 'It must be 6:30,' the time when Gulabi goes to an evening cinema show. He tells someone else that wherever a new film is showing, there you will find Gulabi. Others mention that Gulabi sees today the film she saw yesterday and will see it again tomorrow. It is not that she has any critical or notable aesthetic interest in cinema as an art, but rather, it is the dream-world offered by the silver screen that attracts her and in which she finds fulfilment.

After getting her prawns at an affordable price, she makes it to the cinema in time for the evening show. But a little before this, an element is introduced into the narrative that now converges with the element of Gulabi indulging her love for movies. When Gulabi is setting out in the ferry for the cinema hall in the town, a motor-powered boat moves rapidly in the opposite direction, toward Gulabi's island. It comes to the bank and three young men in flashy Western dress and hairstyle leap out and run to Gulabi's little place, urgently calling her name. This is where the old net-mender redirects them, and the boat then takes them back toward the town. We then cut to a shot of Gulabi settling back in her seat as the show starts. Suddenly there is a rude intrusion as the same young men burst into the front stalls calling out her name. They find her and demand that she accompany them, as her service as a midwife is urgently needed by the daughter of one Kalyani. However, the urgency of an imminent birth is not enough to move Gulabi out of her dream world and she bluntly refuses to go. The young men have strength in numbers, and they simply pick her up and carry her out. Affable and warm-hearted as she is, she is by no means submissive, and when they reach their destination, she refuses to get out of the boat. For her abductors and their superiors, the urgent situation is becoming desperate, so to get Gulabi out of the boat and get her to deliver the baby of Kalyani's daughter they are willing to be more than generous. In short, Gulabi instantly becomes a devoted midwife on the promise of a second-hand television set with a satellite dish to ensure the effective reception of colour movies in her own island home. (There is another television set on the island, but without a satellite dish it gets only black and white reception.) And so Gulabi Talkies is established, and a little later it will be authenticated with a film poster that Gulabi steals from a boy who is pasting them around the town.

Once Gulabi's set is installed, with full colour, she becomes something of a celebrity, and other women on the island, as well as small children, now squeeze into her shack to enjoy free and glitzy entertainment. Mostly it is the women of the village who make up the audience, but sometimes she entertains groups of children, offering them snacks to chew on while they watch, incidentally recalling similar entertainment sessions in *Kraurya*. One morning, she comes quite late to her domestic job in the town, the reason being that she could not miss the programme of film songs on television at 8.00 in the morning, the sort of programme that makes one 'forget the world.'

Curiously, perhaps, while Gulabi Talkies brings people together, it is also an instrument for friction and division. Two old crones watch with interest the new socio-cultural phenomenon but do not take part in it. They are Hindus, and quite pre-modern at that, so '*we* don't go into *their* houses.' Thus, an old prejudice is kept in currency, though it is simply a statement of the way things are, the way they are accepted as being. Rancour is yet to develop.

The village community on this island lives by fishing, with the men going out very early in the morning and coming home late at night. The women, therefore, have a lot of time on their hands away from their husbands. Gulabi's colour television set is a great attraction to them all, especially with the lure of soap serials. And so they crowd into Gulabi's shack, to lose themselves in make-believe people's worlds and make-believe people's problems, joys, and sorrows.

There is a brief scene in which some of the men are discussing Gulabi Talkies and its appeal to their women. Most of them seem happy about their wives indulging themselves in this entertainment, as it gives them something to do in the long hours when the men are absent. Sheena, however, is an authoritarian husband and a bully. The night before this discussion among the fishermen, he is seen coming past Gulabi's shack and sees his wife Kamli in there. 'What's this?!' he roars, and all the women scatter, including Kamli, who can guess what is in store for her. There is an outside shot of Sheena chasing her about, and the next morning's discussion on the beach makes mention of what happened when he caught her. The expression used is 'showing his muscle power to his wife.' He tries to justify his wife-beating, insisting that their women should not go into Muslims' homes, a view with which some agreement is expressed, but Sheena is a notorious wife-beater; his prejudice against Muslims cannot explain away his brutishness.

While Kamli must suffer the strain of a violent husband, two of the women have effectually no husband at all, as one is working in the Gulf and the other is in the army. And then there is Netru, a woman whose husband is working in Dubai, and who is obliged to live with her mother-in-law, Akku. A serial that excites the ongoing interest of most of the women is based on a similar relationship—an attractive young widow called Prafullata, living with her callous and tyrannical mother-in-law. There is a clear parallel here to Netru and Akku. When the satellite dish, dominating the boat on which it is being floated to the island, arrives, to the excited delight of a swarm of young boys, many of the adults rush off to satisfy their curiosity. Netru starts to join them, but is stopped by Akku. 'Your highness need not come. Stay here and get on with your chores.' Netru is submissive and obviously down-hearted. Whenever Gulabi asks her why she looks so sad, the reply is, 'My mother-in-law is still alive.' Netru is held in strict domestic thraldom, is given no opportunity to find happiness of even the simplest kind, and is desperately lonely. Her yearning for escape from a conflicting familial relationship develops as a major narrative element.

Outwardly, the happiest family in the village is that of the fishing boss, Vasanna. Much of the film deals with his ongoing business and financial difficulties, but his house is probably the biggest and best-built in the village, and his family are well cared for. There are, however, arguments with his wife over things that might be important to her, though trivial to him—such as her wish to have a colour television set—and there is also the basis for a very serious falling out with his son at the end of the film.

And, of course, Gulabi's own familial situation is racked with tension and conflict. Her husband, Musa, is her neighbour, living in an evidently better house than the simple shack that is her home. His second wife, Kunhi, is bitter toward Gulabi and is obsessively protective of her son, Addu, from any association at all with her. Musa is content to be detached from all this, although at one point his irritation, caused by the ongoing dispute between the two women with regard to Addu, brings him out in vociferous support of Kunhi and threatening to Gulabi. Gulabi is not one to be cowed by anyone and she fires back at him, 'I am not a dog to be shooed away. You have not yet given me *talaq*.[1] I am still your wife.' There

[1] Divorce.

will be conciliatory gestures, there will be suspected betrayal, there will be Gulabi's solicitous concern for Musa, Kunhi and Addu will flee the village, and the familial relationship among the four of them will always be fractured.

Prominent in the opening scene is Gulabi as a Muslim woman. In her distinctive dress she stands out among everyone else. Yet communalism is not a feature of the film until some way in. Its roots may be set, as seen in the accepted bigotry of the two old crones as well as in Sheena's perception of impropriety in visiting a Muslim's house, but for some time there is no animosity or conflict arising out of communal difference. However, as the narrative develops, circumstances conspire to sharpen dulled antipathy. Quite late in the film Addu calls Gulabi on behalf of his mother to find that Kunhi's father and friends have come to take her away, in order to avoid trouble before it strikes. The rival fishing magnate, Suleman, and Gulabi's husband Musa, his factotum, are vilified on communal grounds as culpable in the failing market success of rival fishing enterprises—notably Vasanna's. When mystery and ignorance come together, rumour develops, and it takes a sadly, though unsurprisingly, communal turn.

We might also note that whenever Pakistani hostility is directed in one way or another toward India, the insecurity of Indian Muslims becomes manifest, and we have evidence of that in this film, which is set at the time of the Kargil War. For the most part, it is war by stealth. When Gulabi's new television set is being installed, she is instructed on how to use the remote control. A report on Indo-Pakistan hostility appears on the news and is greeted by Gulabi's tutor with, 'The news. Some war somewhere,' and he moves straight on to a Kannada movie. There are more shots of television news reports on the strife with Pakistan, which are offered simply as a reminder that this international hostility is building up. Boys in the town collecting money for the war effort are rejected by Gulabi, preoccupied with something else, prompting a passer-by to remark, 'Why waste time asking them?' Thus, there is the perilous potential for nationalism to take on a communalist garb.

Labour conflict is a major element in the film and is based on the rivalry between Vasanna's enterprise and what would seem to be the more prosperous enterprise of Suleman, who never appears in the film but works through his agent, Musa. Musa is actively involved in recruiting fishermen from Vasanna to work for Suleman, something which loyalists might see as treachery, but struggling fishermen may also find tempting. So there is dissension in and defection from the Vasanna camp, along with intended defections to Suleman. Musa is central to this, and Gulabi is guilty by association.

All of these conflicts are synthesised to produce an unsatisfactory conclusion, with rumours concerning Musa. Two narrative elements converge—perceptively, if not actually—to give rise to this. One is the somewhat brief and insubstantial story of Netru, the other is the more tangible story of Musa as a functionary of Suleman's enterprise. In fact, Netru and Musa have nothing to do with each other, yet when simple and unthinking people are confronted with the seemingly inexplicable, strongly tinged with the suspicion of what might well be a hostile Other, distorted perceptions and imaginings can prevail over actuality. In fact, the two narrative elements are developed separately from one another and they converge only in the malice of men's minds.

At the heart of Netru's misery is her acrimonious relationship with her mother-in-law, yet this is not explored in any way. At first it might seem that this is a simple means to show that the television soap is a mirror to life, for whatever purpose. However, the plight of a young woman living with her mother-in-law (and incurring the expense of being kept) is common enough in India to be relatively unremarkable. There is a lovely scene at the water's edge, in which the fever-ridden Netru meets Gulabi, who has come to wash clothes. The young woman complains of her tyrannical mother-in-law, who has forced her to work, even though she is sick. There is an incidental reference to Prafullata, the young widow in the television serial, who is planning to elope, which might give those more prescient in the audience a suggestion of what Netru might do next. However, a stumbling block is put up by the question, 'With whom?' As for Musa, there has been no evidence to suggest that she even knows him.

However, while there is no elopement, Netru does make an escape. She is in the town, selling fish door to door and happily gets rid of her basket of fish for whatever paltry price she can get, finds a secluded place and changes her clothes. A little later, we see her on a bus looking relieved, but her relief is only temporary as a posse has been sent out to look for her—and for Musa.

The posse looks familiar. They are, indeed, the same young men who had come after Gulabi at the beginning of the film, extracting her from the cinema hall to go and deliver Kalyani's daughter's baby. We will meet them again at the end. Apparently, they are a self-styled agency of the conscience of the community, with nothing better to do than interfere in the lives of others—righteously, of course. They take Netru back to the island, where she is rejected by her mother-in-law as well as by a cowed and uncertain gathering of neighbours. They do not know where she has been, where she was going, or who she might have been with, and so, unsure of due propriety, they keep their distance. Once they all retire for the night, they have seen the last of Netru.

As for Musa, his tale is transparent enough. He appears as a major factotum of Suleman, the Mr Big of the fishing world, who is never seen in the film—indeed, there are those who quite plausibly doubt his existence. On the island—Musa's island too, it must be remembered—the major enterprise is run by Vasanna, a personable, genial man, even a touch soft-hearted with those who would unashamedly cadge money from him. Musa's aim is to attract labour away from Vasanna to Suleman, tempting them with material benefits such as job security, better wages, and the like. On one occasion, he takes a group of them for a ride on his boat, impressing them with the extent of the Suleman enterprise whose nets cover a huge expanse of water and bring in tons of fish. Eventually a price war of sorts heats up, with Suleman's fish going for half price and Vasanna's not being sold at all. Vasanna's own men turn against him, suspecting that he is cheating them (he says there is no money, yet they observe that, at least by their standards, he lives in notable style), and so a few more go over to Suleman. It is easy to see how Vasanna might feel threatened by Musa.

Tension spills over into the wholesale fish market, then into the Fishing Society. The complaints are, for the most part, *ad hominem*—'that Muslim is not a local so he should not be allowed to fish here' is the crux of it, answered decisively by 'but he can, because he has paid his licence fee.' In frustration and anger, inflamed perhaps by an element of communal bitterness, Musa is given a sound thrashing. Later a view is put forward that everything would be all right if Suleman were kicked out. And so there is an anti-Suleman rally in the town, which all seems rather pointless when that day's paper carries a report of the government allowing other countries to fish in Indian waters. In the meantime we learn from Gulabi, who turns up to one of her cleaning jobs in a car, that Suleman fears that Musa might be targeted and has directed him to move about in a car for a few days. And then Musa disappears.

The possibility that he feels acute shame at having been thrashed by men of his own village and is frightened of it happening again does not seem to be considered. It is far more dramatic to believe that he has embezzled a large sum of money from Suleman and has absconded with it. There is also a more salacious possibility, for his disappearance occurs at about the same time as Netru's aborted escape. This is all the evidence that is needed to accuse Musa, a Muslim, of running off with a Hindu girl, and it ought to be enough to hang him. It is a tempting thought for some—even for Vasanna—that if Musa is jailed, Suleman might be curbed.

So the seemingly upright Vasanna has been drawn into the intrigue, as we see when he is serving tea to the community-conscience boys, thanking them for their good work in saving Netru from shame. One of them, with mock apology, regrets being unable to catch Musa, because 'these people are very shrewd—he saw us and made his escape.' The fact is that they did not catch him because he was not there. The boys finish their tea, but before leaving, they want to watch the television news, and just a snippet of war footage, juxtaposed with the previous prejudice, is enough to suggest the brewing of something bigger and more insidious than a fisherman's squabble with one ordinary man.

On the same night, having been returned to an unwelcoming village, Netru assures Gulabi that she has had nothing to do with Musa. Then there is a shot of her coming on to a rocky outcrop, with waves beating strongly against it. She sits down. There are shots of the water crashing and foaming against the rocks. There is a shot of a big wave breaking on Netru. There is a cut to a shot of birds in a treetop in the brightness of a new morning.

Curiously, attention now falls on Gulabi. The apparent reason is nothing more than the fact that she is the wife of Musa, albeit spurned by him. The old man of Akku's house demands to know from Gulabi whether Netru has eloped again or committed suicide. Gulabi truthfully says that she does not know, and he hits her. There is probably an element of self-righteousness in this brutishness, as there is in the villagers' turning away from Gulabi. It can be satisfying for some to attribute blame where an explanation is lacking.

Netru, it may be assumed, is dead. Musa has gone into hiding, almost certainly without any of Suleman's fortune. The good, genial, kind Gulabi is now pilloried and removed from the community by the same arrogant young bully boys who removed her from her cinema seat in the early part of the film. It is a very discomforting ending, showing these thug-like nobodies throwing her humble belongings out of her hut, while she gathers them up and replaces them, only to have the procedure repeated, with an astonished crowd of villagers looking on, some of them shame-faced, all of them passive. The leader of the bullies menacingly orders, 'Gulnabi, (*sic*) leave the village right now!' She finds this amusing, for even she had forgotten the Muslim form of her name, being known as Gulabi ('rose') for so many years. But now she is, in fact, a Muslim, no longer a rose. And then, just as they had lifted her out of her seat in the cinema hall and placed her in the boat, they carry her to the boat again and off to who-knows-where. But as Vasanna's son puts it, 'Who are they to decide who will live where?'

The really sad aspect of this ending is Vasanna's involvement in it. It had always been easy to see him as a cool-headed man, rational and generous. However, if one can ride on the back of communalism to claim the prize of personal gain, even the good will be tempted to do just that. His son overhears Vasanna directing that the bully boys are not to be impeded and censuring his wife for expressing the view that injustice has been done to Netru, to Kunhi, and now to Gulabi, for he would hope that Gulabi might divulge the whereabouts of Musa. The boy drives off in his father's van to warn Gulabi away from the thugs, but she characteristically barges headlong into battle, and loses. Vasanna's son asks her what she will do. She is stoic and cheerful in spite of everything. 'So long as women continue to get pregnant, my life will go on.'

As a populist gesture, the bully boys leave the television set and satellite dish behind, and the film ends with the two old crones coming into what was Gulabi's hut, but which is no longer the house of one of *them*, to watch television. They sit back comfortably, enjoying the sight of a cat perched on top of the set, not knowing that the power has to be turned on. The last image of the film is, appropriately, one of the most fatuous ignorance.

The film's atmospherics are well-conceived and deployed. The opening scene in the market, for example, while offering some signs of key features in the narrative that are yet to be unwound, also offers some elements of simple fun, such as the practical joke played by one man in dropping a small block of ice down the inside of another's shirt; the resulting chase results in a third man falling off his bicycle and losing whatever sense of humour he may have had before his fall. The cheating in the fishermen's card school is amusing in its blatancy as well as its clumsiness. The scenes in Gulabi's shack, when it is crowded with avid television watchers, evoke a social joy deriving from both the television programme and the sense of community that is engendered by it. There is also some gentle humour in the passing reference to Kasaravalli's *Mane*, as Gulabi flicks over the channels to find something worth watching. She rejects *Mane*. Like the other films where water is prominent—*Dweepa* and the latter part of *Nayi Neralu*—this one too has its special visual splendour. But along with the atmospherics depicting light-heartedness, much of the visual beauty belies the subtle ugliness that is going on in the minds and hearts of people. The stream is a lovely waterway; it also conveys the engine-driven boat of the young bully boys. The rocky outcrop is majestic, as is the dramatic crashing of waves against it; it also claims the life of Netru. The sea is, as always, beguiling; it also is the basis of most of the human conflict and acrimony in the film.

Although our first observation of Gulabi with Musa is one in which harsh words are exchanged, there would appear to be some marital affection left in the relationship. There is one scene where a group of women are enjoying a movie song and dance number, and Musa comes to the door. Probably feigning that he did not know he would be interrupting, he comes in and again feigns surprise at the television set and expresses his desire to watch it for a bit. Even by the time he sits down, the women and few children have dispersed. Gulabi is taken aback and not at all sure of how to behave. Her friend Ratna urges her to be nice to him, and that comes easily to her. She makes him a cup of tea, and there is a lovely shot of her handing him the glass; not wanting to distract him from his absorption in the programme, she holds it close to his head, allowing the jingle of her bracelets to inform him of her service. There is immediate eye contact, then the sharing of a smile; he holds her hand and she invites him to eat. He asks for her fish curry. Later that night, Addu is sent to fetch his father and it is Gulabi, most surprisingly, who shuts the door against her adored little friend. Musa berates Kunhi angrily and the dinner would seem to be spoiled. However, the mood is resurrected by Gulabi's offer of more fish and television, and then we see her with her head lovingly resting on his shoulder, while Kunhi sits despondently outside.

It is significant to note, then, that feeling like a wife again is very important to Gulabi, and despite the strong suspicion of his apparent double-dealing and her subsequent throwing him out of her shack, Musa is still a significant concern for her. This concern is brought to the fore when the rumour that he has eloped with Netru starts circulating. She goes out looking for him, only to be confronted with the rumour that he has embezzled funds from Suleman and is on the run and the subject of a police investigation. There is a shot of her walking alone, pensively, along the beach at evening, and another of her praying. However, the damage has already been done. As Kunhi's father sums it up, 'Musa should not have got involved with that Hindu girl. Now the whole community has to pay for it.' The truth or otherwise of the rumours is now immaterial.

The Muslim nation of Pakistan is in many ways the worst enemy of India's Muslims, who have to fear not only Pakistani bombs and terrorists but also many members of the Hindu community who identify them with the national enemy because of their religion. When Gulabi talks of people having different dreams, she might well be reflecting a sad shortcoming in Indian nationalism, that the dream that all the people ought to share is not, in fact, common to them all. The dream of a nation in which enmity is cultivated by harassing people and viewing them with suspicion because of their religion is by no means the foundation of a lofty nationalism. It is disturbing that it is held by anyone at all.

The film makes its impression very simply, belying the complexity of its narrative content. There is a great deal in between 'the price of prawns' and 'Pakistan,' and yet all those elements are introduced organically, set to engage with one another and work themselves out rationally. While the Kargil War is the pinnacle of the developing dramatic conflict, essentially mundane matters are allowed to develop in the foreground for most of the film. The foreign Other tries to establish itself, but is often stifled by a simple change of the channel. One of the strengths of the narrative is this careful introduction and gradual establishment of the dramatic pinnacle, lending a particular irony to the final scene where Gulnabi, the perceived enemy alien, is removed from the village in the interests of national security. We might then look back at so many other narrative elements that gradually implanted the notion of fracturing in the family, in the village, in the workplace, in the greater society, and in the nation. It is a narrative rich with human interest, joyful and pitiable, but also one in which a strict philosophical and artistic logic has kept restraint throughout. In this film about fractured relationships, the harmony of narrative structure and cinematic technique is remarkable.

11

Stars Will Fall from the Sky if My Dream Proves False

Undoubtedly the most mysterious and least mundane of Girish Kasaravalli's films is *Kanasemba Kudureyaneri* ('Riding the Stallion of Dream,' 2009). To say that it is the least mundane, however, is not to say that it is the least realistic; its realism remains uncompromised, despite the implications of 'dream' in the title. The substance of a dream may be quite chimeric, but the reality of its occurrence and its effect on the dreamer remain unquestioned. While it is 'modern,' perhaps, to explain dreams away as chaotic or arbitrary workings of the mind in an unconscious state, there are very many people who believe that dreams are not inconsequential mental ramblings but carry meaning, often convey messages, and are a medium through which a higher being, such as a divinity, may actually communicate with the dreamer. Whether or not one considers such ideas medieval nonsense is beside the point; as long as people believe that dreams have powers and properties of significance, then that is all that matters. Our concern, then, is with the ramifications of such a belief. Lest we find this trivial, it is well to remember the damage caused by so many in history who have sought to justify aberrant—or worse—behaviour with the plea, 'God came to me in a dream ...'

Kanasemba Kudureyaneri is manifestly Indian in its ambience and garb. Most of the action takes place in and around Irya's hut, which is surrounded by an open expanse of hard and dry land; thus, it has an obvious link with the soil, seemingly infertile as it may be. Much takes place in the house of the elder Gowda, also physically removed from the village, and in its architecture and décor it carries a manifestation of traditional aesthetics and living style; thus, it has an obvious link to a rich past. The few scenes set in the village make obvious its remoteness from modern urban civilisation, again emphasising the persistence of the traditional in Indian rural life. But the film is also laced with significant references to Hinduism—religious devotion, ritual, values and protocols pertaining to death and funerary procedures—while much of the narrative is built on social inequality, the most salient feature of the caste system.

The structure of the film recognises the centrality of dream in the narrative. After an introductory sequence that is quite empirical in nature, the rest of the film is divided into sections, introduced as in *Nayi Neralu* by title cards, each indicating an emanation of dream, while the section itself traces the dream's implications.

There is a need at the outset to convey some basic information concerning *Siddha*. We are told that they are a nomadic tribe of Karnataka, now greatly impoverished and surviving as street charmers and beggars. For whatever reason, a kind of cult has developed around them, acknowledging them as bringers of good luck, even seeing them as emissaries of death, who ensure that the soul of whomever might die in the presence of one of them will surely be blessed with access to Heaven. Finally there is the simple fact that the community of grave-diggers hails a Siddha as its guru. Fundamental to the film then is the religious phenomenon of *Siddha* and, it would seem, a grave-digger. The opening shot is of a frog, swimming to where a group of women are taking water from a pond. They walk up the steep bank and then toward their homes, and we note a bare, very rugged landscape. The camera comes to focus on one of the women, whom we later meet as Rudri. She enters her very humble hut. From the inside, internally framed by the doorway, we see a man, later to be identified as Irya, coming toward the hut. His clothes are tattered, he is barefoot, and his shirt seems to be blood-stained; he carries a long-handled shovel. Rudri's first question is revealing: 'Did you find any work today?', and a pattern of unemployment and poverty starts to emerge. In reply, he asks her tetchily if anyone had died today, and we might guess that he is a grave-digger. The opening titles then come up. The pre-titles sequence has established a condition of abject poverty and squalor and the occupation of grave-digging, both of which are radical to the narrative that will develop.

The scenes that follow after the titles are actually anterior to the pre-titles sequence. There is a shot of Irya out on the road, his shirt relatively clean, though just as tattered. Driving along on his evidently new tiller is the landowner Basanyappa. Irya now takes to begging, asking Basanyappa to give him 50 rupees and following him into the village. The plea is refused, as Basanyappa sees Irya as an idler. 'His wife works in my field, but he won't.' A big, shiny red car comes into the narrow lane, eliciting an observation that Shivanna has come with his family and positing the opinion that maybe the elder Gowda is critically ill, a possibility that makes Irya's eyes light up.

A woman is painting red patterns on a step nearby, and Irya accidentally upsets her pot of red paint. As a comment on his low-caste status and his inherent unworthiness, she throws the pot's residue at him, so 'bloodying' his shirt. He meekly accepts the humiliation, as people like him have done for millennia.

The car arrives at a traditionally splendid old home, with timber balustrades, columns, and interior balcony and staircase ornately presented. The cows near the entrance underline the rusticity of the place. The visitors are welcomed by the old retainer, Matadayya, whose religiosity is reflected by the marks of devotion on his forehead and the string of *rudraksha* beads around his neck. He is obviously glad to see them, but candid in expressing his regret that it has been a long time since Shivanna has visited, and longer since his wife Hema and daughter Pinki have been there. He tells Shivanna that there has been no change in his father's condition in the last six months. They enter the old man's room and confront a senseless, though apparently conscious, wraith. Their discomfort at the smell is obvious, and Matadayya is embarrassed, but he is also defiantly supportive of the old man. There is no getting around his incontinence in the bed, and although servants clean the room twice a day, the smell would seem to be permanent. While Matadayya has given no offence, Hema still whispers to Shivanna her utter dislike of him. Maybe it is because he pricks her conscience.

A little later she informs Matadayya that Shivanna is the principal of a college and his time is not his own to visit his father as he might like. Matadayya's retort is simple: he can find the time to come and sell his ancestral land, but not to care for his dying father. The last piece of information is that Shivanna needs the money to set up an English school, now apparently a very lucrative business. Two conflicting values have been established: the care and loyalty of Matadayya, and the venality of Shivanna. And then comes the first title card, which reads: IRYA'S DREAM.

The sections which follow, all with 'dream' in their titles, do not relate the details of a dream or seek to explicate it, but rather to briefly state its essence and explore its implications. In some cases elements are repeated, sometimes with slight variations. This is not to be seen, however, as a detective exercise in sifting the 'truth' from apparent inconsistency or minor contradiction, but rather as an examination of how the same reality might be perceived by different individuals. The major elements of these subsequent 'dream' sections are Guru Siddha and the extraordinarily strong faith in which he is held, especially by Irya and Rudri, and how the nature and value of his advent are inflected or modified—essentially catalytically—by the death of the elder Gowda.

'Irya's Dream' opens quite atmospherically. There is the sound of a conch, conventionally believed to herald the appearance of the Guru Siddha, and encased in darkness, a robed figure bearing a flaming torch coming toward the camera. As he approaches, he calls to Irya. There is, then, a cut to morning, the sunny outside world seen from inside the hut and again internally framed by the doorway. Irya gets up, bright, cheerful and optimistic, and thanks Siddha for appearing in his dream. The lore is that when Siddha appears in a dream, someone has died, and for Irya that means a grave is to be dug. Faith in the infallibility of this is based on the fact that the dream 'has never been wrong.'

With the aim of earning a day's wage, Irya goes to the Gowda's house, where he is bribed by Bhimya, the major factotum of Matadayya, to make himself scarce as Shivanna is about to go out on important work. Presumably, the sight of an untouchable would cast an inauspicious shadow over that work. However, Irya is not to be dismissed so easily, nor will he readily believe the assurance that no one has died. 'Stars will fall from the sky if my dream proves false.' Despite Matadayya's charity, Irya will not budge and has to be unceremoniously dragged out.

However, so confident is Irya in the authenticity of his dream that he spends the money given to him by Matadayya in the toddy shop, then immediately sets about digging the grave. He returns to the house, very tired and a little drunk, expecting his wages, but no one will pay him for digging a grave for someone who has not died. We then see him brooding outside his hut, unable to accept that his dream might have failed him.

It is at this point that the reason for Shivanna's visit comes to the fore—the important work that must not be spoiled by an inauspicious sight, and a work that will, quite unexpectedly, complicate what would be the otherwise simple and natural matter of the death of the elder Gowda. The local landowners gather at the house prior to a meeting with the developers who want their land and seek to negotiate a deal with them. Some are excited at the prospect of instant riches; Shivanna is quietly expectant of being able to fulfil his dream of establishing an English school, while Basanyappa—the cotton grower for whom Rudri labours in the fields—declares himself the odd man out, seeing no advantage for himself in the scheme. This is a matter of concern for Shivanna, for if Basanyappa influences others in joining him, there is the distinct possibility that the deal will fall through. As it turns out this worry is unfounded, and they all eventually go off to negotiate the sale of their land. Just as they are about to leave, the old man dies.

For the devout Matadayya there is no problem. Due protocol must be observed, with religious and social propriety demanding a 15-day period of funerary ritual. The matter of the land deals should be put off until due ceremony has been completed. As far as the landowners—and Shivanna and his wife—are concerned, that is out of the question. They persuade Matadayya that their work will be completed by the afternoon, after which the funerary rites may commence. It is hardly a long delay, and Hema offers to stay back and watch over the corpse. It would seem that a happy compromise has been struck, but simplicity is again thwarted when news comes that there has been some unavoidable delay in negotiations and Shivanna and the other landowners will not be back until the next morning.

Matadayya is greatly perplexed by this. There is no denying his own piety and genuine concern for doing the right thing by his old master, but the force of public opinion must not be underestimated either. He earlier warned Shivanna that if word got out that he had been negligent in observing due protocol, the 'villagers would give you a good slippering'—that is, they would thrash him with their shoes, inflicting both pain and humiliation on him, so serious would his sin be considered.

At this point we have the first of several repetitions, with Irya coming to the house to ask where he should dig the grave. There is a slight variation, in that Matadayya gives the money not directly to Irya but to Bhimya to pass on to him. Again Irya will not leave, refusing to believe that his dream is false, and again he is dragged out. The point here is to underline the importance of denying the death, despite its actuality, for the sake of protecting the reputation of the house, especially Shivanna's stake in it. Even the cleaning women have to be kept away, especially now that the smell of decomposition has started to become evident.

'Rudri's Dream' is introduced with an element of fantasy, though one that is quite different from Irya's. The shot is taken where she gathers water at the edge of the dam. The camera concentrates first on a floating feather, which turns out to have come from the head-dress of the Guru Siddha, whose form we now see under the surface of the water. This is enough for Rudri, who rushes home to assure Irya that the Guru Siddha will be coming tonight. Irya is anxious about not having the money to buy meat and liquor to comply with the basic protocol of hospitality required by Siddhas, but Rudri, well aware that times are tough—an awareness that is well-emphasised by the landowners wanting to sell to the factory development—is confident that people will help pay for the appropriate hospitality in the hope of receiving the Siddha's blessing. She turns out to be right.

The cynical grocer is persuaded by another customer to be generous, arguing that the Siddha might bring good luck to the village. Rudri receives an offering of rice from a woman in the street, hoping that the Siddha will bless her sick mother-in-law. Basanyappa's foreman, Budan, gives her 50 rupees for meat. Later Irya brings home some liquor, for which the toddy seller refused to accept payment. The important point here is that the Siddha is widely believed in and respected, and that people, in times of hardship, genuinely trust in his power to make things a little easier for them.

'Rudri's Dream' now engages with Matadayya's predicament. She passes the big house on the way home and tries to convince Pinki to go inside away from the heat of the sun, but Pinki pleads that the stench in the house makes it unbearable to be inside it. Rudri suspects there is a dead rat somewhere, and while she is looking for it, Matadayya, in some degree of panic, assures her that there is nothing dead there and asks her to go away. In reply to his question about what she has in her basket, she tells him that the Guru Siddha will be coming later. Matadayya—the devout and orthodox Hindu—gives her a 100 rupee note, telling her to ask Siddha to pray for 'the forgiveness of all our sins.'

Rudri's preparations for the visit are obviously painstaking, and then they wait—patiently, expectantly—but there is no sign of their exalted guest. The gravest apprehension is uttered: 'our dreams have started failing.' Irya's faith has taken a severe blow and he refuses to eat. Rudri tells him that he will not sleep if he does not eat, and his blunt reply is, 'If I don't sleep, then I won't dream.' He now sees their dreams as being at the root of their undoing.

Meanwhile, in the Gowda house, the smell of death is getting worse. Somewhat emotionally, Matadayya tries to put the blame on Shivanna: 'You went out on business leaving your father's body to rot.' That, of course, is no longer the point; Shivanna did go on his business trip after the death of his father, and the body is smelling worse by the hour—nothing can be done to change any of that. The point now is the problem of time. Matadayya observes to Shivanna that if the truth were told, declaring that the old man had died the day before, Shivanna would suffer a widespread loss of respect, but the loyal old retainer is uncomfortable with the lie that the elder Gowda died today. However, when the short sequence involving Rudri looking for a dead rat is repeated, Matadayya's gift of 100 rupees might be seen in a face-saving light. The Guru Siddha comes when someone dies; if he is coming tonight, then it will be assumed that someone died today. And so the death is announced as having occurred 'a little while ago.'

There is a shot of Irya squatting near the talisman tree—a tree whose presence is prominent throughout the film—trying to sort it all out in his mind. Then the funeral is arranged and Irya goes to the house. His sense of smell tells him that everything is not clearly above board, and when he starts to voice his suspicions, he is ordered out immediately. Obviously, he knows too much and has become a threat to the esteem in which the family is held, so he is again forcibly removed and beaten.

Irya is determined that the truth will prevail, and so he joins the funeral procession. Since a man of great prestige has died, the funeral is not a meagre affair. There is a sequence showing the floral tributes as well as spoken words of farewell to the corpse, and with fireworks, conches, drums and wind instruments the procession wends its way to the grave dug for it by Irya the day before. But Irya's presence in the funeral procession is not wanted. He does, in fact, join it, and there are some close-up shots of him seriously talking to someone or the other. Then there is a shot of Matadayya directing the two henchmen to remove him. They force him away, and he comes straight back. They spitefully rip his already tattered shirt and chase him away again. Defiantly he comes back and again is seen in earnest conversation with one of the men. He is then dragged away and beaten so severely that he will not try to rejoin the cortege.

This marks the end of the section titled 'Rudri's Dream.' Despite the apparent confusion, the narrative is indeed becoming clearer. There ought to have been a correspondence between the death of the elder Gowda and the coming of the Guru Siddha. The old man did in fact die, but it was the day before. The Siddha should have come to Irya and Rudri that night, but he did not. Seeing that the Siddha comes on the same day on which a person dies, it might be argued that because the Siddha did not come last night, the elder Gowda did not die yesterday; as the Siddha is expected to come tonight, then it is feasible that the old man died today. At least, this is the perception that Matadayya wants people to have. Irya, whose sense of smell, particularly as it pertains to decomposing bodies, is acute, has strong doubts about the tidiness of Matadayya's arrangement of things, so as long as he is present in the funeral procession, the acceptance of that arrangement is vulnerable.

The next section, 'And the Dreams Diverge,' is divided into three subsections that are separated for a second or two by a blank screen. The first subsection opens with Rudri at the talisman tree, looking for Irya. She finds him in a semi-conscious state. Other women help her to carry him home, fanning him, washing him, massaging his hands and feet, and applying a poultice to his severely injured leg. This sequence is followed by shots of Irya lying down and Rudri sitting beside him, worried and compassionate. Then there is the sound of a conch and Guru Siddha appears. He is given a frosty reception. Rudri refuses to serve him and he has to serve himself. She even throws a beaker of water at him, accusingly saying, 'Look at his fate for placing his faith in you.' The Siddha then apologises, pleading that over-indulgence had clouded his mind and so prevented him from coming on the day after he appeared in Irya's dream, the day the elder Gowda did, in fact, die. He is then seen internally framed by the doorway, going out into the darkness and the fog.

The next subsection opens in the same way, with Rudri calling to Irya at the talisman tree. She finds him in the same place, but this time his leg seems broken and she binds splints around it. There is a cut to daytime, and Rudri is seen waiting at the side of the road for Budan, who comes on his motorbike to give her some oil and pills. He also advises her to take Irya to the hospital, even assuring her that Basanyappa would take him on his tiller. The despondent response is, 'He feels let down by Siddha and finds no meaning in living.'

There is an interesting cut showing Budan and Basanyappa riding along the road on the motorbike on their way to Irya's hut. It is clearly a daytime shot, but as they enter the hut, it is very obviously night. The deliberate confusion here suggests at least a degree of unreality, but then Basanyappa makes an extraordinary confession, assuring Irya that the Guru Siddha did indeed come on the right day, but that he had him sent away. His intention was that people like Irya would only become self-reliant if they did not have Siddhas and the like to give them false hopes of miracles and semi-divine intervention in mundane affairs. Budan supports him: 'His intentions were good but things went out of control.' Basanyappa then offers to take Irya to hospital, even to meet the expenses, and receives for his courtesy a jug of water in the face from Irya. Basanyappa's face reflects profound resentment, and this time it is Irya who hobbles out into the night.

The final subsection opens in the same way, with Rudri at the talisman tree calling to Irya. This time her call is answered by cries of anguish. When she gets to him, he sits up and laughs, joking that he is really quite all right. His characteristic defiance shows as he promises to reveal the truth. 'You bastards tried to shut me up!'

There is, then, an emanation of pride and self-respect when Irya decides to discard his ragged shirt and beg for a new one. Rudri gives him some money from the fund for feeding Siddha and tells him to buy a new one. The new shirt is, perhaps, an indication of an upturn in their lives, for when he meets Bhimya and his companion on the road, Bhimya remarks that on top of his new shirt, he might get a new house as well, given the deal worked by the landowners and the developers. There is underlying all of this a sense of the reality that people like Irya and Rudri do not experience upturns in their fortunes.

There is a final section called 'Irya Dreams Yet Again.' We see Rudri watering the rock-hard ground and Irya trying to dig it. It is obvious that getting anything to grow in it would take a miracle. While they are working, the Guru Siddha pays a visit. He tells them that they need to dig a pit along a straight line, and starts unfurling a braided cord to determine that line. The cotton seems to be never-ending, as the Siddha walks on and on toward the horizon. This time the dream signifies nothing but a dream.

Much of the narrative of this film proceeds through binary conflicts, or simple assertions of difference. In this context, the basic one is the distinction acknowledged between caste and outcaste society. This is more stated and assumed, and by no means focal. The visually evident abject poverty of Irya and Rudri might well mark the distinction of a particular economic class, but the unanswered contempt in the throwing of a pot of paint over Irya points to his debased social status. He is indeed at times defiant and persistent, but such hints of strength of character are suppressed by his general submissiveness to his lot and, when he can afford it, his escape into drink. The divide between village and city is played out largely on a personal level. When Shivanna's car is driven through the village, its owner is immediately identified, despite having been away for some months. Indeed, it is probably the only car ever seen in that village street. This urban-rural dichotomy is delightfully set up early in the film by the juxtaposition of Basanyappa's harvester and Shivanna's station-wagon. Much is made, particularly by Matadayya, of Shivanna and his family belonging more to Bangalore than to the village, and Shivanna sees his future in the essentially urban and globalist world of English-language education. The much cosseted and disarmingly forthright little girl is patently out-of-place in this rural environment, engaged in solitary play or complaining blatantly about the pervasive smell. The discord that often seems to prevail between Shivanna and Matadayya neatly personalises the broader tension between religion and expediency, which also embraces in some ways the urban-rural dichotomy. In the rural world, where time seems to move more slowly, religion is more central to life than in the cities, which have so many modern and secular distractions. And of course, the purpose of Shivanna's visit is wholly secular and materialistic; naturally, expediency is central to his values. When a conflict emerges between funerary propriety and commercial dealings, we might also note a conflict between the traditional and the modern where, ironically, the outcaste Irya has a position of potential power. There is also the distinction between the traditional religion of Matadayya and the popular religion of Irya and Rudri; however, that distinction is somewhat obscured by the sympathy for Rudri of many more orthodox people, including Basanyappa and

Budan and even Matadayya, although his sympathy might be more strategic than genuine.

Kanasemba Kudureyaneri might seem notably more mysterious than mundane, and this is in some part due to the technique of telling the same story through different characters. It means that the audience needs to be alert to variations in perception, in emphasis and even in fact, but it does not imply a mystery which has to be unravelled in order to get to the truth. Once certain keys are recognised, a fairly simple basic narrative emerges. Beyond that, the film is concerned with matters that are very much mundanities. Even the Siddha, despite his exotic appearance and elaborate heralding, is mundane enough to confess to over-indulgence in drink and to be treated with a degree of contempt, even having water thrown in his face. The actualities of the death of Gowda are in no way mysterious, despite the arcane protocol to which Matadayya would unquestioningly submit. Indeed, the picture of the body before death and the description of the smell surrounding it are flagrant in their effect, as is the picture of the corpse when *rigor mortis* is setting in, along with the continuing reference to the smell.

There is much in the film's atmospherics that might suggest mystery, but underneath there is a simple story about deception and seeking advantage. Much of the story is shared and interpreted variously; a significant part of it is kept concealed. And just as the dream aspect of the film is perceived variously, so too might the reality—or the mundanity—of the film appeal in a variety of ways to an audience.

12

Acting is Not in My Nature

According to Hindu mythology the god Vishnu had 10 incarnations, each with a particular moral purpose and directions to act in certain sets of circumstances. One such avatar is Kurma, the tortoise, serving to support on his back Mount Mandara in the Churning of the Ocean, an endeavour which took something like 1,000 years and which saved the world from evil. Kurma is remarkable here for his singularity of purpose, steadfast faithfulness and patience. While conflict between gods and demons has a significant place in mythology, it might also be symbolically discerned in human history. In the conflict with foreign imperialism, which was central to India's freedom movement, a Kurma was needed to patiently provide a moral basis with similar singularity of purpose and steadfast faithfulness. It is an easy symbolism to identify Mahatma Gandhi as Kurma, a man who saw the freedom struggle as essentially a moral endeavour. In contemporary India, conscientious nationalists and social commentators have frequently lamented a serious moral decline in society, where the historical equivalents of demons take the forms of corruption, greed and self-interest. Such a decline produces a call for a renewed moral leadership, a Kurma or, let us say, a Gandhi. This is a constant undertone in Girish Kasaravalli's 2011 film, *Kurmavatara* ('The Tortoise, An Incarnation').

One of the truly great lives in human history is that of Mohandas Karamchand Gandhi (1869–1948). However, of considerable historical significance is his death at the hands of a right-wing Hindu fanatic. How people in India and throughout the world reacted to this shocking assassination and its ramifications for the newly independent nation is the subject of a very thought-provoking book by Makarand R. Paranjape, *The Death and Afterlife of Mahatma Gandhi.*[1] Richard Attenborough also sees the death of Gandhi as having some special significance to warrant its bookending his epic *Gandhi* (1982). There is great dramatic impact in this, especially in the visuals of the masses following the funeral procession. Kasaravalli also sees the death as significant enough to open his film, but he does not repeat it in full at the end, nor does he seek to exploit any dramatic impact or insinuate epic import. The point he wants to make has been set up at the beginning and carefully established throughout the film, allowing it to end at the entry into the garden, having gone a long way toward answering some important underlying questions.

This central point bears the suggestion that, with the murder of Gandhi, so much of value in the national psyche—honesty, decency, compassion, justice—was diminished, for the removal of Gandhi created a moral void, allowing corruption to flourish in its multitudinous forms. Along with this suggestion is borne an innocent, almost tentative, musing at the possibility of some kind of avatar of good coming into that moral void. For admirers of Gandhi and those who would place him on a high pedestal in history, his assassination was shocking enough, but particularly sad has been the rapid dwindling of his memory among the people to whose freedom and well-being he devoted his life. Indeed, it is a somewhat perverse irony that the most frequently seen image of the great man is on currency notes. With the dimming of that memory, Gandhian moral values, fundamental in his view to making a worthy society, faded too. His famous philosophy and discipline of *satyagraha*, or 'the force of truth,' has been gradually superseded by expediency, exploitation and the blatant exercise of power, especially against the weak and humble. And so the question of Gandhi's continuing relevance to contemporary India, dealt with so thoroughly in Paranjape's book, is presented forcefully, albeit much more microcosmically, by Girish Kasaravalli in *Kurmavatara.*

---

[1] Makarand R. Paranjape, *The Death and Afterlife of Mahatma Gandhi,* Routledge, 2014.

The opening titles are intercut with some important visual images. There is a close-up of a pocket watch and a hand cleaning it with a cloth. Then there is a close-up of a simple spinning wheel and a hand turning it. Finally a hand is seen to pick up a pair of round, wire-rimmed spectacles. As the hand starts to polish the lenses, the owner's face comes into the picture, lending a negative significance to this brief presentation of images—the man is *not* Gandhi. But while Gandhi himself is not with us, these readily recognisable iconic signs of him do suggest an invulnerability to extinction. Gandhi might be dead, but the historical value of such a man might be believed to live on. So these few visual images establish the import of the film, which is loosely about Gandhi, but more about the meaning and value of Gandhi.

There is a more lengthy sequence intercut with the opening titles, and this portrays a deception. In the style of a biopic or historical drama, we see two young women coming to take an elderly man out of a house and into a garden. The glasses are being worn, the pocket watch is consulted, and the spinning wheel is put aside by the elderly man, who is very much a Gandhi look-alike. What follows is familiar to many as the exterior of the Birla mansion in New Delhi. Gandhi, now frail, is walking very slowly, supported by the two young women. A crowd is assembling, some are coming forward to touch Gandhi's feet, and the cry goes up of 'Victory to Mahatma Gandhi!' The somewhat militarily clad figure of, apparently, the murderer Nathuram Godse steps up to Gandhi, greets him reverentially, then steps back and fires three shots into his chest. But before we get a chance to feel the shock of this horrible brutality, the deception is revealed with a cut to 'Maulana Azad,' 'Nehru' and 'Patel' on a balcony looking on and applauding—not Nathuram Godse's wickedness, of course, but the merit of what has been, in fact, an act. All these people are actors doing what they are doing in front of a film crew who are making—as 'Maulana Azad' tells 'Sardar Patel'—a tele-serial on Gandhi, pointing out, perhaps on Kasaravalli's behalf, that theirs is a small budget tele-serial and should not be compared with the big budget multinational productions that have become so well-known. Slightly disturbing, perhaps, is the fact that the actor playing Gandhi does not get up when 'Cut!' is called, but remains on the ground, clutching his heart, his face contorted in agony. An ambulance is called and the few remaining titles are shown. It might seem that the actor, perhaps under the strain of work, has suffered a heart attack. This scene will not be repeated in full at the end, but by then we will have a very good idea of what ails the actor.

The film now opens with what turns out to be a flashback and continues on from it up to the entry of Gandhi and the two young women into the garden. In this opening scene we see a car entering the driveway of a vast garden in front of the imposing edifice of a grand building—a connection with the Birla mansion and garden, not narrative but purely aesthetic, has been maintained. The car pulls up at the entrance to a government department and two young men get out and enter the building. The momentary prominence of mobile phones suggests a remoteness to the spinning wheel, though it is Gandhi who is on their minds. They have come to meet a clerk, Ananda Rao, who might be a credible Gandhi look-alike, to replace the one who has had to pull out of the tele-serial they are making. They meet with a peremptory rejection from Rao.

Important here is the introduction of Ananda Rao as a potential Gandhi. It is possible to discern a visual resemblance, and we learn of Rao's singular devotion to his work, being told that he always leaves the office late at night. A high shot, taken of Rao after the others have all left, emphasises his solitariness. Another snippet of Gandhian resemblance is his attendance at a prayer meeting on the way home.

We see him arrive at his very humble, lower middle-class home, first doting on his sleeping grandson, Abhi, by affectionately caressing his face and putting a cone of sweets or puffed rice in his hand. He then serves himself his meal. But then the boy wakes up and tells him that he should enjoy what is left in the box of goodies—Chandan, the TV director, determined not to accept Rao's rejection, had come earlier with a bribe. Rao's son and daughter-in-law—Jayu and Kamala—are extremely enthusiastic about Chandan's offer, but it is soon made quite obvious that their sole interest is in getting their hands on the not insubstantial amount of money that the old man would be paid. They seem venal and selfish at the beginning and, as the film progresses, prove themselves categorically to be just that. Rao's affection for his grandson would seem to be his Achilles heel. Jayu argues that the money could be invested in Abhi's future so that he might pursue a professional career, something that had not been possible for himself. He later blames his father for his limited education, but Rao pleads that so much was not possible on his meagre salary, a salary that remained slight, given his scrupulous avoidance of corruption. 'And where did that get you?' counters his son. Some people at this stage might be thinking of the moral basis to the drawn-out clash between Gandhi and his son, Harilal. Nevertheless, Jayu wins this battle, given Rao's fondness for his grandson.

So there is a cut to Rao in a make-up room, being fixed with a bald pate; he wraps a shawl around himself, puts on the wire-rimmed, round-lens glasses, then walks across the screen with a staff. Visually, he passes the screen-test, and there is, at this stage, no indication that his utter lack of experience as an actor will cause immense stress to himself, his family, Chandan and other members of the company.

His first venture in the portrayal of Gandhi is in conference with Azad and Patel, learning of the threats of the intransigent Jinnah in his campaign for the establishment of Pakistan. Chandan is concerned that Rao does not show any appreciation of the gravity of the situation, tutoring him with such nebulous advice as to be 'more emotionally charged.' One might wonder about the value of Chandan's counsel to associate Gandhi's emotion at the prospect of the partition of India with Rao's own emotion at the death of his wife, but this allows another window to open up on Rao, as Jayu tells Chandan that his father showed no emotion when his wife died, putting his job before spending time with her in her last days when she was dying of cancer. We might remember Gandhi's deep and constant love for Kasturba, but we will also remember that his public work always prevailed over his private life. Chandan does not see this vestige of similarity between actor and character, but rather makes tactless humour about Rao, describing him as 'weird.' Rao tries to defend himself by quoting the *Bhagavad Gita's* injunction to treat joy and sorrow as one, only incurring moral pedantry from Chandan and some sharp humiliation that brings a tear to Rao's eye. Chandan is able to exploit this in the interest of his own interpretation of Gandhi in this particular scene. We are starting to see Chandan becoming more and more boorish, more and more of a bully, and we might marvel on noting Rao's constantly respectful and quiet approach to him, in spite of the man's arrogance.

There is a scene in which a very pensive and introspective Rao walks into a public park and children's playground. Jayu follows him in to learn that his father does not want to act any more and will give back the advance that he has been paid. Rao asks Jayu about his mother's suffering in her last days, and Jayu is not at all sparing in candour in answering his questions. Rao's sense of guilt becomes manifest, and the truths with which he has just been furnished will continue to trouble him. We might well assume that there is no possibility of Jayu allowing the advance payment to be returned, but at this stage it does not become a matter of argument. Of poetic interest in this scene is the discovery of a tortoise wandering about the playground, and Abhi picks it up and takes it home. It seems to inspire some response from the brooding Ananda Rao, who tells his grandson the story of the Kurma avatar of Lord Vishnu. Kamala does not see any moral dimension in the new pet and simply orders that it be kept outside. To read something symbolic in this would not be going astray. However, the tortoise is not used in the film as any kind of focal symbol; it is more an occasional visual reminder of the possibility of moral redemption, for which Kamala and Jayu never see the need.

In the earlier discussion on *Bannada Vesha* it was noted that in India there is often a popular conflation of actor with character. Actors-turned-politicians, such as N. T. Rama Rao, have been able to successfully exploit to great political advantage their backgrounds as deities or epic heroes. In Mrinal Sen's *Akaler*

Sandhane,[2] a cataclysmic lack of tact is shown in asking a village girl to play a prostitute in a film about the Bengal Famine. And so in *Kurmavatara* it should come as no surprise that Ananda Rao will undergo some degree of public transformation due to his association with Gandhi. Even on a relatively minor level, we will see later that the pet shop proprietor, Iqbal, in being cast as Godse, will stir up what might have been the makings of communalist friction, and so is removed from the role. Despite his renowned dedication to his job, the clerical Rao must take time off from his office to enable the theatrical Rao to pursue his new work. It might be expected that his boss in the office would discipline him in some way, but in fear that this might be taken the wrong way in public, he congratulates Rao and expresses his pleasure at his playing the role of Gandhi. He also delights in the fact that an old pin-up girl of his, Sushila, is playing the role of Kasturba, and gives Rao a diary (almost defunct, as the year is drawing to a close) to give her as a mark of his admiration for her.

It is Kurma who, as it were, brings Rao to Iqbal. A simple and effective narrative connection is made by Rao's visit to a pet shop to buy food for Abhi's tortoise. He is recognised by Iqbal as the TV Gandhi. A coincidence now emerges as Iqbal tells Rao that he is the son of Mohammed Ghouse, a former boss of Rao, who has been in retirement for some years. Rao responds by acknowledging the warm affection with which he remembers the older man. Iqbal has a photograph taken of himself and Rao, and requests the clerk-cum-actor to try to arrange a small part for him in the serial.

It is through Iqbal that Rao meets Suresh, who later prevails upon him to be by his side at a meeting over a dispute with the municipal council. The perceived Gandhi persona then is to be exploited in the hope of achieving a desired outcome in a disputation with local government. The dispute concerns the council's refusal to renew the licence for his shop without the bribe of 3,000 rupees. Rao is embarrassed to learn that the official reason for refusing to

[2] 'In Search of Famine,' 1980.

grant the renewal is that the shop is a tobacco shop, situated near a school. Rao's embarrassment is justified, although the matter of the bribe remains a live issue. Apparently Suresh is successful and Rao is brought home in an auto-rickshaw, bearing gifts. While Jayu is delighted, Rao is dismayed to find 500 rupees among them. The notion of remuneration for moral action is evidently repugnant to him, as indeed it would have been to Gandhi.

It is in regard to activism in local government that Rao's office boss puts his foot down, ordering him, as a civil servant, not to engage in agitation with local government. He obviously misses the irony of his injunction, 'Limit your Gandhi to the TV screen!'. To limit in this way is to minimise Gandhi and his teachings. Indeed, for many, it is to banish, for one does not have to turn on the TV at all, let alone watch the channel that is screening the Gandhi serial. The sentiment is clearly implied that what is confined to the realm of entertainment is that which does not matter; let it into the real world and it can become a nuisance, or worse.

There will be further requests from neighbours and friends of Jayu for Rao-cum-Gandhi to support them in their disputes with the municipality, and Rao will judiciously turn them down while he is able to define himself clearly as a clerk, as a family man, and as an actor in a particular role. Nevertheless, he will continue to be stopped in the street for photos and autographs. The almost reclusive clerk is becoming a public figure.

At his first meeting with Chandan he expresses his ignorance of Gandhi, who has never been relevant in his chosen walk of life (making him, incidentally, one of a great many half a century or more after the Mahatma's death). He is given the role of Gandhi nevertheless, but soon that ignorance becomes apparent, as does his lack of acting experience. Jayu then brings him some books on Gandhi and his philosophy in the hope that his father might bring more credibility to his role. Initially this might be heartening to Chandan, but in fact, it will turn out to be a thorn in his side. As Ananda Rao studies and thinks about Gandhi more and more, not only is his own ignorance diminished but his growing knowledge also highlights the limitations of Chandan's expertise on the subject. Chandan seems to be able to justify compromising historical accuracy in order to achieve dramatic effect, but Rao is concerned that such creativity might be offensive to Truth. Here, and in subsequent disagreements of the kind, Chandan dismisses him ungraciously. Later, when they argue over Gandhi and the Kasturba–Harilal dispute, Chandan reacts with further nastiness, yet is forced to admit to his assistant that Rao is probably right. During their altercation on the appropriate degree of emotion to be shown by Gandhi, Chandan lectures Rao with the extraordinary statement: 'Everyone has his own version of Gandhi. This is *my* Gandhi. Just do as I tell you.' A well-known and towering public figure is not to be owned and then manipulated to suit the owner's interests, but is to be learnt from, to be inspired by, and to be followed. One might suspect that Chandan is making up with bombast what he lacks in learning and talent. However, Rao now reads Gandhi instead of attending prayer meetings, and it would seem that his reading starts opening up a window on himself. 'As I started playing Gandhi, I realised how much I had wronged my wife and my son,' he admits to Sushila.

There is a shot of Ananda Rao sitting on a hill above the city, looking down on the world, as it were. The ebullient and self-possessed Rao is becoming more brooding, more introspective. He has always been an upright man, and his distancing himself from any corrupt practice, his devotion to honest work, his putting duty before self and his attendance at prayer meetings are all indications of a life guided by truth and notions of what is good. Now it would seem that the personal morality that had so long been internalised is being examined and extended into a broader social context. It is increasingly applicable not only to himself but also to his relations with his family, his superiors on the set and in the office, and even with Gandhi himself, for it is only right to portray the man honestly, notwithstanding any shortcoming in acting talent.

It is possible to approach any set of teachings as one might approach a smorgasbord, taking what one is disposed toward and rejecting that which is unappealing. Thus, the appearance of a Gandhian look-alike in a council office, where there has been mention of paying bribes for services rendered, can spark a certain action;

and being there, not perceived as a Gandhi look-alike but known to be a civil servant, can spark an appeal to a different propriety. Suresh might rightly oppose the demand for a bribe, but he is cunning in not revealing to his 'Gandhi' the true reason for the council's discomfort with his shop. Jayu also picks and chooses, encouraging his friends' admiration for his father's revival of *satyagraha,* and having them believe that he can lead them in an agitation for better roads and clean water, for example. At home Jayu tries to persuade his father to change his mind, though Rao suspects an ulterior motive. There is a shot of Rao reading Gandhi late one night, and then a cut to a shot of Jayu at his computer, a mass of money figures on the screen. Ananda Rao goes to his son's room and tells him that helping people is certainly good, but accepting commissions for that help is not. It is now clear that Jayu and Kamala are using the old man for monetary gain. Jayu patronisingly disparages his father's study of Gandhi, which he, in fact, had instigated. In fact, Jayu has earlier admitted to having signed a contract for his Gandhi-look-alike father to do a TV commercial for washing powder. Again it is just an appearance of a photographed face associated with an inane commercial, though cheap and venal nevertheless.

When we first meet Ananda Rao, he is wearing the standard Western-style trousers and shirt. As he becomes more and more imbued with Gandhian thought, there are a number of incidental shots revealing a gradual change in this appearance. The first of these sees Rao in a shop purchasing a *khadi kurta,* or Indian-style homespun shirt. He still wears his Western trousers, however. A little later, we see him wearing a different *kurta.* Soon we notice that the trousers have been discarded in favour of the traditional Indian *dhoti.* There is also a brief sequence showing him buying a new pair of glasses, choosing plain-rimmed, round-lens ones. Given that the *dhoti* is tied in a style not characteristically Gandhian, it would seem that Rao is not attempting a Gandhian metamorphosis so much as he is trying to identify, outwardly as well as inwardly, with the traditional Indian values espoused by the great man.

One person from whom Rao gets no carping criticism and who makes no demands on him is Sushila, the actress playing Kasturba.

She is an accomplished actress, notably lacking in flamboyant ego, quiet, gentle, understanding and sympathetic. On set they are married, and off the set they form a warm friendship. She gives him advice on acting, he shares with her his growing understanding of Gandhi. She is, we are told, some 10 years older than he is, yet she too confesses an ignorance of the Father of the Nation, pointing out that she has worked in cinema all her life to the exclusion of all else. She has not even married and raised a family. Given the obvious loveliness of their friendship—and its therapeutic value for Rao—it is very sad that Jayu and Kamala should sully it by accusing Rao of cultivating a scandal by his association with Sushila off the set, and by visiting her at her home. He pleads that he finds peace when he is with her, which provokes Kamala's selfish retort, 'Can't you find peace in this house?' His candid reply motivates his son and daughter-in-law to stand on whatever dignity they can contrive and move out to Kamala's parents' place, leaving Ananda Rao alone.

The petulant walkout is prompted by more than Rao's friendship with Sushila. There is an earlier scene in which Rao and Jayu are sitting in the back seat of a taxi, going home, Jayu gleefully counting his father's money—50,000 rupees. This apparently innocent act blows up into something quite sinister after Jayu refuses to give the money back to his father, determined to invest it on the stock exchange and give it back after it has brought in a windfall. Rao counsels against such naiveté, but Jayu is deaf to his reason. In his determination to get and invest money, Jayu suggests that his father demand a 'fat advance' on the threat of withdrawing from the serial. Characteristically Rao replies, 'Is that ethical?' Jayu is steadfast in his refusal to return the money to the man who earned it; Rao refuses to eat until he gets his money back. Eventually Kamala plays the peacemaker and gives him the money. How she intends to get it back to Jayu is not made clear, for the move to her parents' house occurs in the meantime, as do further developments.

The role of Iqbal as the killer of Gandhi occurs, naturally, right at the end of the serial, and it is in the later part of the film that a fuss blows up about his being cast in that role. Misgivings are first aired when Iqbal's father and former boss of Ananda Rao,

Mohammed Ghouse, comes to visit Rao. They go to a teashop, where Ghouse confesses to Rao his discomfort at his son being cast as Godse. He does not offer much of an explanation, still less of an argument, but circumstantial evidence does help to establish Ghouse's unease. Again we might note the potential for conflation of character with actor, so it could simply be that he does not want his son to be associated with the truly wicked act of murdering a good man. But there is more to it. Gandhi was a devout Hindu and Iqbal is a Muslim, and so there might be in this a sniff of communal tension. Moreover, Godse was also a Hindu, a member of a right-wing extremist organisation with successors in contemporary India. And so the bullies who want Iqbal removed from the role come with threats to Chandan, complaining that one of their religion should have been given the part. While Mohammed Ghouse might not want the shame of his son being associated with Nathuram Godse, the bullies (whose leader has to be reminded of the killer's name) do not want a Muslim to be associated with what they see as the credit pertaining to the crime. It is sad that one of the major planks of Gandhi's social philosophy was to dispel Hindu–Muslim friction, but that decades after his death communal tension is still a live bomb that is waiting to go off in many parts of the country. However, it is not really due to a concern for communal harmony that the decision is made to take the role from Iqbal but the fact of the bullies' threats to damage immensely expensive equipment and the producer's fear of losing money. Nevertheless, the communal reality is still there. There is a lovely shot at the end of Rao's visit with Iqbal to Tatayya, the old freedom fighter, who declares with regret that he can do nothing to help in getting the bullies to rescind their threats. 'No one listens to me any more.' A crestfallen Iqbal is consoled by Rao in an exceptionally warm and affectionate embrace, suggesting the lovely irony of the melding of the Hindu 'mahatma' with the Muslim 'would-be killer.'

The narrative direction that will take us to the final shot in the film—though seen only at the beginning—is now given form. Disappointed as well as lonely, Rao is seen in the empty house with only the tortoise for company. He decides to take it to Abhi at his son's in-laws' house. His reception there is exceptionally frosty and punctuated with bursts of hostility and plain rudeness, most notably from Kamala. After some moments of tension he learns that Jayu has been arrested and locked up on charges involving the issuing of post-dated cheques. Curiously, Kamala and her parents see Rao as the villain. If he had not been so mean in refusing to part with his money, everyone would have been happy. Jayu has probably acted more naively than criminally, but Rao pleads that he had always had cause to worry about the integrity of his son's actions, about which he was so secretive. No one is moved by this, and Rao is quite brashly told by Kamala to leave and to take the tortoise with him as she does not want it—again there is a gentle irony in this. As he leaves the house, Rao presents a figure of great sadness. He now has to deal with the invidious problem of the conflict of morality with family happiness. Can joy be brought back to the little boy only by indulging his father's shady deals?

Rao visits his son in the lockup and is greeted with 'Your beliefs and ideologies have finally won.' Jayu says this accusingly, as though good had no right to prevail over shady expediency. There is a long moment of silence as Ananda Rao looks pityingly and lovingly at his son. He offers to pay 50,000 rupees immediately, but as the court will be closed for the weekend, they will have to wait a few more days. Suresh then learns that as a required First Information Report has not been filed, another 10,000 rupees 'will do the trick.' This is another severe blow to Rao, who is appalled at the prospect of paying a bribe. In a later scene Sushila expresses her sympathy for the terrible dilemma in which Rao finds himself. If he pays the bribe, he betrays his dearly held moral principles; if he stands for principle, he loses his family. After this nothing more of the dilemma is verbalised; all Rao's emotional and moral anguish is read from his face and his actions. He goes to Iqbal's shop to find his father there in his son's absence. Mohammed Ghouse tells him to leave the envelope he has brought for Iqbal on the table. Rao's trembling hand and the tremor in his voice make it clear that the envelope contains the 50,000 rupees as well as the bribe. His son has brought him down.

Rao's mood has become very introspective as the end of his shooting approaches, and this is shown in several shots, such as a high shot of him lying down, lost in thought, and the shot from the spinning wheel to the seated Gandhi, his face similarly drawn. Clearly, his mind is troubled and far from the job at hand, shooting the last scene of the film. Needless to say, the work does not go well, the final scene needing more than a dozen takes before Chandan is satisfied. The tension is added to by Bhuvan, a big name actor, gracing the set with his star qualities as the replacement for Iqbal. He arrives almost in caricature, wearing sunglasses, talking on a mobile phone and waving to his admirers. He treats Ananda Rao patronisingly, even rudely, and enjoys a brief chat with Chandan about how bad an actor Rao is. At this point Rao approaches Bhuvan and makes what might be thought to be the conclusive confession of the film, admitting that he is, indeed, a bad actor and that it was a grave mistake for him to have tried to play Gandhi. 'Now I've lost even the moral right.' We now have the explanation, if one were needed, for his collapse in the enactment of the shooting. As we saw the end at the beginning, the final titles roll just as Gandhi and the women step out into the garden.

There have been more than 20 feature films made on some aspect or other of pre-independence India involving the character of Gandhi; there have been relatively few focussing on Gandhi himself. There is Attenborough's classic biopic, of course, and a very well-made film on Gandhi's early life by Shyam Benegal, *The Making of the Mahatma* (1996), is a worthy addition to the Gandhi filmography. An American film, *Nine Hours to Rama* (directed by Mark Robson, 1963), deals specifically with the assassination, while *Gandhi, My Father* (directed by Feroz Abbas Khan, 2007) deals with the very sad relationship between Gandhi and his son, Harilal. There have also been a few imaginative workings of the Gandhi persona, such as A. Balakrishnan's *Mudhalvar Mahatma* ('Welcome Back, Gandhi,' 2014), a popular film which has Gandhi returning to contemporary India, and the great commercial success that was Rajkumar Hirani's *Lage Raho Munna Bhai* ('Carry On, Munna Bhai,' 2006). It is the latter that might be said to bear some similarity to *Kurmavatara*—as well as a world of difference. There is the openly confessed ignorance of Gandhi in the central character, and there is the keystone element of gradual conversion to Gandhian values that is based, as in *Kurmavatara,* on studying books on and by Gandhi to obviate the confessed ignorance. Whereas Munna Bhai enjoys an ultimate gain in the love of a beautiful young woman, Ananda Rao loses everything. *Kurmavatara* is far more dense, and examines character development much more thoroughly and incisively, and here lies the strength of Kasaravalli's film. Nothing happens by miracle or short-cut in the development of Rao. As the film progresses, he is revealed increasingly as a troubled soul, more and more alone and, in the end, sadly lonely. More than anything, it is the unquestionable credibility of this character that gives to the film its compelling strength.

13

India is the Biggest Story of All

Two years after making *Kurmavatara,* Girish Kasaravalli made the first of two feature-length documentaries. While both works bear the marks of a master filmmaker, they also offer insight into Kasaravalli the intellectual. One is on a writer, the other on a fellow filmmaker, and while the subject of each is prominent, both films paint a substantial picture of Kasaravalli the filmmaker as thinker, comfortable in the intellectual pursuit of interrogating art, the artist, and his world.

Ananthamurthy—Not a Biography but a Hypothesis (2012) is an exploration of the mind and work of eminent Kannada writer and thinker Udupi Rajagopalacharya Ananthamurthy (1932–2014). Much of the substance of the film is given in commentaries by a number of experts familiar with the writer's work and his significance in the continuing history of Indian society. These talk-to-the-camera pieces are short enough to avoid heaviness and substantial enough to be informative and provoke creative thinking. One might also note the visually appealing physical settings in which Kasaravalli places his commentators. There are also a number of talk-to-the-camera pieces featuring Ananthamurthy himself, reading from his own poetry or expatiating his thoughts, and given their worth as primary material, these pieces are invaluable, as they also provide a wonderful window into the writer's personality. There are many simply visual passages presenting Ananthamurthy's (and Kasaravalli's) Karnataka—its architecture, its gardens and jungles, its rivers and its rain. One segment of the film is based on Ananthamurthy's novel, *Samskara,*[1] and several segments are

[1] The film was made in 1970 by Pattabhi Rama Reddy.

dramatised extracts from the novel *Bharathipura* and the short story *Prashne*. There is also a brief interview with Ananthamurthy's wife, Esther, and many visual snippets of his domestic and family life. The film does get a bit weighty at times, and so all this variety effectively mitigates that potential to detract from the film's appeal. Nevertheless, there can be no avoiding the fact that the appeal of any work on a prominent intellectual is likely to be more particular than popular.

The film has a beautiful pre-titles sequence with a first-person commentary given by Kasaravalli himself. The opening shots are above the cloud and fog that are hanging over a lush, green valley, and then there is a focus on the monsoon sky and the rain falling on the luxuriant jungle. Kasaravalli's voiceover then tells us that his memory of a childhood in Karnataka is dominated by the monsoon. He recalls the dense greenery, the paddy fields and the sparse housing, noting that his life out of school-time was necessarily a solitary one. In that solitude he would lose himself in Kannada literature, and in this pursuit as a boy in the 1960s he encountered the man who would change his life. He met U. R. Ananthamurthy in the pages of his story, *Ghatashraddha*. So great was the story's impact on him that he gave up his study of pharmacy to train to be a filmmaker and, in a relatively short time, make his own *Ghatashraddha*. The first shot of Ananthamurthy is of a smiling, jolly man seated on a swing, suggesting, perhaps, the extensive happiness for Kasaravalli that came from that literary encounter. It is not until almost 15 minutes into the film that a title card tells us what might have been revealed at the beginning (though the placement of it is neither here nor there): Ananthamurthy's writings include six novels, 42 short stories, five collections of poetry, 14 collections of socio-cultural essays, a play, and a number of translations. The simple facts speak to a considerable degree of fertility and a variety of forms; the expert participants in the documentary will attest to the quality and value of the work.

The opening titles are accompanied by a vertical sequence of photographs that move upward on the left of the screen, depicting Ananthamurthy in the presence of luminaries, enjoying the company of family and friends, and being feted. The easy impression is of a happy man and a man of significance and value. In the pre-titles sequence, Kasaravalli started by establishing the importance of Ananthamurthy to his life through *Ghatashraddha*, and now he is suggesting the man's importance both in a domestic sense and in the public and national forum.

There are some shots placing Ananthamurthy in the context of his home and his marriage, and then he reads one of his poems in which the monsoon prompts memory and the natural world fuses with the erotic. Poetry is the most difficult literary form to translate, and a worthy translation needs more than a competent subtitler. Here, and in other poems presented in the film, the rendering into English may be technically correct, but the product is not a good poem in English. Hence, it is difficult for those not familiar with Kannada to significantly appreciate Ananthamurthy as a poet.

Two pieces of expert commentary follow, both aiming to encapsulate a notion of the value of U. R. Ananthamurthy. The first is given by the renowned political psychologist and social theorist, Ashis Nandy, and the second by the eminent social scientist, Shiv Visvanathan. Nandy is quite assured in declaring Ananthamurthy to be one of the foremost intellectuals of independent India. He recognises the great variety of sources of his thinking, and also notes the originality of his method of marshalling his ideas in the language of literature. Visvanathan describes him as a man of 'outrageous experiments,' citing his extraordinary ability to link the local with the global. He notes the man's many-sidedness—academic, socialist activist and administrator (noting his long list of directorships and chancellorships)—and hails his combination of all this as the mark of a storyteller for whom 'India is the biggest story of all.' He concludes, intriguingly, that India is not a geographical term, 'but a metaphor.'

There is a brief visual interlude of Ananthamurthy at home with some of his family, and then the film proceeds to a new expert commentator, whose ideas will be taken up by Ananthamurthy himself. The literary essayist and critic, C. N. Ramachandran, sees Ananthamurthy as a 'staunch modernist,' most notable for his exposure of arcane and often corrupt religious traditions of India, the divisiveness of caste, and the pointless rituals that cloud Hindu society. There is a visual blend to Ananthamurthy's study where he himself takes up the point, claiming that his works are well-founded in reality and set in historical time.

He then comments specifically on his great novel, *Samskara*.[2] This work is an excellent example of C. N. Ramachandran's vision of Ananthamurthy uncovering Hindu obscurantism. *Samskara* looks at the customs and habits of a community of Brahmans and candidly exposes their superstitions and prejudices, venality and hypocrisy, rivalry and bloody-mindedness. It also comes to focus on one man's mid-life crisis. Ananthamurthy describes it as both realistic and allegorical, having an epic quality emanating from the mystery of so much in village life. The writer tells of the need to steer between writing that is too realistic, so becoming banal and prosaic, and too symbolic, so becoming vague. He aims to give 'a sense of being in time and beyond time.' His comments are interrupted by a clip from Reddy's film where we see, in stark black and white, Chandri rushing to the house of Praneshacharyra to inform him of the death of Naranappa, a wayward Brahman whose past deeds—including keeping the low-caste Chandri as a mistress—and their seeming impropriety form the substance of the contentious uncertainty that is at the core of the first half of the novel.

From the top of an archway in a high stone wall the camera slowly comes down to show two men sitting before another archway, with greenery in the background and the foreground. The writer and academic N. Manu Chakravarthy acknowledges that Ananthamurthy works within historical time and other frames of reality, but argues that the writer is therefore trapped in the temporal; in locating his narrative in historical time, he makes it clear that the moment has 'eternal manifestations.'

There is a cut to a pan shot, moving from the left of screen over lush green treetops and the intricately tiled roof of a large house. A group of children are playing around an ancient sculpture. There

---

[2] 1965. English translation: *Samskara. A Rite for a Dead Man*, tr. A. K. Ramanujan (New Delhi: Oxford University Press, 1976).

is only the sound of birds and then temple bells. Ananthamurthy's voiceover is talking about his forebears, and a black and white photograph appears, showing his parents. The camera takes in the outer buildings and the adjacent jungle as Ananthamurthy relates how they were culturally rich but monetarily very poor. He speaks of his mental growth during his high-school and college years when he confronted Darwinism and then Gandhi, noting particularly Gandhi's temple entry movement on behalf of the Untouchables. Then came Leninism and frequent engagement with communists. He also makes the point that ideas were discussed for their own sake, with practicalities not having much appeal.

Interest now turns to the novel *Bharathipura*.[3] To suggest the everyday aspect of the novel there is a close shot of rain falling in a puddle on a broken road, and a pair of bare legs with sandaled feet coming toward it, then jumping over it. This is the central character of the novel, Jagannatha, who, we are told in this cinematic representation of some of the opening chapter, preferred to jump over puddles rather than to walk around them. We are also told that nearby is the temple town of Bharathipura, as the camera looks down and extensively over an actual town of similar appearance. We note mossy roof tiles, walls with patches of plaster missing, and a labyrinth of roads and lanes at irregular angles, and we are told of unpleasant smells. Women are cooking throughout the day in smoky kitchens, while men sit and watch the pilgrim visitors to the town. The narrator tells us that Lord Manjunatha—the god of the temple of Bharathipura—has 'spread his tentacles' throughout this town, and the question asked is: In such a place, is any action possible that might make one feel part of history? Jagannatha, recently returned from some years in England, is seen reading from a letter that he is writing to his English friend, Margaret, in which he declares that life is no longer creative in Bharathipura, a place where nothing ever happens. He blames the hold of Manjunatha—'a cancer'—over the town, and for creativity to occur, the cancer must

[3] 1973. Susheela Punitha's English translation goes by the same name (a town).

be destroyed. 'Unless we destroy God we will never be creative.' We might discern a similarity with *Samskara,* which develops the notion of the stultifying stranglehold of religious tradition on the human condition.

After a little more of Nandy and Visvanathan, we are given an indication of Ananthamurthy the activist with some very brief clips of him involved in the 2001 movement to save the river Tunga and a protest meeting in 2002 against illegal mining. There is then a picture of him addressing a Booker Prize programme in 2013. All of this leads into some commentary from S. R. Vijayashankar, whose opening words, heard over a shot or two of some items of classical Indian sculpture, acknowledge that although Ananthamurthy was a teacher of English literature throughout his life, he was never actually taken by Western ideas, but was greatly attracted to Indian philosophy. However, there can be discerned in his work an urge for fusion: of East and West, politics and individualism, socialism and existentialist philosophy. He also stresses the importance in the work of Ananthamurthy of the difference between Western and Eastern societies, as seen in the distinctions of two social ideals: the 'civilised man' (or gentleman) in the West and the 'saint' in the East. The former suggests the external aspect of a person, while the latter focusses on the internal; moreover, with the latter, there is a harmonious integration of the external and the inner self.

There is a cut to a title card announcing *The Wrinkles on Grandpa's Shoulder, 1989,* followed by a shot of an old man, his upper body bare and revealing a very wrinkly pair of shoulders, followed by a shot of a little boy with a bubble pipe being taken along on the shoulders of another old man. Shots follow highlighting paths—walked on, run along, cycled on—through fields and forests, in sunshine and in rain, all symbolising memories of discovery and guidance, mapped out by the wrinkles on an old man's shoulder.

H. Raghavendra Rao says that Ananthamurthy explores his own experiences through his fiction and interprets the external world in his poetry. (There is a shot of some of his books on the coffee table.) It is more usual the other way around—fiction for the external and poetry for the internal. Conventional aspects of poetry—rhythm, lyricism, emotionality—are underplayed in his verse, which, Rao holds, is controlled more by the intellect. Rao then asserts the uniqueness of Ananthamurthy's poetry in contemporary Kannada literature.

There is a short sequence of Ananthamurthy happily presiding over a family gathering, and then N. Manu Chakravarthy returns to the screen to talk about Ananthamurthy the thinker, as distinct from the creative writer. He says that his writing is exceptionally perceptive of the spirit of the times, and there is much in his language that is subversive of tradition and any uncritical acceptance of it.

Another title card comes up: *Ideas of the Backyard and the Front Yard Enrich Indian Literature.* A right to left pan shot takes in paddy fields and jungle and houses tucked away in between, finally coming to rest on the courtyard of a magnificent home in the traditional style, rain constantly dripping. It is here that Ananthamurthy's voiceover tells us that 'backyard' and 'front yard' belong to a metaphor he uses when talking about literature. On the veranda is a group of about 10 men sitting engaged in conversation or reading the newspaper. The talk, we are told, is of 'important' things—politics, epic philosophy, and the like. The camera passes through an inner room in which children may gather before moving into the backyard where a number of women are drawing water from the well, washing kitchen utensils and talking about domestic affairs. On one level it is a truly sexist distinction, representing the privileged position of men and the servile role of women; however, Ananthamurthy describes the backyard as the 'real world' and the front yard as the 'world of ideas.' The backyard develops its own epics which in time blend with those of the front yard. He describes the regional languages of India as being invigorated by the backyard. N. Manu Chakravarthy takes up the idea, pointing out that non-mainstream literature—that of the developing world, of tribal and Dalit people, for example—can be described as backyard literature. For Ananthamurthy it is important that the long-suppressed voices of the backyard be heard. Shiv Visvanathan applies the theory to Ananthamurthy the storyteller, who must be a perceptive listener and maintain a love for gossip. Thus, as Visvanathan concludes, the writer becomes part of the story.

There follows a brief interlude with the camera behind a seated Ananthamurthy looking through glass doors into his garden, absorbed in classical music, a shot that gives a lovely suggestion of Ananthamurthy's quest for harmony. The sequence concludes with a shot of Ananthamurthy's reflection in three panes of glass, as S. R. Vijayashankar asserts the three aspects of Ananthamurthy's persona: teacher, activist and thinker. The thinker searches for metaphors and new concepts. The metaphors pervade his creative work while the concepts form the basis of his critical writing, and he mentions Ananthamurthy's original style of blending tradition and modernity. (Here, the commentary accompanies a very happy photograph of the speaker and Ananthamurthy.) Thus, the old no longer remains old, nor does the new remain new but makes way for the renewal of the old. Hence, the classical is given new life in the modern.

Attention is again directed to *Bharathipura*. A dramatisation of a small part of the novel shows the same actor as seen earlier walking through the architecturally impressive temple of Manjunatha—the focal point and foundation of the economy of the town of Bharathipura—musing over his belief that no social or cultural progress is possible within the constraints of traditional religion. Jagannatha then reveals his view that significant change would be initiated if he led a party of Untouchables into the temple. There are some very appealing visuals in this sequence: various shots of the temple, both internal and external, its colonnades and roofing, the house set at the end of the jungle facing lush greenery, more rain, and Jagannatha sitting by the fast-flowing river. Then we return to book-lined studies, with Ashis Nandy expressing the view that Ananthamurthy's views would be more appealing to an African or Asian reader than to a Western one, and then the Bengali critic Samik Bandyopadhyay mentioning Ananthamurthy's overarching interest in culture, especially the connection between 'the culture of the community' and 'the culture of history.' He expresses the belief that Ananthamurthy is still looking for a realm of shared experience beyond the barriers imposed 'by the so-called civilising process,' where culture 'does not degenerate into dogma.'

There is a cut to a shot of Ananthamurthy at work, and then comes the voiceover of the eminent litterateur Ashok Vajpeyi, declaring Ananthamurthy to be a champion of the dignity and freedom of literature. From this comes Ananthamurthy's belief that writing itself is action, particularly social action. He refers to the prominence of Indian writing in English, noting that the best literature is, in fact, written in the writer's own language, and this does not exclude the less well-known languages, such as those of the tribal people of India. This is immediately taken up by Ananthamurthy, declaring that the choice of language in which one writes is not just a cultural choice but a political one. He asserts here that Indian democracy depends on the multiplicity of the nation's languages.

There follows another domestic interlude, with Ananthamurthy and his wife admiring the greenery beside their terrace. We learn from Esther Ananthamurthy's voiceover that her husband comes from Brahman orthodoxy while her family was liberal Christian, and she talks a little of the dissension between the two families over the couple's proposed union.

Ananthamurthy then remembers his grandfather's interest in cowrie shells as an aide to the prediction of the future, and the pleasure that children take in playing with the shells to cultivate manual dexterity that can be quite remarkable. Just as the shells fall without design or purpose, sometimes the randomness of words creates unintended meanings. A title card, *Negotiating Poetry: a leap into the unknown ... 2009*, introduces the reading of another poem, one which expresses the fascination of a child for cowrie shells. The accompanying visuals focus on a little girl playing very skilfully, tossing and catching the shells as they fall to the floor. One interesting shot here shows the shells turning into alphabetical characters as they reach the floor, underlining the association of cowrie shells and words in the mind of Ananthamurthy with a focus on the notion of chance, of randomness.

The camera focusses for a few seconds on a couple of waves in the river progressing downstream, then draws back to reveal the big rocks on the bank. The voiceover is of C. N. Ramachandran, who is speaking of the changes wrought on Indian society by globalisation and liberalisation, leading Ananthamurthy to launch a strong attack on the West and its values and interests. There is a cut to a title card carrying an image of the face of Ananthamurthy, and a caption comes up on it: *WRITING IS A POLITICAL ACT, NOT A MERE CONTEMPLATION.* Ananthamurthy appears now to articulate a very subjective theory of literature, declaring that any idea may be used to explore the self, becoming a pursuit of truth and inviting the reader to critically engage with it. Good writing is more questioning than didactic.

Another title card introduces the short story, *Prashne* ('Quest,' 1960). This dramatisation concerns the blind old Shankarayya who, in deference to his Brahman tradition, will not condone the marriage of his niece to Ranga, a man presumably of a lower caste. After the death of his sister, he has brought up the girl, Sharade, with great affection, but now, it would seem, he will deny her the ultimate happiness in marrying the man she loves. Ranga, in soliloquy, questions the value of tradition (and, perhaps, of Shankarayya himself) in noting a number of tangible things that have had their day: the camera takes in the great timber pillars and beams of the old house, the safe placed in a corner, an idol of the god Ganapati, the clock slowly ticking life away; Ranga declares them symbols of evil and death as the camera focusses on a nest of spiders. He asserts that everything should be destroyed after it loses its utility. And finally Sharade, also in soliloquy, searches her mind to find peace in her uncle's faithfulness, in Ranga's love, in love in general, ultimately submitting to the simple subjectivity that is awoken in her heart at the sound of his voice. 'I can't live without him.' The essence of the story is a confrontation of tradition with modernity and the quest for harmony. Sharade's wish is not for one force to triumph over another but to find a way in which she might find happiness with both her uncle and her beloved.

Title cards appear now to inform us of the major awards won by Ananthamurthy, and some of the important positions held by him in universities, the Indian Institute of Social Sciences, the Sahitya Akademi, the National Book Trust, and the Film and Television Institute of India. Another title card announces Kasaravalli's first film, *Ghatashraddha* (1977), which was based on Ananthamurthy's 1962 story. The voiceover now belongs to Kasaravalli himself. He reminds us that the story started a more than 40-year association with the great man—'individual, writer, thinker and cultural force.' The voice comes over a brief scene in *Ghatashraddha,* a shot of Kasaravalli sitting on the floor of the temple where *Bharathipura*'s Jagannatha had sat earlier, and during a family gathering in Ananthamurthy's home, also seen earlier. Kasarvalli acknowledges his own growth in admiration of Ananthamurthy's intellectual originality, referring to his holistic thinking in which metaphors of history and tradition reflect social complexities and provide a link between past and future. This kind of approach has greatly influenced Kasaravalli's own thinking. 'While my first film was inspired by his story, my later works were inspired by his concepts.'

Ananthamurthy then speaks of the complexity of time, noting how we live in the present but respond to the past and aspire to the future. He sees that all responses to the present must be political and ethical. Further complicating the issue is the particular temporal and ethical framework innate in a piece of literature, and the need to be true to it as well as to the greater reality. Shiv Visvanathan sees the natural corollary of this as the battle against globalisation, a battle that is yet to be won.

A title card announces *A Need to Learn ... 1985,* and Ananthamurthy is seen reading from that poem. The film comes to an end as the poem articulates the urge to freedom, seeing its light as important, as is the shade that comes with its fading. It sings of compassion, and of patience and timeliness.

In *Ananthamurthy: Not a Biography but a Hypothesis,* Kasaravalli has tried to worthily represent U. R. Ananthamurthy, and to do so by means of a commendable film. The man is presented well indeed. His intellectual stature and his literary creativity are easily established, while his consequence as a social activist is well alluded to, although it could have been a little more widely explored. No doubt the film is an introduction to one of the great minds of contemporary India; however, a major strength in this introduction, quite apart from the tributes and analyses of experts and the presentation of literary extracts, is Kasaravalli's care in showing the essentially personal side of the man. Kasaravalli makes perfectly plain his own admiration and affection for him, and his film enables us to share that esteem, accepting the arguments for his eminence but also taking into our hearts an immensely likeable man. The Ananthamurthy who appears before the camera here is natural and relaxed, utterly without affectation, displaying a sense of humour, a ready compassion for people *as such*, and an avuncular gentleness that makes one instantly warm to him.

Kasaravalli's tribute to Ananthamurthy is truly an excellent film. The quality of a documentary film will always be limited by the quality of the sources with which it is presented. Too many still photographs, or too much use of talking heads, for example, can detract from the cinematic nature of the work. Moreover, literary material does not readily offer itself as effective cinematic material. Nevertheless, Girish has succeeded here in two fundamental endeavours: to present a digestible amount of balanced substance, and to do so in a way that does not allow the cinematic nature of the work to be minimised to any extent. Variety of presentation is of great importance, and even more so is the essentially visual nature of cinema. The great variety of visual richness in this film is remarkable and is, apart from its substance, its greatest strength.

14

One of the Finest Filmmakers in India

Girish Kasaravalli made the second of his two feature-length documentaries in 2015. *Images/Reflections: A Journey into the Imagery of Adoor Gopalakrishnan* is no mere tribute to the eminent Keralan director; it is an invaluable insight into the mind, craft, and aesthetics of one of India's finest filmmakers. It is by no means common for an accomplished filmmaker to make a substantial documentary on another filmmaker, yet it is indeed Girish's own exceptional talent that has helped shape his response to Adoor's cinema, to creatively question his colleague, and to represent him and his work in such a way as to make this documentary a remarkable contribution to the appreciation of Indian cinema.

Stylistically the film is very similar to the one on U. R. Ananthamurthy, though some differences might be discerned. The second documentary is a little more formally structured than the first, and it has slightly fewer and less extensive expert comments. Moreover, the expert commentary and the commentary from Adoor Gopalakrishnan himself are more readily accessible to the understanding of most viewers than the more complex and sometimes esoteric material in the earlier film. Nevertheless, there are still the book-lined studies—though some of them are decorated with film posters—in which luminaries present their views, and Kasaravalli exploits the natural beauty of Kerala every bit as much and as lovingly as he does that of Karnataka in the earlier documentary.

The pre-title sequence suggests a deference to tradition, quite appropriate to a filmmaker whose works are set in a society that is very much determined by tradition and are, in many ways, trying to break away from it. We see Adoor lighting an oil lamp from which all the other lamps will take their light in the evening. The tradition would involve the members of the household silently saying their prayers. The image of the lamp is maintained on the right of screen as the titles appear on the left, after which the opening shots portray another aspect of tradition. Women are seen arranging blossoms according to colour in concentric circles while female voices are heard singing; this, we are told, is part of the Onam festival. There is a cut to the streets, where crowds of people, elephants, and decorative lights all attest to the joyousness of this Hindu harvest festival, the biggest festival in Kerala that runs for 10 days in the month of Chingam (from mid-August to mid-September). A voiceover summarises the mythological basis of the festival, concerning jealousy of the gods and the annual homecoming visit of the popular, ousted king, Mahabali.[1] Lights are lit and paths are decorated to welcome the much-loved king. Kasaravalli's voiceover explains that the celebration of Onam is a fitting introduction to a study of Adoor Gopalakrishnan, whose work is so imbued with 'traditional forms and modern expression.'

There is a cut from a blaze of Onam lights to the inevitable book-lined study. Kasaravalli's voiceover offers an opinion: 'In a way, Adoor Gopalakrishnan's films defy any simplistic depiction of the real.' The camera moves along the shelves from left to right, toward a desk on which columns of books are stacked high; it zooms in, slowly, to reveal Adoor working behind the mass of books. His voice, belonging to another shot, is heard at first, raising the issue of the nature of reality. The starting point of the creative process, he says, is an experience, then comes the memory of that experience. However, memory will often 'flower into imagination'—thus, there will not be an exact reproduction of the experience or the memory of it. Reality, then, is multi-layered. Now we see the first clip, which is from *Anantaram* ('Monologue,' 1987), where the old cook offers quite a challenge to the little boy, Ajayan, at an age where he is coming to terms with reality.

All that has been seen so far is introductory. The rest of the film now follows on from this, structured in five chapters. A title card

[1] The autumn Durga Puja in Bengal has a similar homecoming element.

announces, 'Chapter 1. Adoor Gopalakrishnan, *Kathapurushan* of this film.' 'Kathapurushan' means 'protagonist' and is a reference to Adoor's 1996 film of that name.[2] The chapter opens with a shot of Adoor seated in a spotlight, surrounded by darkness, perhaps suggesting solitariness or singularity. There is then a tribute from the Bengali filmmaker, Mrinal Sen, who describes Adoor as 'one of the finest filmmakers in India' and a revolutionary in every sense of the word, though this latter attribution is not substantiated. The renowned Mumbai director, Shyam Benegal, corroborates Sen's view, praising Adoor's films for their content as well as their style. He notes the contemporary history of Kerala as the substance of Adoor's films, and the simplicity with which he deals with it.

There are some shots of Adoor the busy director—tending a prop, helping an actor with his *dhoti* and another with her shawl—as a bridge to the next commentary, this time by Gouridasan Nair. He notes that Adoor has been influenced much by Gandhi and by socialist principles, but his concern for political arrangements, both public and domestic, demands an engagement as well as a detachment, and it is a mark of his genius that he can effectively marshal both.

There is a cut to a shot of Adoor reading, then to one of him eating, his wife coming to stand beside him. We then move to a well-lit library, where the eminent historian K. N. Panikkar speaks of the significance of historicity to Adoor's films. He notes that the main movements of his time, with which he has engaged, have been the Renaissance, the National Movement and the Left Movement, all of which have engendered structural changes in family and society, and have sought to stem exploitation. His films do not necessarily deal with such changes directly, but 'they form the background in which his ideas take shape.'

There is a visual of Adoor setting up a shot, then another clip from *Anantaram*, in which Ajayan spins round and round, becoming dizzy and falling to the floor. The dialogue tells us, 'The story does not end here. I think there is a lot more to be said.' There

[2] The English subtitled version is called 'Man of the Story.'

is a shot of Kasaravalli and his cameraman reflected in the glass of a French window, through which Adoor appears as the title card announces, 'Chapter 2. *Mukhamukham* ("Face to Face") with Adoor Gopalakrishnan.'[3] The chapter is what its title says—Adoor and an interviewer addressing certain issues, with illustrative film clips interspersed.

The chapter opens with the camera tracking down a country lane, then turning into a beautiful old home in the traditional architectural style—Adoor's ancestral home, we are told. Kasaravalli raises the matter of history and politics in cinema, and Adoor makes the point that in his films, history is not to be narrated or reproduced; what is of interest to him are the effects of historical processes on his characters, as well as on himself. Indeed, well within the first decade of his life, the Second World War had come to an end, the Quit India Movement and the struggle for freedom had led to Independence, the Direct Action campaign and other divisive urges had brought about the Partition, and Mahatma Gandhi had been assassinated. And so much was to come.

We cut here to a clip from *Kathapurushan*, where three policemen come to Kunjunni's press to search the premises. When asked for a search warrant, the officer responds with a brutal thrust of his baton into Kunjunni's stomach. The clip shows that at that time, at least, the protectors of society might also have been described as its oppressors. Adoor goes on to reject the view that a political film must be didactic and replete with slogans, declaring that the working of politics in everyday life, subtle though it may be, is far more common than we might think. As Adoor and Kasaravalli are seen rummaging through film posters, Adoor cites *Vidheyan*[4] as an example of 'the colonisation of a man's mind' and a metaphor for the colonisation of a country. The clip we are shown reveals the landlord, Patel, in all his crass brutality and the Christian convert, Tommy, as pathetic and servile, at the receiving end of Patel's cruelty. Patel is supported by his toadying henchmen, who laugh and berate

[3] The film was made in 1984.

[4] 'The Servile,' 1993.

on cue, faithfully lending support to the thuggery of their boss. Adoor's point about metaphor is well-illustrated.

There is a brief shot of Adoor sitting at his desk talking to another interviewer, and then there is a cut to a canal, a boat being paddled along it followed by another boat that carries Kasaravalli and Adoor. The topic now is the characterisation of Adoor's women, who are generally presented as strong and forthright. Adoor refers to the matrilineal tradition in Kerala as partial explanation for this. As he declares that his female characters have been strong people, we are taken to another canal and another boat, in a clip from *Naalu Pennungal*.[5] A woman comes to take home her older sister, who has elected to live on her own without the support of a man. The inevitable appeal to popular opinion is made—'What will people say?'—but the woman is quite emphatic that she likes living alone. Then there is a cut within the clip to the woman trying to turn away a man from her locked door, reneging on a previous invitation in order to strengthen her self-sufficiency and independence. 'It should not be impossible for a woman to make her life without a man,' she pleads.

This sequence is followed by a cut to a room cluttered with numerous framed photographs, film posters, trophies and books; Adoor's face is noticeable in some of the pictures as a spotlight moves about the room, suggesting a blend of the man and his work. Then there is a shot of Adoor seated on a veranda, seen through Venetian blinds. He is again talking with Kasaravalli, this time about cinematic technique and technology. Adoor stresses the importance of keeping up with ever-improving technology. He points out that technology is an objective means to an end, whereas technique is more personal, the subjective utilisation of technology. Some of what is seen here are voiceover shots of Adoor engaging with technology while shooting a film.

Part of his style, as Adoor would have it, is a minimalist approach to filmmaking. He is now in his study, where a strong

---

[5] 'Four Women,' 2007.

electric bulb shines over the desk, picking out the vicinity around it. He is talking with the documentary filmmaker, critic and academic, C. S. Venkiteswaran, and makes the very important point that a minimalist technique helps to ensure that every element in a shot can be of some significance. A clip from *Mukhamukham* gives excellent illustration of this point. Sridharan, an erstwhile political hero but now mysteriously fallen from grace, his abasement highlighted by his addiction to alcohol, sits down alone in a tea-shop. A former associate follows him in and demands to talk with him. Very little talk ensues, however, but this brilliantly directed scene speaks volumes on tension, mystery and frustration, pity and disappointment, since such elements as the face of the proprietor, the barely touched glass of tea, the accusatory-yet-flat delivery of the interrogator, the profound speechlessness of Sridharan, the stark interior of the shop, and the religious pictures on the walls, all fertilise the thinking of the audience. A brief shot of a small group of men gathered outside and observing Sridharan in serious silence is especially telling.

Through the window we see Adoor listening to Kasaravalli mention the shift in narrativity from Adoor's early films, with their linear narratives, to the later ones, which are more 'episodic and austere.' Adoor acknowledges this with words such as 'going straight to the core of the subject' and 'getting involved in the essentials and not in the peripherals.' Kasaravalli wonders if Adoor's minimalism is at all due to Gandhi, for whom he has expressed a notable admiration. Readily confessing this admiration, Adoor recalls that it started when he was a schoolboy, wearing homespun cloth and spinning yarn. He describes Gandhi as 'a man for all seasons.' Here there is a cut to a shot of yarn being spun in a clip from *Nizhalkkuthu*,[6] which becomes a shot of the shooting of the film, with Adoor himself demonstrating how the spinning-wheel is to be used.

C. S. Venkiteswaran takes up with Adoor the question of storytelling in his films. Adoor tells him that 'in a way, all my films

[6] 'Shadow Kill,' 2002.

are about storytelling.' A shot of Adoor at the keyboard leads to the title card announcing, 'Chapter 3: Adoor Gopalakrishnan as seen by Naalu Pennungal (Four women)'. Of course, the four women are not those of the film of that name, but women more intimately connected with Adoor's life and work. The first of these is a cousin, Bhanumathy Kunjamma, whom we meet while she is sitting on a veranda, stringing a garland of marigold blooms. She tells of the inauspiciousness at the birth of Adoor—continual rain and thunder, a protracted labour and a breech delivery. A clip from *Kathapurushan* then depicts the protracted breech delivery of Kunjunni, and the grave concern of the women attending it. The babe is smacked and duly howls, heralding a burst of joyful ululating. Adoor's daughter, announced very formally by title card as Aswati G. Dorje, IPS,[7] is at first seen engaged in some family banter with her young son and two of his friends. She goes on to talk of her father growing up in a very big extended family, which included aunts who were playwrights and wrote for acting cousins to perform. She talks of characters in Adoor's films who were inspired by family members, and then there is a brief clip from *Kathapurushan* and its allusion to the death of Adoor's mother. The next testimony comes from the actor Maheshwari Amma, announced by her stage name, K. P. A. C. Lalitha. She talks of Adoor's perfectionism and his unfailing cool-headedness on set. An interesting quirk is his refusal to divulge the ending of a film to his actors until they come to shoot it, being careful to prevent them from interpreting it their way rather than his. There follow some stills of her from roles in earlier films as she declares herself the female artist who has performed the most with Adoor, having acted in five of his films. Perhaps the most unusual role was that of Narayani in *Mathilukal*,[8] who is not seen but only heard, as shown in the extract from the film that follows. The fourth woman is a friend, the eminent film administrator and writer, Uma da Cunha. Her professional association with

[7] Indian Police Service.

[8] 'The Walls,' 1989.

Adoor was as his English subtitler, and she speaks of his rigorous perfectionism in this vital aspect of communicating his work to a non-Malayali audience. (Subtitling is an aspect of Indian cinema that is treated all too casually by many filmmakers). She also makes the very important point that despite profound cultural differences, Adoor's films are by no means inaccessible to non-Indian audiences, given the simplicity of his technique of developing a narrative and the essential humanity of his characters. This is corroborated by a lovely excerpt from *Kathapurushan* that deals with the affectionate friendship of the children as they learn a very complex alphabet.

Chapter 4 is headed with the title of Adoor's first film, *Swayamvaram*.[9] His voiceover tells us that *Swayamvaram* means making one's own choices, and the title card carries the words, 'Adoor Gopalakrishnan on His Own Choice of Film Techniques'. The first choice concerns the use of music. Adoor, sitting on a veranda, raindrops falling in the foreground, affirms the importance of music in cinema, but warns of its potential to be a distraction. Three excerpts from *Elippathayam*[10] illustrate the effectiveness of non-melodic, atonal music; the sound heard here might also remind us of Shrikant Prabhu's very haunting title music for this documentary film. Closely connected is the second choice, the use of sound. There is a clip from *Oru Pennum Randaanum,*[11] dominated by the sound of women beating coconut shells. Adoor points to the effect certain sounds might have on the meaning of a scene. The filmmaker can, of course, communicate to his audience through sound other than dialogue, and natural sounds too can enhance meaning, as is suggested by the wind in the treetops that look down on Kaliyappan and his house in the clip from *Nizhalkkuthu*.

The next choice has to do with scripts. At the outset, Adoor makes it clear that his scripts do not provide solutions or answers, but in them he presents problems and leaves the audience to think

[9] 'One's Own Choice,' 1974.

[10] 'The Rat Trap,' 1981.

[11] 'A Climate for Crime,' 2008.

about them. This, of course, requires a more meaningful engagement with a film than is usually the case. There is then a clip from the end of *Swayamvaram* where Sita, now alone, is feeding her baby girl. From outside comes the sound of a storm, made ominous by the stark black and white photography. The constant point-of-view shots of the door, suggesting the possibility of an unwelcome visitor, enjoin the viewer to think more fully about what the future might hold for Sita and her little girl. The director does not minimise that experience by offering any 'help' but, as in all of his films, leaves it open-ended.

The next choice is on his characters, who, Adoor insists, are not odd or out of the way but simply caught in unusual or difficult situations. A clip from *Kodiyettam*[12] shows the film's hero—or anti-hero—Shankaran as assistant to a truck-driver, heartily enjoying a silly contest on the road between the truck and a car whose driver wants to get past. The contest is settled by a tyre blowout. Adoor quite rightly points out that it is easy to see the faults and deficiencies in Shankaran as definitive, without seeing the qualities that make him as ordinary as any of us.

The final chapter is announced as 'Chapter 5: Anantaram, a postscript,' and aims to discern the extent to which Adoor's work has reflected the crises and the changes of the turbulent times covered by his films. The chapter starts with an excursion to the factory where *Mukhamukham* was shot. One P. R. C. Nair tells us that he was 37 when *Mukhamukham* was released and was a member of the factory's trade union, which was opposed to the film in the belief that it was antagonistic to the interests of the working class. Now, 30 years later, he realises that the film was indeed sympathetic to working-class concerns. 'It's only now I realise the vision of the film,' he says, noting the loss, as he puts it, of political and economic direction in Kerala in recent times. The camera takes us on a tour of an obviously long-deserted factory, with some of the accusatory dialogue from an earlier clip from *Mukhamukham* heard in the

[12] 'The Ascent,' 1977.

background. Gouridasan Nair talks about change in society and the economy, change that can be either deliberate or imperceptible.

We are taken to a house similar to that in which *Elippathayam* was shot. We are able to see the traditional style of architecture, the ornately carved timber balustrades, cornices, ceiling beams and columns. Though now abandoned, the house still suggests the grandeur of past times, when a privileged few lived elegantly on the labour of others. As we look around at what remains of the house, snatches of dialogue from *Elippathayam* are heard over, deploring the hard times into which the comfortable classes would seem to be sinking.

There is then a captioned shot of the house that was used for *Naalu Pennungal*. Decay and disrepair are evident, and then there is a cut to a comfortable living room, with the critic Maithili Rao talking of contradictions in the matrilineal system, in which women are actually trapped, citing *Elippathayam* as an excellent example. She describes the film as 'an indictment of both feudalism and the matrilineal system,' and suggests that Adoor, being so familiar with the past and the present, might be anticipating greater freedom for women in a more modernised social structure.

Kasaravalli's film then ends with a clip from *Anantaram*, showing Ajayan as a little boy counting the steps of the *ghat* down to the water. As he waits on the bottom step, a voiceover offers us the apposite words from that film, 'I am not sure if I have told you the complete story. There may still be things I have forgotten to narrate.'

The closing titles are preceded by cards listing the major awards, national and international, won by Adoor Gopalakrishnan, and major international retrospectives of his films. Given the form of such a presentation and the time given to it, one is overwhelmed by the abundance of honour.

As was the case with the documentary on U. R. Ananthamurthy, Kasaravalli has tried to represent Adoor Gopalakrishnan by means of a worthy film. The filmmaker comes across somewhat more readily than the writer; it is possible that thinking in cinematic images makes one's expression more direct, more concrete. Moreover, when Adoor is expressing abstract ideas, he often has visual corroboration from a film clip. While Adoor is gentle and urbane, he is also less ebullient, and he appears as much more of a filmmaker than a personality. There is a little less of Adoor's family and a lot more of his Kerala, for that, after all, is what his films are about. Kasaravalli is able to clearly and simply establish Adoor's basic ideas on the essentials of filmmaking, but of even greater interest is his focus on the substance of Adoor's cinema. His deep and extensive engagement with the recent and continuing history of Kerala gives him fulfilment and animates his films. He is presented by Kasaravalli as a profound thinker on cinema and society, and on the marriage of the two. As for the second of the two endeavours, it can be said that a documentary on a filmmaker is likely to be more cinematic than one on, say, a literary figure, mainly because of the ready source material that is itself cinematic. Almost all of Adoor's films are effectively used to illustrate many of the points he makes and the ideas he expounds and, in addition, there is a balanced presentation of the interviews, commentaries and context shots. In all, it is an excellent documentary by a master filmmaker on a master filmmaker.

15

And Finally ...

That Girish Kasaravalli belongs with a small handful of the leading filmmakers in India is corroborated by just a cursory glance at the awards and honours his films have brought him. Even his diploma film, *Avshesh*, won a National Award in 1975, and since then four of his films have won the National Award for Best Feature Film and six have been judged to be the best in Kannada in their respective years.[1] Of course, awards are usually controversial and will rarely gain universal agreement; however, it might be of passing interest to note that the legendary Satyajit Ray picked up six Golden Lotus Awards for Best Feature Film from a total of 29 films, so Kasaravalli's four from among 14 suggests a creditable comparison.

Girish Kasaravalli is a quintessentially Indian filmmaker. His narratives are all built around themes and characters drawn from his contemporary India; in fact, the scope of his sources may be narrowed even further to his native Karnataka where, in fact, all his films are set. It is of course possible to discern certain prominent themes in his work, but it must also be acknowledged that while any one of his films might give an impression of simplicity, its narrative will also be marked by complexity and contain a number of layered or interwoven themes.

Notions of tradition and change are treated in all of Kasaravalli's films, sometimes prominently, sometimes incidentally. *Ghatashraddha* deals focally with aspects of cultural heritage which, when examined closely as it is here, will be its own cry for change. Under the aegis of custom and lore, so much that

[1] See Appendix 1.

is undesirable—hypocrisy, cruelty, and the stultification of the spirit—is allowed to prosper. The darker nature of tradition dominates in *Nayi Neralu*, where injustice, callousness and sheer cruelty are significant elements in the dynamics of the narrative. Recondite protocols are adhered to, superstition is rampant and, as in *Ghatashraddha*, the spirit of the individual is relentlessly stifled. Venkatalakshmi finds freedom from such oppression only in the form of self-imposed exile.

In these two films, tradition is specifically a Hindu inheritance. However, there are variations on this. In *Bannada Vesha, yakshagana* bears certain affinities to the 'great' tradition, yet is very firmly entrenched in the 'little' or localised popular tradition. Nevertheless, one assumes the social strictures of the other, thus substantiating the importance Shambhu gives to the time-honoured social inequality innate to the caste system, an unjust inequity that he sees as fundamental to his struggle to prosper in his chosen profession. The ill-effects of social discrimination on children, seen in flashbacks and implied on behalf of the young Shankara, also highlight injustice and a need for change.

Central to *Dweepa* and *Kanasemba Kudureyaneri* is a localised and popular religious tradition that would seem to be more heterodox, not based so much in scripture but deferring largely to superstition. However, the lore of *nema* in *Dweepa* and the customs of *siddha* in *Kanasemba Kudureyaneri* hold sway over their adherents as strongly as does the more orthodox Brahmanism over the majority community. There are several threads of tradition running through *Kanasemba Kudureyaneri*, none of which seems to have the same deleterious effect on the individual as we find in *Ghatashraddha* or *Nayi Neralu*, except for the obvious foregrounding of caste and the economic and social depression presupposed by it. Change, in fact, is implied in economic terms in the submission of Shivanna and the other landowners to the lure of profit, as they sell their lands to a factory development agency. In *Dweepa* the basic elements of the drama are the *nema* tradition and the march of progress. The latter conflict is by no means informed: the traditionalists have no argument with which to confront the modernists, and the modernists need none—other than the likelihood of death by drowning—to prevail over the former. Ultimately, some unknown official, for whatever reasons, makes certain decisions and the threat passes, and because of the unknown factor the passing of the threat is easily ascribed to divine will. Nagi may have done all in her power to show that human action can prevail over traditional faith, but her husband does not have the breadth or depth of mind to understand that.

Mane and *Kraurya* might be said to be more secular in their thematics, but in each film there is significant deference paid to orthodox tradition. The ritualistically daubed landlord in *Mane* is visibly orthodox, yet religion in any accepted form does not seem to have much relevance to his life of pursuing material profit. Similarly, the iconographical religiosity of the old woman bears no significance to the working out of the narrative. The more worldly yet no less religious Aunty tells a familiar tale of traditional prejudice against women as she recalls her failed marriage—a failure due entirely to the inferior man that other men chose for her to marry—and the alacrity with which unprincipled men will brand and exploit a single woman. Except for Rangamma's occasional allusions to the epics, *Kraurya* is even more secular. However, the major turning point in the narrative progression is made by a deferral to the religious tradition that threatens the raining of curses, should the elderly widow live in her own house for the first 12 months after her son's untimely death, and this deferral is made with minimal controversy and resistance.

Tradition is an underlying notion in *Tai Saheba*, though again not at all in any religious sense. There is, of course, the matter of the first wife of Appa Saheb renouncing the world and ensconcing herself in a temple, but this is a peripheral issue, not a central one. The underlying traditional value here is the privileged position of men in upper-caste society, a value which, in its inconsistency, would tend to draw India closer to the medieval than the modern. It is not enough to alert men to the feudalistic nature of their exploitation of women for pleasure, but it is also essential for women, following the lead of Tai Saheba after Nanu, to rebel against men's notions of entitlement and to reject the debasing idea that women exist purely in the interests of men.

Hasina presents a conflict set in the Muslim community, but being a conflict between a woman and the power of men, it is hardly any different from films with similar themes set in the Hindu community. It is significant to point out that the nastiness of Yakub, while not shared by the other men in the film, is effectually supported by them. The basic dynamics of the narrative assume the suppression of women, particularly those of lower economic status. However, the *muthavalli* is a man and the *jamaat* is all male, and while all the power over the community is in the hands of men, inferior people like Yakub will thrive and women will be vulnerable to them. Women will prosper only when they have a voice, as is most effectively made clear by the ending.

A number of films are concerned with inequality in various guises. The traditional social organisation of Hindu India, the caste system and its innate hierarchical arrangement ensured a society that was essentially unequal. Social inequality due to caste is evident in *Bannada Vesha,* where contrasting reactions to caste oppression are seen in the headstrong Shambhu and his weak and submissive father. The ugliness of caste prejudice and callousness is underlined when such attitudes are directed at children. Shambhu's father probably learned at an early age to accept such ill-treatment, whereas Shambhu himself resents what he rightly sees as unjust and unwarranted. The harsh treatment of Irya in *Kanasemba Kudureyaneri* can be condoned simply on the basis of his lowly social status, a status which also ensures his being condemned to the most menial, unsatisfying and ill-paid work for his living.

Economic inequality as militating against social cohesion is presented in *Mane* by the mysterious shed people. They are presented as a socio-economic fact; as people, they are a mystery, significant to the film only insofar as they present a contrast of sorts to Rajanna, which highlights his particular moral quandary. Aunty is a victim of what might be described as moral inequality. Her unmarried status, in popular perception, raises the issue of her morality, which is easily devalued. Simple economic inequality besets Tabara, his wife and their adopted son in *Tabarana Kathe.* Working as a clerk in local government service all his life, Tabara, like Ananda Rao in *Kurmavatara,* has maintained respectability, but with penury to accompany it. Of course, a career in the bureaucracy might bring substantial monetary rewards if one is cunning enough to exploit opportunities, but Tabara and Rao are both singularly incorrupt, and so remain considerably less well-off than their morally questionable colleagues might be.

Economic inequality is evident in *Gulabi Talkies,* though not to any remarkable extent. Gulabi herself is a midwife, but well-paid work in that field depends entirely on others, and so she is obliged to supplement her meagre income by working as a domestic help and this, in fact, is neither here nor there. However, the most insidious kind of social inequality gradually reveals itself in this film as communal inequality, and as it plays itself out on Gulabi in particular, it is fired by perceived economic inequities in the fishing industry. Early in the film there are indications of communal difference, which certainly do not necessarily amount to inequality, but later circumstances conspire to prompt members of the majority community, in particular the otherwise upright Vasanna, to find it opportune to exploit those differences in order to seize an economic advantage. Simple numbers will ensure the efficacy of this endeavour.

In some 10 of Kasaravalli's feature films there is at least one woman in a focal role. In *Tabarana Kathe* and *Bannada Vesha* the woman is notable for her stoic stalwartness. In *Tabarana Kathe* Appi labours to play her role in support of her small family, though in time becomes more of a victim than an agent, and from stoic stalwart becomes stoic sufferer. Shambhu's mother is the victim of economic and social misfortune, yet she stoically accepts her lot as both mother and father to her small family. The most piteous of Girish's women, a representative victim, is Yamuna in *Ghatashraddha.* She is representative of her sex, being presented here as illustration of feudalistic male values that would privilege men and demonise women. Like Appi and Shambhu's mother, she accepts her lot and suffers without complaint. Unlike them, however, she does fall into despair, as seen in her suicide attempt and her ultimate acceptance of defeat in submitting to the abortionist. The final shots of her illuminate the end of her pathetic plight, brought about by the shamefulness of a male-dominated and legalistic tradition.

The elderly woman in *Mane* is also a silent sufferer, having been tricked, we are told, by the wily and ostensibly devout landlord. However, in this film we also meet two women who are determined to be agents rather than victims. Aunty has proven herself to be self-reliant and self-sufficient in a world where men make the rules, while Gita is not prepared to go along with her husband's personal prejudices but resolves to be led by her own perceptions of what is good and worthy. Tai Saheba is, for the most part, a model of the traditional wife, faithfully serving her husband as the unquestioned master of her world. But as Nanu grows up, she sees herself as the one called to fight against traditional values, to ensure happiness not only for him but for the many women like the girl he wants to marry.

Nagi in *Dweepa,* Hasina, and Gulabi are obvious agents. In carrying the burden of two inept men, and later the well-meaning but impractical Krishna, Nagi is affectionate and caring, but she must also be pragmatic. When she finds herself left to her own resources, she proves her mettle and strength of character in the face of fearsome odds. Hasina is constant and resolute, bearing herself with dignity and pride. Gulabi, a simple and exceptionally good-natured woman, suffers the blows of injustice and petty prejudice, yet right to the end her optimism and good faith are in evidence and we can be sure that they will sustain her. Of some interest here is Rangamma in *Kraurya.* She, like Nagi, Hasina, and Gulabi, is a strong and determined character. She does not suffer defeat, but is ultimately brought down by age coupled with disappointment. However, her being female is not so significant, for the character might easily have been written as a man and, with a little tweaking of the scriptural directives, the narrative might have played out in exactly the same way.

Being female is vitally significant, however, in the case of Venkatalakshmi in *Nayi Neralu.* She is a part of an orthodox household where familial positions carry particular demands and responsibilities. She has been a wife and, when the film opens, is a widowed mother. Undoubtedly she was a duteous and faithful wife, satisfying her mother-in-law's fastidious concern for formalities, and we see her as an uncomplaining and still young woman, suffering the harsh self-denial of the orthodox widow's regimen. The particularly strange dynamics of the narrative then give her the opportunity to be a self-determining woman, complete with personality and sexuality. We see her gradually weaken in her deference to her mother-in-law as she strengthens in her understanding of herself. Ultimately she has a victory of sorts against the stultifying tradition that all but destroys Yamuna in *Ghatashraddha*.

While there might be causes to be pursued through the women in Kasaravalli's films, this is not so with children. In some films they are integral to the narrative and in others they simply reflect the fact that children are a part of our lives. They may be connected to broader issues while not being intricately involved in them. In *Tabarana Kathe* the fact that Babu is an adopted son tells us a little more about Tabara and Appi. He is a good, simple and loving boy, which makes the crisis of his disappearance so disturbing. The boys in *Bannada Vesha* remind us of the cruelty of social inequality while illustrating the character development of Shambhu and offering a caution that Shankara may well be a vehicle for the same reprehensible tradition. In *Mane,* the child being whisked away by his mother before Gita can return his ball to him and the missing child in the devastation at the end of the film serve well to highlight the dangers of social disintegration. Pinki's childish innocence offers some light in the shadowy confusion of interests in *Kanasemba Kudureyaneri,* while adding to that confusion with her candid sense of smell. Addu's role in *Gulabi Talkies* is simply to be adorable and so bring out one of the many endearing aspects of Gulabi, while Vasanna's son, in a perceptive moment, offers a moral insight that is sadly lacking in his elders. The very sensitive direction of the three little girls in *Hasina* provides the emotional cohesion for that film as well as a point of reference by which a number of the adults may be critically interpreted. While the majority of the children in *Kraurya* are simply indications of innocence and joy, Murthy, of course, is central and recalls Nani in *Ghatashraddha* in his untutored care for an older woman. Both boys are untainted by experience, at times naïve and overawed by that which they are too young to understand, but are morally sound agents of hope. There are no angels among Kasaravalli's children, for the emphasis is on the essence of childhood: innocence, simple joy and faithful dependence. In reality the angelic could be but an artifice, and so it is happily done without. Also happily absent are the negative emotions and values that besmirch so much of the adult world.

Kasaravalli acknowledges in his films the fact that many people suffer for want of a voice. They are not understood because they are unable to articulate their problems and their needs. There are also those whom society does not deem worthy of being heard and who, by various means, are kept silent. For example, Yamuna in *Ghatashraddha* is stifled due to her sex and her extramarital pregnancy; she is no match for the power of male-dominated tradition. In *Tabarana Kathe* Tabara is kept down by the power of vested interests and the frighteningly irrational entanglements of local bureaucracy. When he does eventually find his voice, buoyed by his righteous rage, it is too late to be of any advantage. Tai Saheba is representative of Indian women long suppressed by tradition, eventually finding the opportunity to be articulate, but only in exchange for personal suffering. Like Tabara, Hasina is heard only when it is tragically too late. Venkatalakshmi in *Nayi Neralu* is a very sad case of a woman who is almost crushed by the strength of the traditionally imposed discipline on widows, subsequently to be suppressed even more by the confusion that emanates out of superstition and delusion. And Ananda Rao in *Kurmavatara* speaks the thoughts of one of the greatest thinkers of modern India and is not heard because of the vast cocoon of self-interest that inures people against hearing what he would want to say.

Society suppresses those whose voices might threaten the comfort of the strong and privileged, and it also quite cruelly alienates such perceived threats. *Mane's* shed people are at first alienated to the night and then to a place where alienation will assume a much more terrible nature. In *Dweepa* whole communities are removed from their ancestral land by the force of modern development, while individuals are alienated from one another. Nagi is belittled because of the arcane values of her husband, while Krishna is harshly rejected due to the same values and the emotional confusion that stems from them. Gulabi's sin by association has her cast out at the end of *Gulabi Talkies*, addressed by the exclusive appellation of 'Gulnabi' in a callous act of cheap populism perpetrated against a good and large-hearted woman. Venkatalakshmi can find freedom and peace only in exile, Tai Saheba must embrace jail, and the morally upright Ananda Rao is alienated by his fellows and even by his own family. In all his films Kasaravalli shows a profound empathy for those whose lot it is to be overlooked.

There are also some metaphorical agents of alienation. In *Tabarana Kathe* the mountains of files so often seem to be barriers, as are the fundamental trappings of the theatre—masks, make-up, costume—in *Bannada Vesha*. The prominence of water in *Dweepa*, *Nayi Neralu*, and *Gulabi Talkies* is certainly a sign of separation. In *Dweepa* it is a formidable barrier that separates people from one another; it also ensures a significant degree of isolation for Venkatalakshmi; and it is the means by which Netru and Gulabi are each taken away, though with quite different effect. The factor of age both alienates and embraces in *Kraurya*, but it is Rangamma's rejection, enforced by her fateful look in the mirror, that ultimately breaks her.

In four films, a very real and human metaphor of alienation is to be seen in the form of bureaucracy. Here the bureaucratic world appears very much as a world unto itself. It has power and authority, which might inspire awe or even fear, and it has its own ways and mysteries, which imbue it with a distinctiveness that cannot be easily broached. The nightmare that is the *tehsildar's* officer in *Tabarana Kathe* is almost surreal, and it is frightening because it is not so. The plainly suggested impenetrability of the Corporation office in *Mane* is complemented by the aggressive brusqueness of the official who hears Rajanna's case. While the clerks in the Relief Fund office in *Dweepa* are courteous, and one of them even listens with apparent sympathy, it is impossible for Gunappa to engage with them because of the systemic gulf between him and them. Before his entry into the world of acting, Ananda Rao is, in fact, somewhat alienated from his family by his obsessive devotion to his bureaucratic career. Later, as an emergent Gandhian, he is given an official directive to leave Gandhi to television—this from a man whose sensibilities run to presenting an ageing actress with an almost defunct diary as a token of admiration.

While there is disaffection and estrangement, there is also a vision of meaning that spreads to broader horizons. On the surface, *Bannada Vesha* is purely local Karnataka, steeped in local folklore and religion, but one does not have to go deep to find notions of universal interest—social inequality and chips on shoulders, personal rivalry and attendant bitchiness, the delusions of ego and the illusionary nature of identity. *Dweepa* has a similarly local visual appeal, with an even more esoteric local religious practice, but the universal notions of the cost of so-called progress, the rivalry of the human and the natural worlds, petty human jealousy and the ascription to God of what seems beyond us, are all plainly dealt with.

Closely related to the binary of the local and the global and often part and parcel of it is the binary of the mundane and the mysterious. In every one of Kasaravalli's films we will find the recondite attached to the ordinary. In *Mane* the housing complex known as the *chawl* ought to offer a most unremarkable, simple life, but how do we interpret the mysteries that prevent that simplicity from being manifest? In *Tabarana Kathe* such mysteries might be more easily interpreted, but to Tabara they are just as baffling as whatever it is that impedes Rajanna's happiness in *Mane*. Every element in *Kanasemba Kudureyaneri* is everyday rural Karnataka—superstition and religious gurus, the co-existence of the supernatural with the natural, death and funerary protocol—but when they all mingle and merge under the auspices of dream, the mystery is manifest. And in the contemporary world of *Kurmavatara*, why should a colossal historical figure have descended into irrelevance and his simple words of good moral sense gone unheeded?

The films of Girish Kasaravalli present significant themes and creative ideas. They present us with a world that is rich in interest, often colourful and even at times exotic. They tell absorbing stories simply and with no political intent, giving viewers the freedom to engage with them to whatever extent they want. Yet Kasaravalli's greatest strength lies in the presentation of his characters. He is very much a lover of people—all kinds of people, but especially little people. The isolated, exploited, confused, ill-treated and humble are his protagonists, while the strong, wealthy and privileged are often in conflict with them. However, his antagonists are not all bad (obviously Yakub is an exception), and Kasaravalli is careful not to be niggardly in distributing redeeming features. The *muthavalli* is pompous and self-obsessed, but he can also apologise; Appa Saheb has used women basely, but he has also fought for the rights of the lowly and dispossessed; Chandan is an opinionated bully, but he can also admit that he is wrong. The credibility of Kasaravalli's world relies on a balance of the endearing and the negative, and so in his presentation of people we may discern a meticulous and, indeed, truly loving attention to detail as characters are drawn with great concern for individuality. One senses behind Kasaravalli's characters the presence of a benign, loving and largely forgiving creator. The 12 feature films discussed in this book, along with the two documentaries, are testimony to a man steeped in humanity.

Appendix 1

*Filmography**

***Avsesh* ('The Ruins')**—Diploma Film
1975, Hindi
Camera: Jehangir C
Editor: Mithika Taneja
Music: B. Chandavarkar
Produced by: Film and TV Institute of India
Cast: Girish Murudkar, Ananth M. Oak, Rukmini Govindan, Mallesh, Rameshwari Talluri, Abha Dhulia, Sashibala Saxena

***Ghatashraddha* ('The Ritual')**
1977, Kannada, B&W
Based on a story by U. R. Ananthamurthy
Screenplay: Girish Kasaravalli
Camera: S. Ramachandra
Music: B. V. Karanth
Editor: Umesh Kulakarni
Art director: K. V. Subbama
Produced by: Sadananda Suvarna
Cast: Meena, Ajit Kumar, Jagannath, Ramaswamy Iyyengar, Narayana Bhat, Suresh, Shantha, H. S. Parvathi

***Tabarana Kathe* ('The Story of Tabara')**
1986, Kannada, Colour
Based on a story by Poornachandra Tejaswi

* The dates given here are the dates of the granting of censorship certification

Screenplay: Girish Kasaravalli
Camera: Madhu Ambat
Music: L. Vaidyanathan
Editor: M. N. Swamy
Art directors: Srinivas, Mohan
Produced by: Girish Kasaravalli
Cast: Charu Hasan, Nalina Murthy, Santosh Nandavanam, R. Nagesh, Madhava Rao, Srinivas, Jayaram, Vaishali Kasaravalli, Sathyasandha, B. S. Achar, S. G. Jamadar, Mallige Nagaraj

***Bannada Vesha* ('The Mask')**
1988, Kannada, Colour
Screenplay: Ramachandra Dev, Girish Kasaravalli
Camera: G. S. Bhaskar
Music: B. V. Karanth
Editor: M. N. Swamy
Art director: T. B. Srinivas
Produced by: Doordarshan Kendra Bangalore
Cast: Sridhar, Smitha, A. B. Jayaram, Shantamma, A. R. Chandrashekhar, Umesh, Narayan Bhat, Sripad Rao, Lokanath

***Mane* ('The House')**
1989, Kannada, Colour
Based on a novel by T. G. Raghava
Screenplay: Girish Kasaravalli
Camera: S. Ramachandra
Music: L. Vaidyanathan
Editor: M. N. Swamy
Art director: John Devaraj
Produced by: Girish Kasaravalli
Cast: Naseeruddin Shah, Deepti Naval, Rohini Hattangady, Mico Chandru

***Kraurya* ('The Tale of a Story Teller')**
1995, Kannada, Colour
Based on a story by T. N. Sitaram

Screenplay: Girish Kasaravalli
Camera: S. Ramachandra
Music: L. Vaidyanathan
Editor: M. N. Swamy
Art director: Suresh Anagalli
Produced by: Nirmala Chitgopi
Cast: Vikas, Renukamma Murugod, Swathi, H. G. Dattatreya, Vijaya Ekkundi, Ashok Hegde

***Tai Saheba* ('The Lady of the Manor')**
1997, Kannada, Colour
Based on a novel by R. S. Lokapur
Screenplay: Girish Kasaravalli
Camera: H. M. Ramachandra
Music: Isaac Thomas Kottukapally
Editor: M. N. Swamy
Art Director: Ramesh Desai
Produced by: Jayamala
Cast: Jayamala, Suresh Heblikar, Shivaram, Harish Raju, Sudha Belvady

***Dweepa* ('The Island')**
2001, Kannada, Colour
Based on the novel by N. D'Souza
Screenplay: Girish Kasaravalli
Camera: H. M. Ramachandra
Music: Isaac Thomas Kottukapally
Editor: M. N. Swamy
Art director: Sashidhara Adapa
Produced by: Soundarya
Cast: Soundarya, Avinash, Vasudev Rao, Harish Raju

Hasina
2004, Kannada, Colour
Based on a story by Banu Mushtaq
Screenplay: Girish Kasaravalli
Camera: S. Ramachandra Aithal, G. S. Bhaskar, Chokkalingam

Music: Isaac Thomas Kottukapally
Editor: M. N. Swamy
Art directors: Sashidhara Adapa, Ravi
Produced by: Chiguru Chitra
Cast: Tara, Chandrahasa Ullal, Purushottam Talavata, Ritu, Chitra Shenoy, Bhodhini, Soundarya

***Nayi Neralu* ('In the Shadow of the Dog')**
2005, Kannada, Colour
Based on a novel by S. L. Bhyarappa
Screenplay: Girish Kasaravalli
Camera: S. Ramachandra Aithal
Music: Isaac Thomas Kottukapally
Editor: Manohar
Art director: Ramesh Desai
Produced by: Abhishek Patil, Basant Kumar Patil
Cast: Pavitra Lokesh, Sringeri Ramanna, Rameshwari Varma, Ananya Kasaravalli, Ashwin Bolar

Gulabi Talkies
2008, Kannada, Colour
Based on a story by Vaidehi
Screenplay: Girish Kasaravalli
Camera: S. Ramachandra Aithal
Music: Isaac Thomas Kottukapally
Editor: Manohar, M. N. Swamy
Art director: B. S. M Kodagu
Produced by: Amruta Patil, Basant Kumar Patil
Cast: Umashree, M. D. Pallavi, K. G. Krishna Murthy, Ashok Sandeep, Poornima Mohan, Praveera

***Kanasemba Kudureyaneri* ('Riding the Horse of a Dream')**
2009, Kannada, Colour
Based on a story by Amaresh Nugadoni
Screenplay: Girish Kasaravalli, Gopalakrishna Pai
Camera: H. M. Ramachandra Halkere
Music: V. Manohar

Editor: M. N. Swamy
Art directors: Ramachandra, G. N. Kamble
Produced by: Amruta Patil, Basant Kumar Patil
Cast: Vaijanath Biradar, Umashree, Sadashiv Bramhavar, Shivaranjan, Pavitra Lokesh, Soundarya, Purushottam Talavata, Basavalingaiah Hiremath, Akki Chennabasappa, Sawant

***Kurmavatara* ('Tortoise. An Incarnation')**
2011, Kannada, Colour.
Based on a story by: Kum. Veerabhadrappa
Screenplay: Girish Kasaravalli
Camera: G. S. Bhaskar
Music: Isaac Thomas Kottukapally,
Editor: M. N. Swamy
Art director: Sashidhara Adapa
Produced by: Amruta Patil, Basant Kumar Patil
Cast: Shikaripura Krishnamurthy, Jayanthi, Apoorva Kasaravalli, Harish Raj, Cheswa, Rashmi Hariprasad, Goa Dattu, Praveen Rabakavi, Sumukha Bharadwaj, Vikram Soori, Nanjunda, H. G. Somashekar Rao, Akki Chennabasappa, Babu Hirannayya

Ananthamurthy. Not a Biography but a Hypothesis
2012, English, Kannada (English subtitles)
Subject consultant: N. Manu Chakravarthy
Script adviser: Gopala Krishna Pai
Script: Girish Kasaravalli
Camera: G. S. Bhaskar
Music: Bindu Malini
Editor: Mohan Kamakshi
Produced by: V. S. Kundu

Images. Reflections. A Journey into the Imagery of Adoor Gopalakrishnan
2015, English, Malayalam (English subtitles)
Script adviser: Gopalakrishna Pai
Script: Girish Kasaravalli
Camera: Sunny Joseph

Music: Shrikant Prabhu
Editor: Mohan Kamakshi
Produced by: V. S. Kundu

Appendix 2

National Film Awards

National Award for Best Experimental Film:

1975: *Avsesh*

National Award for Best Feature Film:

1977: *Ghatashraddha*
1986: *Tabarana Kathe*
1997: *Tai Saheba*
2001: *Dweepa*

National Award—Special Jury Award for Non-Feature Film:

2013: *Ananthamurthy. Not a Biography but a Hypothesis*

National Award for Best Film of Family Welfare:

2005: *Hasina*

National Award for Best Screenplay:

2009: *Kanasemba Kudureyaneri*

National Award for Best Feature Film in Kannada:

1988: *Bannada Vesha*
1989: *Mane*
1995: *Kraurya*
2007: *Gulabi Talkies*
2009: *Kanasemba Kudureyaneri*
2012: *Kurmavatara*

Karnataka State Film Awards

1977–78: *Ghatashraddha*
Best Film
Best Director

- Best Script
- 1986–87: *Tabarana Kathe*
    - Best Film
    - Best Director
- 1989–90: *Mane*
    - Special Jury Award
    - Best Script
- 1995–96: *Kraurya*
    - Second Best Film
- 1997–98: *Tai Saheba*
    - Best Film
    - Best Director
- 2001–02: *Dweepa*
    - Best Film
    - Best Director
- 2004–05: *Hasina*
    - Best Film on Social Issues
- 2005–06: *Nayi Neralu*
    - Best Film
    - Best Director
- 2007–08: *Gulabi Talkies*
    - Best Film
    - Best Director
    - Best Script
- 2011: *Kurmavatara*
    - Second Best Film

Filmfare Awards

- 1998: *Tai Saheba*
    - Best Film
    - Best Director
- 2006: *Dweepa*
    - Best Film
    - Best Director

2009: *Kanasemba Kudureyaneri*
Best Director

International Honours

1977: *Ghatashraddha*
South Asian Cinema Foundation's 'Excellence in Cinema' Crystal Globe Award

2001: *Dweepa*
Best Film at Moscow Film Festival

2004: *Hasina*
Best Film on Social Issues, Asia Pacific Film Festival, Berlin
Best Script, Best Film of Human Interest, Barcelona Film Festival

2006: *Nayi Neralu*
Best Film at KARA International Film Festival, Karachi
Best Indian Film, OsianCinefan Jury Award
Best Indian Film, MAMI International Film Festival, Mumbai

2007: *Gulabi Talkies*
Best Indian Film, OsianCinefan Festival of Asian and Arab Cinema
Jury Award, Asian Film Festival, Vesoul
Best Script, Lavente Film Festival, Italy

2009: *Kanasemba Kudureyaneri*
Best Film, AsiaticaFilmmediale, Rome
NETPAC Award, AsiaticaFilmmediale, Rome
INALCO Jury Award, Asian Film Festival, Vesoul
Screened at Imagine India Film Festival, Madrid